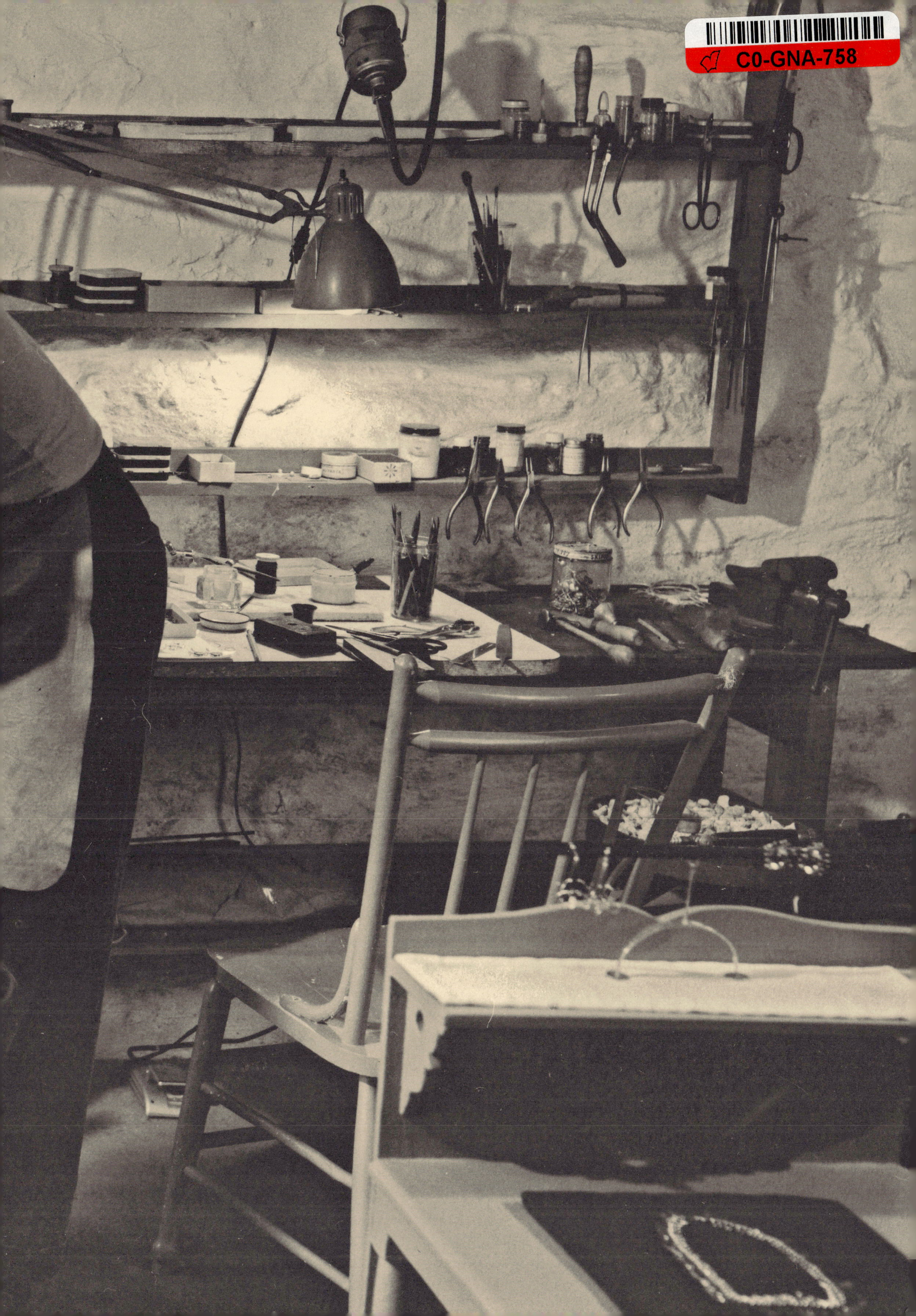

HENRY SHAWAH

HENRY SHAWAH

GOLDSMITH & SCULPTOR

ENDPAPERS: HENRY IN NANTUCKET STUDIO, 1957
(DICK WILLIAMS PHOTOGRAPHY)

To the memory of Lee Day Gillespie (1927–2004),
a treasured friend and patron for more than 35 years,
who has brought strength to my work and cheer
to my heart.

CONTENTS

FOREWORD

Agnes Gund

A little more than twenty years ago, I received my first piece of jewelry fashioned by Henry Shawah. It was a beautiful ring purchased for our engagement by my husband-to-be. Daniel had a friend, Adam Solomon, who knew Henry and his artistry and had fortuitously introduced them. It began a more than two-decade relationship with the wonderfully curious, "wacky," yet elegant Henry. Over that period of time, Daniel gave me numerous items—for an anniversary, a birthday, or a special holiday he would surprise me with a brooch, earrings, a curio box—all manner of things that provoked joy and wonder from friends and myself. Little did I know that I would amass quite a collection of Shawah works. My interest and appreciation of his creative genius developed and grew as new works entered my life. Each work brought another note of fantasy—whimsical, surreal creatures, miniature replicas of classic sculptures, and some wonderful, unique artistic expressions that popped out of his fertile imagination. The works are timeless not only because Henry works with timeless materials—like gold, silver, and gemstones—but also because his concepts are so bold and unique.

One piece that still delights me, and others, every time I wear it is a gold pin in lotus form presenting a beautiful emerald nestled in a baroque pearl. I always show the reverse of the pin, as it has a gloriously etched lion on it. Henry said when he made it for my Leo birthday that it was a secret picture for me to enjoy. A number of his artworks carry these secret images somewhere on them.

Henry's objects usually offer something unexpected. His playfulness abounds. Another item I enjoy looking at daily displays a Matisse-like silver female fashioned after the familiar *Blue Nudes* cut-outs of the 1940s. She lies languidly on a box that was crafted by a Japanese artist, with her arm extended and her heart-hand serving as the lock of the box.

Besides acknowledging that Henry is a masterful goldsmith fashioning delicate strands of gold into incredible figures and forms, and incorporating the most unlikely stones, one marvels at his imagination. Henry creates *sculpture* mainly

on a small scale. He works in a traditional manner—with a hammer to fashion the gold. The finished product, whether worn or displayed on a plinth, requires "up-close" observation, eliminating the peripheral element involved in looking at large sculptures.

The one thing that both Daniel and I have agreed upon with respect to Henry is to give him free range. Henry's strong need to be free to express himself is ever evident in his work. His wit and imagination need to be unfettered so that his lyrical, abstract language is able to come through. Henry refers to some of his figures as "primitive." That word might be used in reference to some items, like an exquisite pin that I own portraying a "magical" fishlike creature that contains elements of a contemporary fish and something unidentifiable.

On first encounter, Henry's work might appear simple because of the delicate lines involved, but upon closer inspection, one realizes that there are various levels figuratively and literally within which one can engage the individual objects. It is this quality that makes his works of art timeless and unique.

Among the many unique works created by Henry is a truly memorable sculpture of an eagle that I liked so much that I acquired it from Henry and donated it to the White House during the Clinton administration. I was pleased to give this piece to the nation because the international and exceptional caliber of Henry's work echoes his stature as an artist.

Henry has an affinity for the Japanese aesthetic and has emulated the rare technique of melding/layering silver onto gold. It is evident in many of his unusual and stunning objects. The Japanese have a tradition of giving their extraordinary artists national status. In my estimation, Henry is a national treasure.

Agnes Gund
President Emerita of MoMA
December 2008

PREFACE

There is one process everyone in the arts must follow. It is the road to finished expression. How we get from A to Z depends on life experiences, education and training, the physical dexterity of the practitioner, and both the nuances and the major factors that make us what we are. These combined elements prepare the road, sometimes full of bold curves, toward our intended expression.

A good example is Francisco Goya, whose artistic expression was largely the product of the terrible events unraveling in Spain during his lifetime. Another example of artistic daring closer to my own time and circle of friends is the ceramicist Judith Motzkin, who forces her porcelain forms to defy the laws of gravity; then, to really prove her worth, she fires the pieces in a raku kiln, where survival is a touch-and-go proposition at best. Or I think of Maria Callas, whose voice gets to where it is going with seemingly little regard for the trip. Her voice may falter, but the grand result is obvious. Damn the torpedoes—full steam ahead!

I don't know whether the battle is with ourselves or with the medium in which we work—probably a combination of both. Dylan Thomas's admonition—"Do not go gentle into that good night"—hardens our resolve. Where I fit in is anyone's guess. I do know that if you want to make an eagle, you'd better feel and act like one. If one fears the medium, it will show up in the work as something stilted and lifeless. Instead I go to the gold as if I am the master. Sometimes the gold wins, and I have to remelt it and begin all over again.

I work as a traditional smith. I cast my own ingot or work from a bar, and by using various hammers and simple tools forge the gold into different forms. With the exception of my torch, polishing wheel, and flexible shaft, the tools I use are the same as those used by goldsmiths throughout history. I find it very exciting using ancient techniques for present-day expression.

Henry Shawah
November 2008

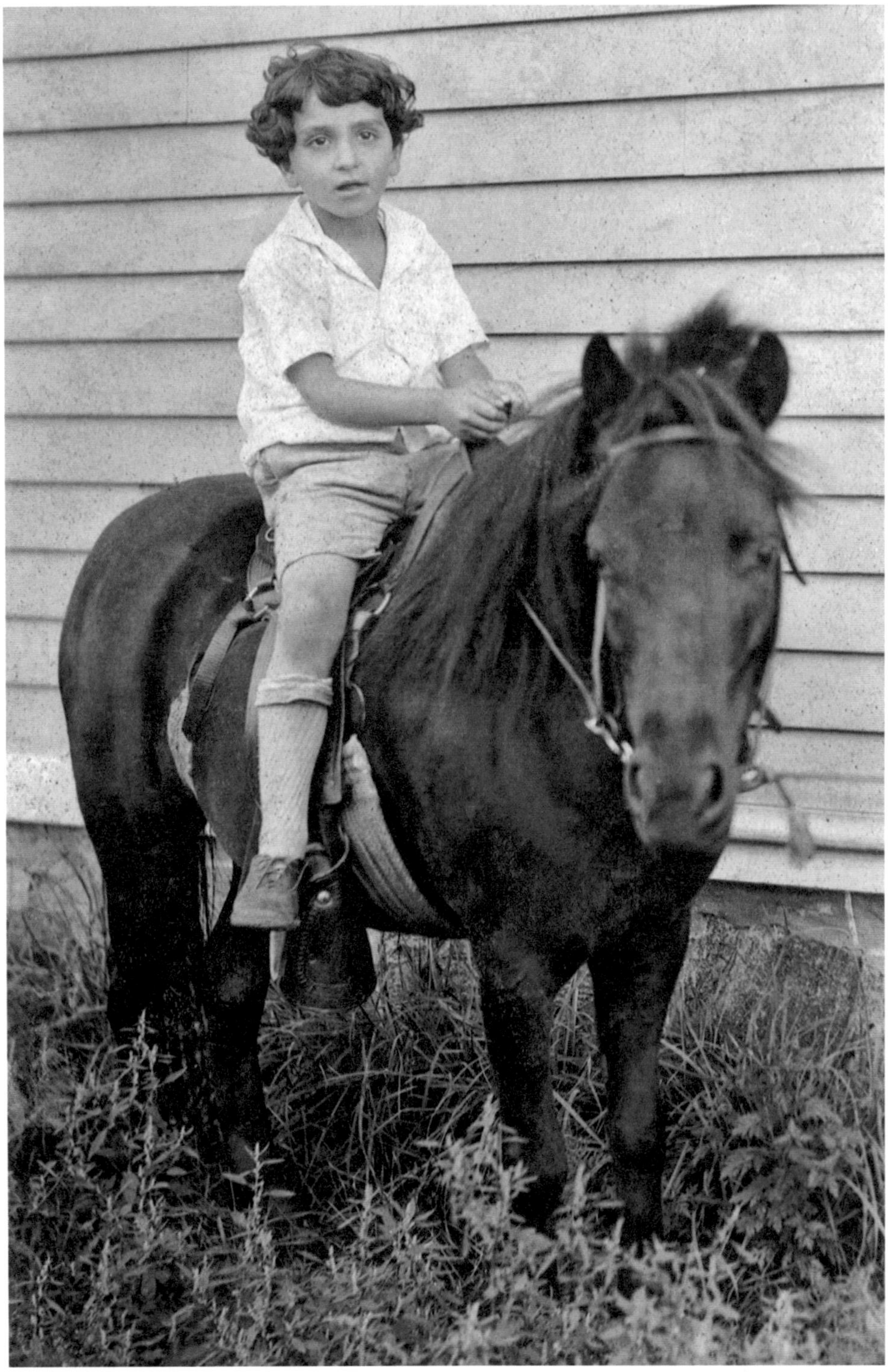

HENRY ON A PONY, C. 1927

CHILDHOOD

In many ways we were no different from other children growing up in Bridgeport, Connecticut, in the late 1920s and 30s. We played "ring a liveo" and "tin-can policeman," and we made guns from the ends of orange crates that fired thick rubber bands sliced from old inner tubes. We built tents out of potato sacks and formed clubs in empty garages. We lived in fear of the Summer Street Gang but learned to swear at them from a distance in Russian and Polish. We yelled "Esh tou perkwa," which we were sure meant "Go to hell" in—in some language. In fact growing up in the south end of Bridgeport meant your fluency in foreign languages consisted of fat round swear words that flew off your tongue in Russian, Polish, Greek, Arabic, Yiddish, and good old American. *American!* We were geniuses compared to our parents, who, poor things, struggled and struggled with this language that seemed to come from another planet. At home we spoke Arabic and English. Our parents were turn-of-the-century refugees from the northern part of Syria, which to their horror had become the southern part of Turkey and the scene of death marches and unimaginable deprivation. They were treated the same as the Armenians in that regard.

We, their children, were the beneficiaries of the WPA arts program. Bridgeport had a symphony orchestra led by Frank Foti. Alec Demis and I saw our first stage play at age ten or so; it was about an airplane that exploded on the stage. In the summer the orchestra played evening concerts in Seaside Park. And I remember our constant walks around the bandstand—not so much to hear the music from a different venue but to see what the girls were doing on the other side. We learned about sex from Alec's older cousin, Charlie. Men put their "thing" in the "thing" ladies had between their legs and that was called sex—we laughed and laughed at such a bizarre idea until with horror we realized that's what our parents did. Needless to say we tried sex—sometimes called Hospital or Doctor. But we never realized the pure joy of sex until we experienced the "feeling," usually self-induced.

Our aunts all had large bosoms, to which we were clutched during visits or when we needed comforting. Comfort and that wonderful smell of rose water. My brother played the violin and hated to be kissed. We all danced and clapped our hands and sang popular Arabic songs taught by our recently arrived immigrant relatives and neighbors. And when we kids were alone, my brother played popular songs of the thirties, led by my sister. We sang, getting the words from large printed song sheets: "You and I are never left alone on necessity..."

FATHERS

Our fathers were wonders. Mine took us fishing and made me a whistle from willow growing on the lake banks. And when we were very small and lived in Norwalk, we would sit in the back of my father's grocery store, near the stove, where he told us stories in Arabic and sang to us many of the parts. One of the songs went, "Oh, beautiful daughters of Abu Ziloof. My eyes are upon you. May your steed drink crystal water even though the stream is cloudy." And once when he went to New York to buy supplies for his store, he brought back a big teddy bear for me. And, for all of us, oranges that he said were the largest and most beautiful in all of New York.

I loved watching my father shave and prayed for the day when I would shave. PaPa did the whole scene: the cup, the shaving brush, the rich lather on his shaving brush, and then the gold-colored safety razor gliding over his face, carefully avoiding his mustache. After each swipe the razor was shaken clean in a cup of hot water. Then he took apart the razor by unscrewing the handle and thoroughly rinsed each of the three segments in hot water, drying them on the towel. Next came the facial rinse-off and the final splashing of cold water over his face. After drying, he would form the towel over his hand and sprinkle powder from a tall red can that had an alluring female face on it. He'd pat his face with the powdered towel, and the ritual was over. It was beautiful.

My first shave came when I was home alone. Everyone was at my sister's house across the street. I had watched the fuzz over my lip grow and thicken, and come the day when it had to be removed, I followed my father's ritual. I couldn't wait when I had finished to run across the street to my sister's and confront our whole family with, "I shaved!" No bells rang and there was no applause. To this day I do feel let down that there wasn't more excitement about my first shave.

SHOES WITH CUBAN HEELS

You never saw PaPa when he wasn't dressed properly. He was quite dapper, with his handlebar mustache beautifully groomed, ends twisted and forming perfect Cs. He was very handsome, and I'm sure the ladies flocked to him. My mother used to say, "Your father, your father, he overcomes women like sleep."

PaPa spent lots of time teaching us how to buy good clothes and shoes, pointing out the supple leather and the lasting qualities of the shoes he had just bought. I think I was about twelve or thirteen when my father took me downtown to buy a pair of shoes for me. It was the era of the tango, and I was obsessed with the idea of dancing in the Cuban or South American style with gorgeous black-haired ladies. But no one who did the tango would consider shoes unless they had a Cuban heel. Cuban heels were about twice the height of ordinary heels—which helped you prance around the ladies and stamp your feet. Dear lovable PaPa made my dreams come true. He bought me the black shoes—Cuban heels and pointy toes. I regret to this day there is no record of me in knickers wearing fancy shoes with Cuban heels. I don't recall a single comment from my older brother or sister when this apparition appeared before them. I think there was probably a lot of sniggering and joking, and I suppose I am blessed not to recall their exact comments.

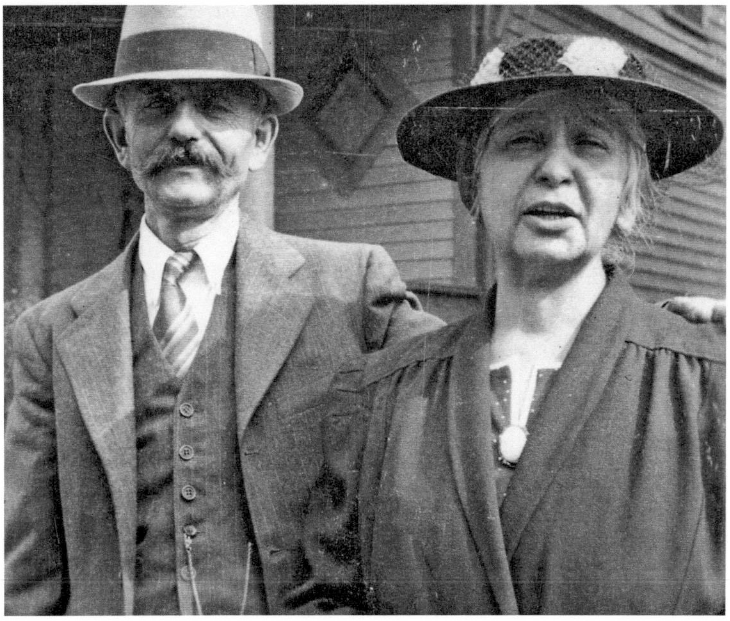

MAMA AND PAPA

PARENTS' STORIES

Since it looked like we were never going to see the land of our heritage or meet our grandparents, we would gather around the stove inhaling the delicious, pungent smell of the toasting orange peel, which was our winter incense, and listen to our parents tell stories. My father was best at the Arabic classics and loved comical fables and tales. Our mother was the family historian, who told us about the lives they had lived in the old country. How they washed their clothes and draped them over fragrant bushes to dry and how, when they were brought inside, the house would smell of the gardens. How the meals were prepared; how the bread was baked in a *tenoor,* a round brick and clay oven with an open top heated by embers in its base; how the flatbread was stuck to the inside walls to bake. In the warm weather the family would literally move out to their gardens. Men tended the small herds of sheep, hunted, and took care of the gardens. Women raised silkworms, baked, looked after the children, and crocheted laces.

Here is a typical story told by my mother:

> *My dear children, during the spring and on special holidays we girls wore our best clothes, and high above the Mediterranean, swings were strung in the trees along the bluffs. As we swung, we sang, one girl picking up the tune and passing it to the next. And after the tune had passed from girl to girl, we would all join in.*

I always thought this must be what heaven was like.

This is my father's story about the bear:

> *My dear children, light of my vision, listen to your father's story. There was and there was not a woodcutter who lived high up in Mount Moosa. It was also where a large and fearsome bear lived—fearsome and not so fearsome, but very curious and almost friendly. Everyone said the bear's main object in life was to mate with the beautiful women in the village. One day the woodcutter was splitting a long log from a tree he had felled. He drove an iron wedge into the log,*

opening a large split, when his wife called him to dinner. He left his work and headed home. Who should come passing by but the bear. He ambled as bears amble and looked at the log. "What has this foolish man done?" asked the bear. "Does he know this iron wedge is splitting this beautiful log?" He squatted over the log, one leg to the right and one leg to the left and in a most helpful manner grasped the iron wedge and with all his strength gave a mighty pull. Out came the wedge. A thunderous snap followed by a mighty howl. The split closed on the bear's ample testicles, and they were locked in the tree forever.

This story reminds me of another story PaPa told us children about my godfather, who was a wonderful cranky guy and the bane of his wife's existence. Fortunately, she was a woman of great humor. She was doing the laundry in the old-time washing machine with roller wringers. My godfather couldn't resist bending over the machine to tell his wife she wasn't doing the laundry properly—when what should happen? His tie got caught in the roller wringer. He was being dragged closer and closer to the machine, his necktie rapidly becoming a noose. His eyes started to bulge. His wife, hysterical with laughter, barely released the wringer in time.

AMTI BARBARA

Weddings and christenings were great events for all of us. Always music, dance, and food—or in proper order, food, music, and dance. I wonder what our "American" neighbors thought when our female relatives recited honoring poems and ululated to greet the bride and groom. Unfailingly, the beautiful Italian wife of a relative would have a seizure at these affairs, and all the ladies would gather around to protect her modesty and help revive her. My Aunt Barbara said Italian ladies always had seizures because they ate too much macaroni. But then why didn't Ami Mike's Italian wife ever have seizures, Amti Barbara?

Amti (which in Arabic means "aunt" and is a respectful form of address to older ladies) could be a fearsome woman. And it seemed whenever we visited her she was sitting in her big rocking chair smoking her water pipe. She was large and strong and worked in the local foundry, inspecting iron pieces for proper castings. Her favorite curse was "salama bitch," and she didn't hesitate to apply it to all except little children. Her husband was a rather small, frail alcoholic who sold bananas from his pushcart. I never knew why he was nicknamed Suttle ("the bucket," in Arabic), unless it was because he rattled on and on like an empty bucket in his pushcart. In any case, *suttle* was not a complimentary term. Everyone liked him, though, because they marveled at how he got along with Amti Barbara. When he was home, you could hear Amti Barbara's "salama bitches" bouncing off her poor husband. With all his problems, he maintained a fierce sense of humor. At a wake being held for one of his cousins, the cousin's brother faced the dead man in the coffin and wailed in a voice of despair and sorrow, "Brother, Brother, where, oh, where have you gone?" The Suttle's quick reply, "Dear cousin, he's gone to the miller's to grind some wheat." The assembled mourners covered their faces to hide their laughter.

FRANK FACHINA

Frank Fachina was our local butcher. His wife, Mrs. Fachina, in summer was the guardian of the lemon-ice tub outside the shop door—a green wooden barrel about four feet tall and fifteen inches wide with a metal insert surrounded by chipped ice. For two cents we could have a lemon ice in a pleated paper cup, which once empty we would turn into a chef's hat by covering the opening with our lips and giving it a puff or two. Mrs. Fachina always greeted us with, "How's a you mod, how's a you fod?" and I think we made up "How's a you brod? How's a you sis?" In her hand she held a stack of holy pictures—saints and angels—like a deck of playing cards. She kissed each one, raised it to her forehead, put it at the back of the deck, and went to the next saint. This went on all day.

Mr. Fachina growled from inside the butcher shop. He was a fearsome man when provoked, either by alcohol or youths or picture-kissing wives, and was known to chase undesirables with his cleaver. The Summer Street Gang never taunted him—or Mrs. Fachina. For they knew their fate was sealed should they tangle with Frank Fachina or his wife. From inside the butcher shop, somewhere at the back, would come the garlicky smells of Italian cooking. Who was responsible for these aromas, which were so awesomely delicious you wanted to roll on the floor like an ecstatic dog? We never knew, because Mrs. Fachina was always somewhere at the front of the shop, in both hot and cool weather, kissing, kissing, and kissing.

Next to the butcher shop lived the Pollotti's. Mr. Pollotti once gave Bolous, a boarder in our neighbor's house, such a punch he fell to the sidewalk and just lay there. I think Bolous had made a pass at one of the Pollotti girls. We ran home to tell our parents, who were all sitting on our front porch, that Bolous was down and breathing heavily, but in our faltering Arabic what came out instead was, "Bolous is leaking air!"

IM HABIB

We all loved Im Habib—but cautiously. An elderly neighbor who sold linens and ladies' underwear door to door, she never hesitated to embrace us, and what kisses! It was like firecrackers going off in your ear. Sometimes we ran away in self-defense before she could reach us, cautioning our friends, "It's Im Habib!" We scattered like sparrows in a field, and we could hear her calling, "Come my darlings and angels, let me see your beautiful faces!"

My father tells of a visit he made to Im Habib. He had heard she was not well. He was amazed when he entered her kitchen to see slices of a whole loaf of bread toasting on the surface of her coal stove. "Im Habib, are you expecting company?" my father said, eyeing the toasting bread. "No, love of my vision," she said, "I feel sickly and don't want to die on an empty stomach."

SCHOOL DAYS

We all went to Prospect School and marched out at 3:00 p.m. to a Sousa march played on the big hall Victrola by our classmate Grace Visconti. I could never figure out how she got the job except that her family specialized in fine Italian lace—whereas our mothers worked at Howie Manufacturing Company making garter buckles on old foot presses and speaking in Arabic and other foreign languages above the clatter of the shop.

Miss Previance, to us a totally other-worldly personage, appeared in our schoolroom to give us music lessons. She wore a quivery pince-nez and black lace dresses that had long and short parts at the hemline. As she warbled new songs to us with her whole being—*warble warble* went the voice, wobble wobble went the pince-nez.

All around in Miss Walter's fourth-grade room were pictures of musical instruments representing a full symphony orchestra. We learned their names and listened to the sounds on the Victrola. I was very good in that department—maybe because in the first grade I sang with the Bluebirds instead of the Pigeons. However, it was in the same room that I failed reading and had to be held back. Reading! Reading! Why can't we just have pictures?

The next move was to Miss Doherty's room, grade five. Love, oh love, oh maddening love. Who could be so perfect, so beautiful? Presents, presents for Miss Doherty. She was sweet, and I still remember her smile as she accepted a piece of jewelry, probably my sister's. What she taught evades me, but what I learned—oh, what I learned—the sweetness, the hopefulness of love.

Then we went to Miss Johnson's room for sixth, seventh, and eighth grade—she truly loved us and we loved her. She was tough but caring, and her auto license plate was HMJ, for Helen M. Johnson—some lady. She said I could make things with my hands. I won first prize, which was one dollar, in the contest for the best play. And we put on the play for our parents and visitors.

Then came great shame. It was the height of the Depression. The bank repossessed our house, and we had to move to four rooms over a store. We left behind our home of several bedrooms and the beautiful blue-and-gold wallpaper that covered our living-room walls with golden wheat sheaves and was the joy of my father and mother.

Even though my father coughed up blood from time to time due to a previous tuberculosis infection and my mother worked on a foot press at Howie Manufacturing Company, it wasn't all that bad. My brother found a good job as a machinist and my dear sister, who was married several years earlier to a loving and hard-working man, helped when she could. And joy of joy, I was excused from high school algebra. "He will be in school for the rest of his life," they said. So I took art and biology instead and loved both and did well.

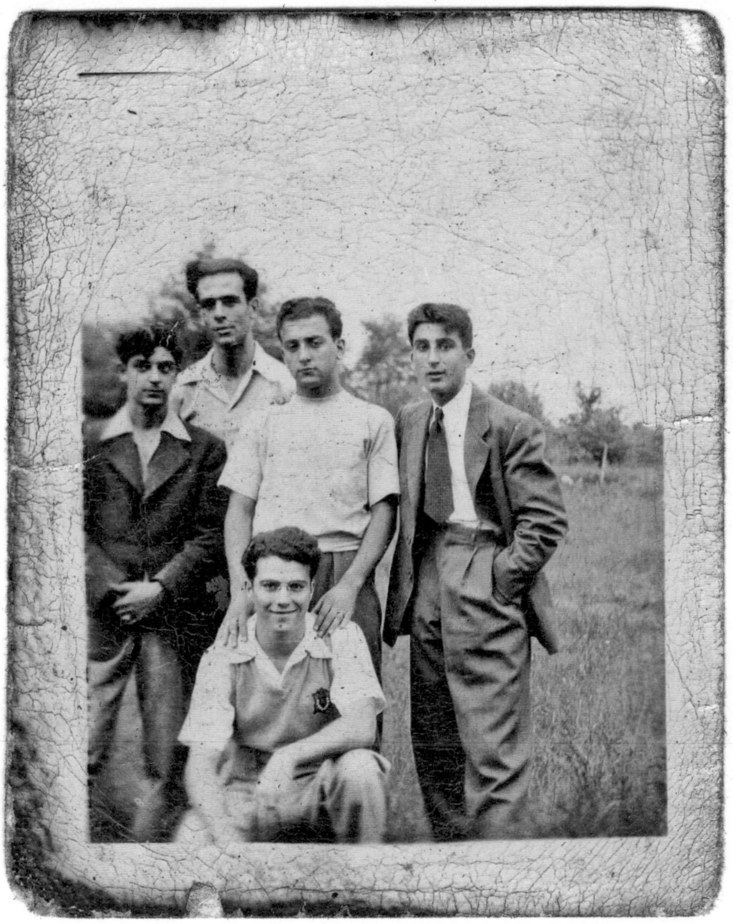

OUR TEENAGE GANG, LATE 1930S

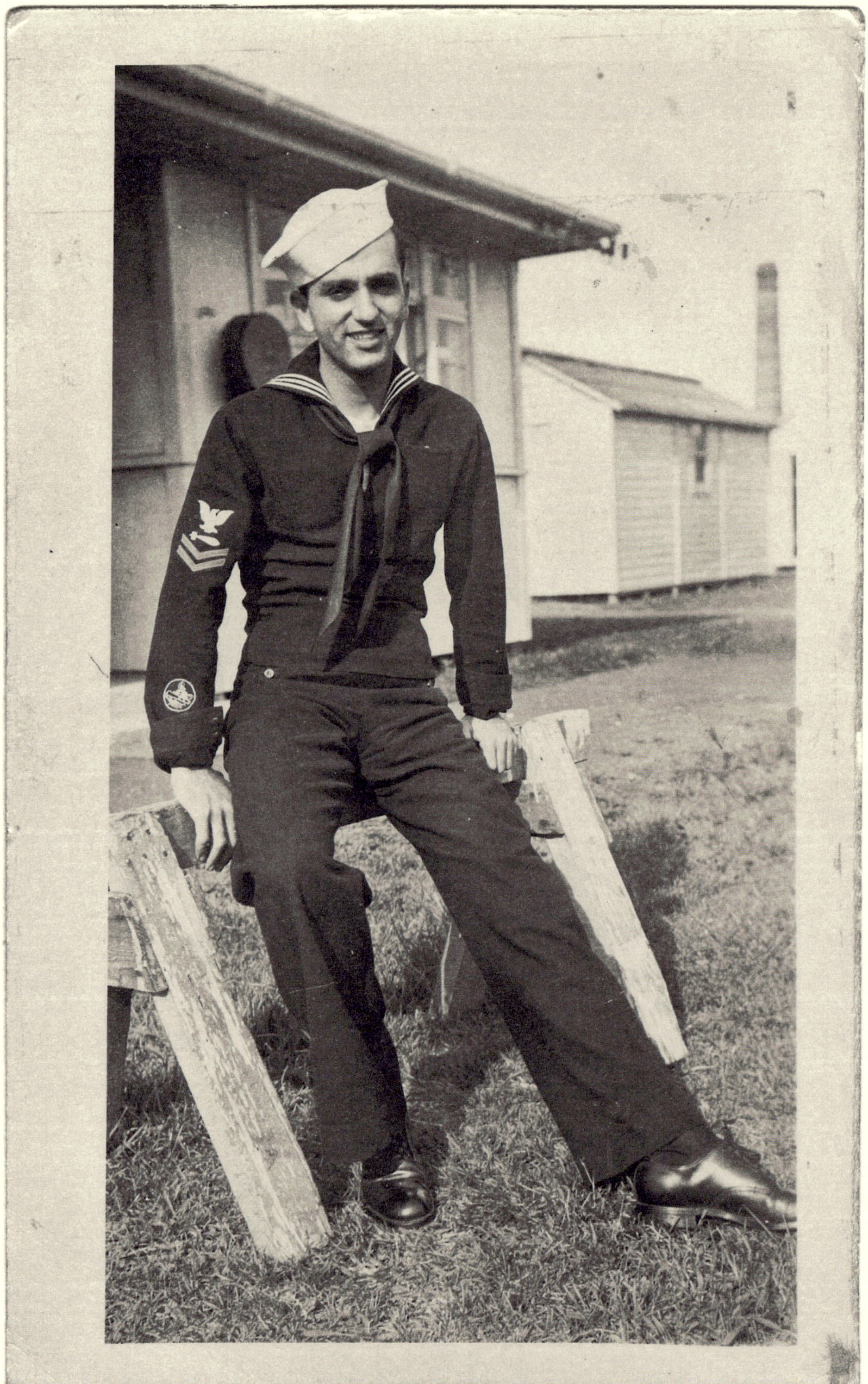

HENRY ON BASE, NEW ZEALAND

NAVY YEARS, 1942–1945

WAR

Strike the flint
that burns the sun
Our lighted way
a walk on fire
Our ashes sift
through dreams of kill
that eat our hearts
to
standing still

After high school graduation, it was time to think about war. When my brother was called up in the first draft, we hung a service flag in our window. Later my buddy John Kassib and I, swayed by Charlie Baker, who had enlisted in the Navy and said it was great, enlisted too. But John was sent to Newport, Rhode Island, and I was sent off to the Great Lakes. John joined a submarine crew and I joined a PT squadron and headed for the Pacific. Miracle of miracles, I eventually ran into my brother's army outfit in the South Pacific. We had our pictures taken together to send home. We were all spared death and serious injury except for our friend and cousin Louis Gramesty. As a tail gunner in a B27 shot down over Germany, he was held in German prison camps and suffered the horrors of his experience long after he was liberated.

My Navy career began in New Haven, Connecticut, where all the recruits were lined up for physical exams. It seemed there was no end of blood. It was on the technicians' gowns and spattered over examining tables near a line of chairs where the weak of heart sat with their heads between their legs—recovering from the sight of blood and needles. Then there were the very weak, lying prone on cots, having mercifully passed out. We were prodded and pushed, our hearts listened to. It seemed every aperture in our bodies was explored. Then it was back home to await the results of the exams—were we in or out? Soon enough we were back to New Haven from Bridgeport, where we were shipped to the Great Lakes Naval Station, all of us now apprentice seamen, the bottom of the bottom.

It was November 1942 when we arrived at the Great Lakes. There were no pea coats to keep us warm. Our barracks, newly completed, had no hot water, and heat was definitely minimal. We marched and went to training classes in the shivering cold wind coming off the Great Lakes, wearing only our shirts and thirteen-button pants.

Our leader, mentor, and confidant was a wonderful schoolteacher, then a Navy chief. When we were out in the open shivering, he was too. He never wore his coat, and we loved him for it. We all hacked and coughed. You'd think we would soon be dead of pneumonia but youth prevailed. We all survived and our chief prepared us for the tests that would determine the school choices we'd have. Most passed with flying colors. I chose torpedo school, and I was sure I'd at last be with my buddy John at the torpedo station in Newport, Rhode Island.

Worse luck, there was a torpedo school at Great Lakes, and there I stayed for many weeks. I made great friends and convinced a group of four or five of us to volunteer for PT boat duty. We finally were sent to Newport for PT training, but by then John had already left for submarine school. Next we were off to Boston, and then to New Orleans on assignment to our new PT squadron, the boats built by Higgins. There were three types of PT boats: Higgins, Huckins, and the elegant Elcos made in Rhode Island. Well, you can't have everything, and at least the Higgins boats were a lot better looking than the Huckins.

Our cruise training complete and our boats shipshape, we were off to Florida on a shakedown. But first the glories of New Orleans; wonderful people, super foods, and the joys and, I think, arrogance of dating a nurse ensign. Not too sure it was something the Navy approved of. But it was dinner at La Louisianne, a fancy restaurant, and oh, my gosh. Florida here I come.

Our stay in Florida was brief and our twelve-boat squadron headed for Panama via Jamaica. Oh, Jamaica, Jamaica. Sex. Sex. Sex. No virgin sailors left.

In Panama, we were loaded onto the decks of two enormous tankers, and we headed for the Pacific, not daring to think about being torpedoed. Our half of the squadron, six boats, was on the deck of the Esso Richmond loaded with high-octane gas. We arrived in Espiritu Santo, Vanuatu, and then at our base in Bougainville, Papua New Guinea, an unbelievably beautiful place with an active volcano that sent up wisps of smoke as we sped over the blue-green waters to our night patrol areas. It was like riding a surfboard—were we on the water or flying? Whatever it was, it felt great. That is, until we realized there was a war on, and the enemy was trying to shoot us out of the water, and sometimes (oh God!) the calm beautiful water was a monster threatening to devour our small plywood boats and us. A seventy-eight-foot plywood boat in a fifteen-foot sea was like a cork on Niagara Falls: three powerful twelve-cylinder Packard engines pushing us up the crest of the waves—and dropping us down. It was half like flying, half like being thrown off a cliff. The choice: pray or sing—but don't piss your pants because then you will be cold all night.

SOON WE DROWN, SOON WE DIE

And then the waves
that break the sun
crack our way
beyond the top,
and drop us in
the rock and sand.
To count our youth
among the dregs

Discharged from the military, I realized I no longer had the Navy sheltering me. It was home to a sick father and a mother still working in Howie's buckle factory. My brother was also back, and with the exception of my sister, who had married before the war, we were all to live in four rooms over the grocery store. Panic. Panic. How could I live at home? How could I afford to go off on my own?

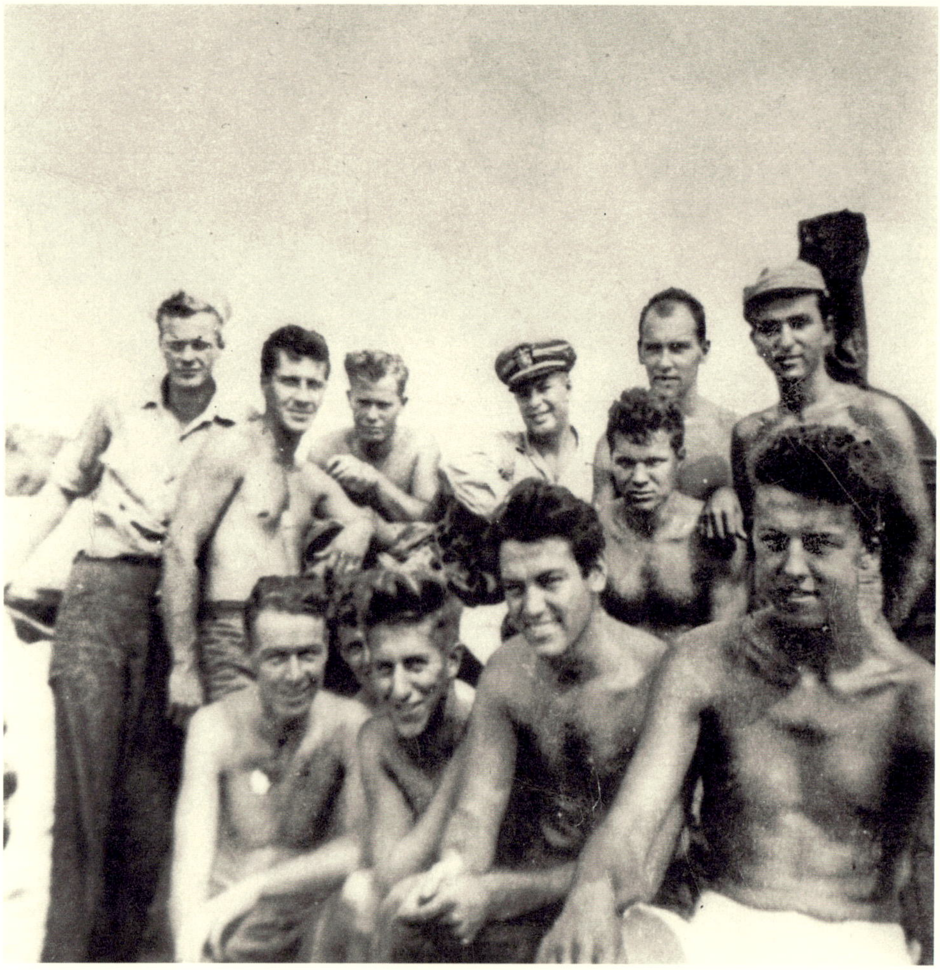

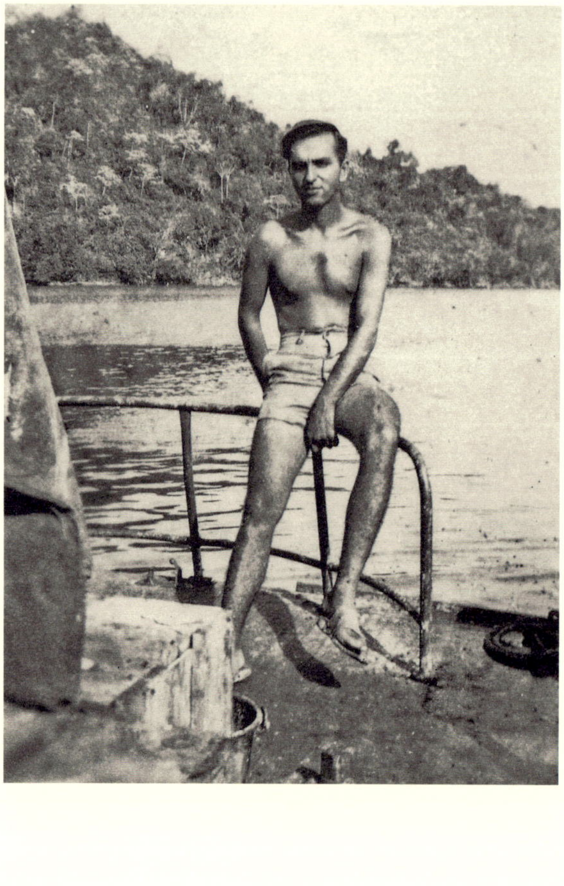

ABOVE: CREW OF USS PT 286, SQUAD 23, IN BOUGAINVILLE, THE SOUTH PACIFIC, 1943 (HENRY AT FAR RIGHT, TOP)
LEFT: HENRY AT THE STERN OF PT 286

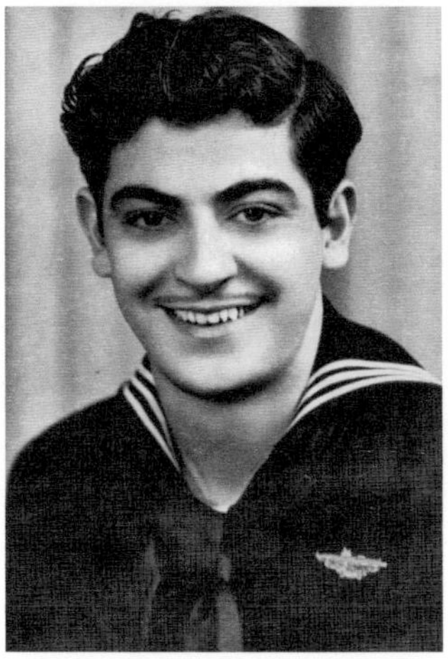

LEFT: BEST BUDDY JOHN KASSIB, 1943

BELOW: HENRY AND BROTHER GEORGE MEET IN SOUTH PACIFIC, 1944

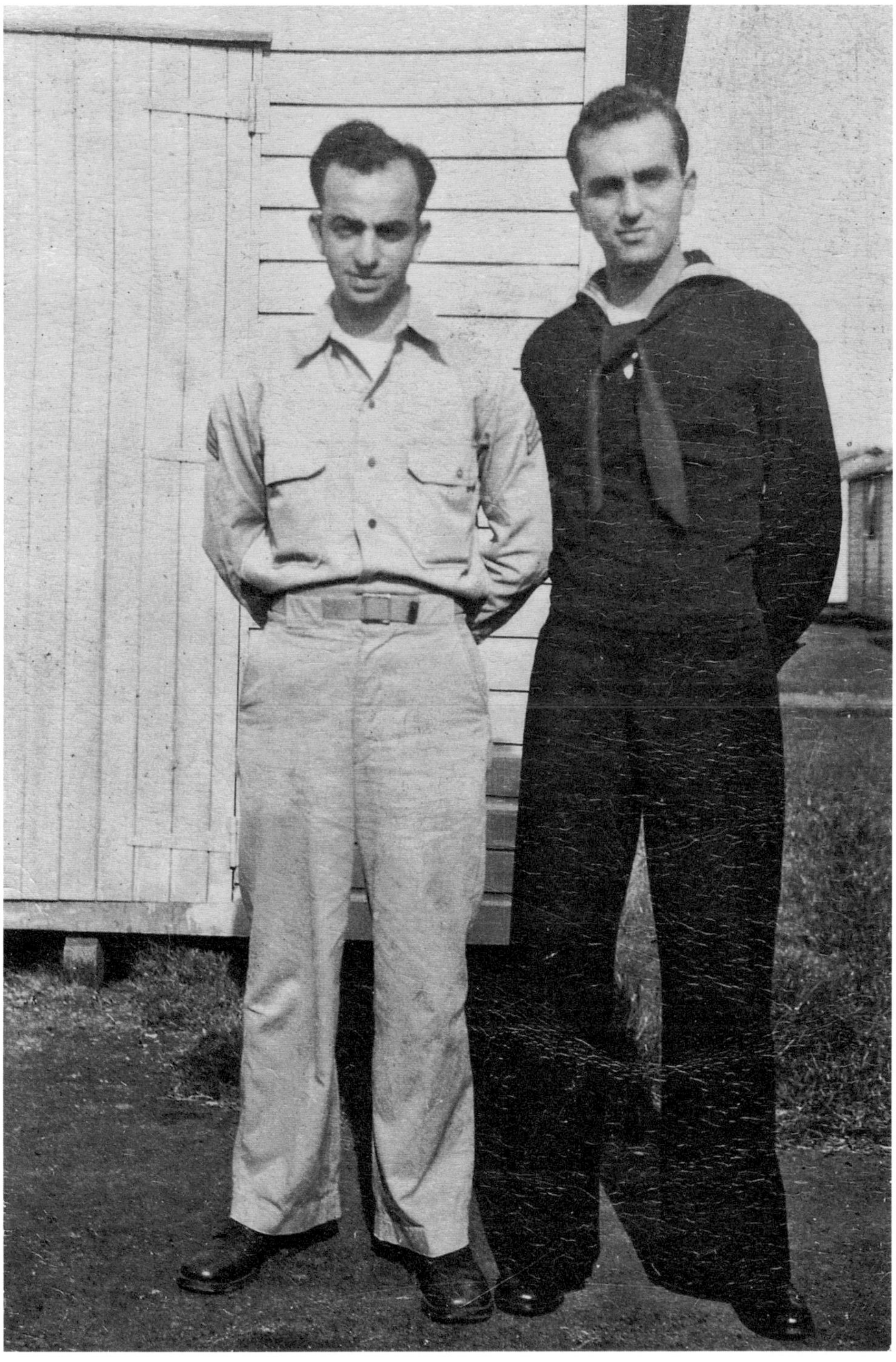

ART SCHOOL AND TEACHING

Lucky guy, I was accepted at Pratt Institute when I finished my Navy duty. The war was over and we were all heroes. I cringe with guilt when I think of how different it was for the Vietnam veterans. At Pratt the returning servicemen were easily spotted—wearing remnants of uniforms. There was a great shortage of civilian clothing. However, I'm not sure we did it because we couldn't afford proper clothes. I think we really wanted to impress the ladies. Here we are, gals, returning heroes.

I registered in an interior design course, the closest I could get to architecture, considering I'd never make it through architecture with my appalling math skills. Interior design was really interior architecture taught by a brilliant group of teachers. Our department head was Konrad Wittman, one of Germany's state architects who left Hamburg in the late 1930s. I think it was really my awakening to the arts—real hard work—but here were these guys Picasso and Matisse and the music and the field trips and the actors. I think if our classwork and assignments were not so demanding we all would have turned into vagabond artists. I daydreamed about becoming a sculptor, but fortunately or unfortunately there was no such course at Pratt.

I left Pratt in 1948 with a three-year certificate in interior design. Because during the war I was stationed in Boston at the Navy's Fargo building, I thought that Boston might be a great place to work and live. Friends snuck me into the Harvard dormitories, and by day I schlepped my portfolio from place to place and finally landed a job at Irving and Casson A. H. Davenport, designing ship interiors.

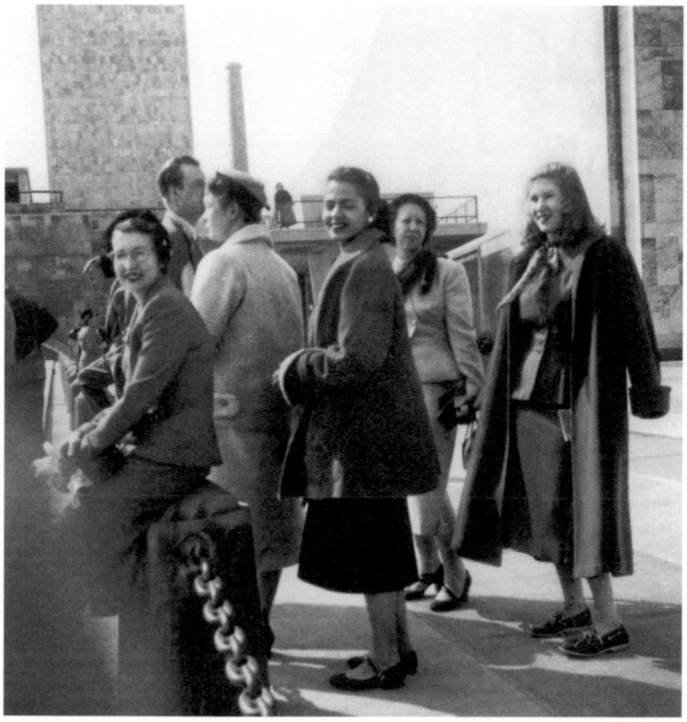

HENRY'S BOSTON UNIVERSITY STUDENTS ON A FIELD TRIP TO NEW YORK, 1953

Irving and Casson was like a Medici workshop. Logs came in from all over the world and left as church interiors, St. John the Divine and I think St. Patrick's Cathedral. Finished furniture filled the Newport mansions, and Pellegrini the sculptor created statues for churches and public places. When I would visit his studio on the top floor of one of Boston's famous buildings, he would say in words brushed with Scotch whiskey, "Just remember, I make the best Jesuses in the country."

Next I worked for an architect as a draftsman and taught an evening design course at Vesper George, a now-defunct art school. Then it was back to Boston University for a BS in art education and an invitation to stay on to reorganize and teach a course in interiors.

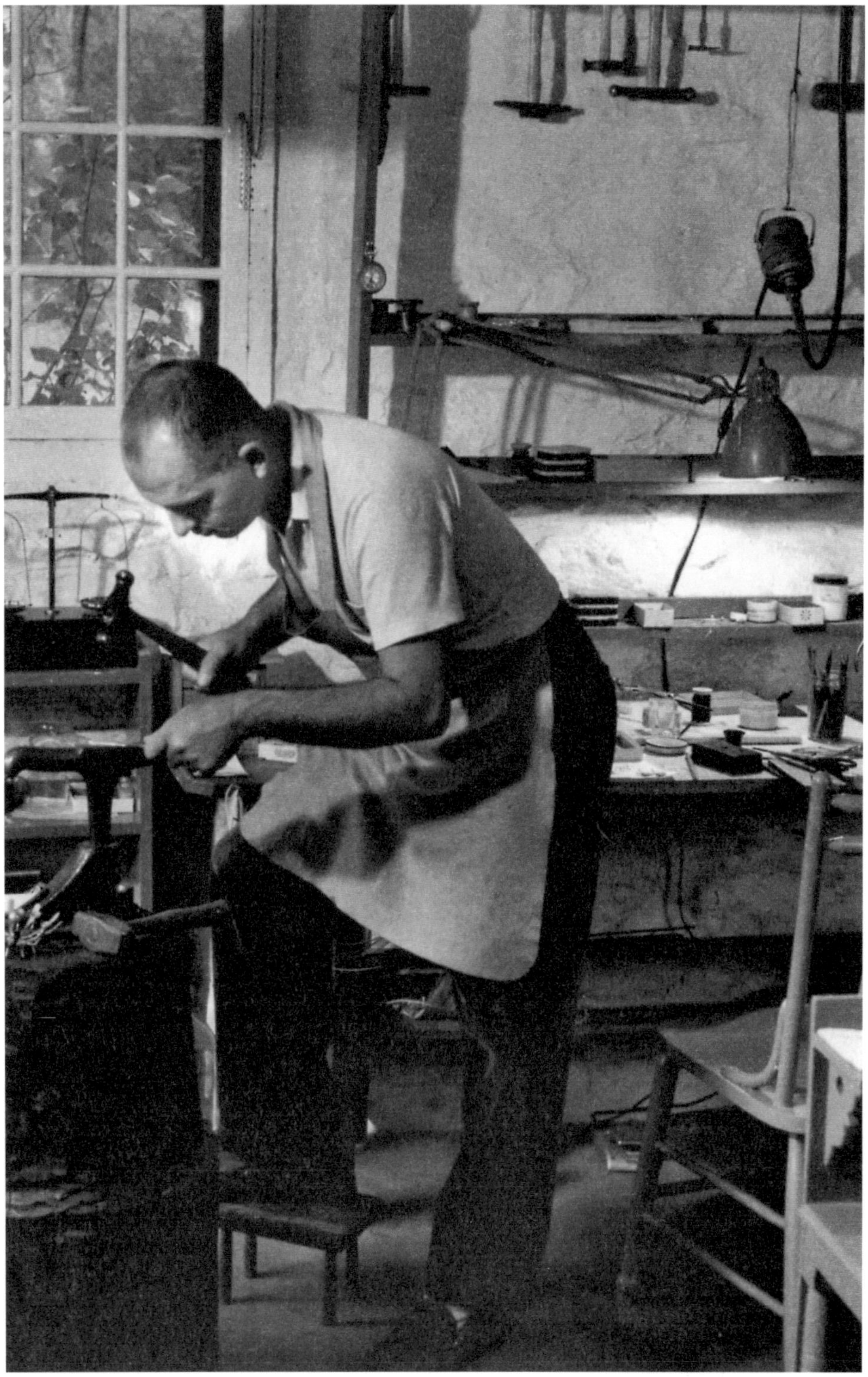

HENRY AT WORK IN HIS NANTUCKET STUDIO, 1957

NANTUCKET

It was during my teaching stint at Boston in 1953 that I took a share in the back of my friend's gift shop on Nantucket Island and began my first serious attempt at making jewelry—in between surf fishing, collecting stones, etcetera. I took my work to Georg Jensen in New York that fall, and miracle of miracles, they bought several of my pieces and displayed them in their Fifth Avenue window. All my relatives from Brooklyn made the trip to Manhattan to see their cousin's work in Jensen's window.

I often wonder if I take my work too seriously as art. After all, it is "only" jewelry. And then I turn to sculpture, a more legitimate art form, and then I reverse it and make sculpture into jewelry. Jewelry or sculpture, I find this inner debate is resolved if I see that my work gives people pleasure or wonder, in the best of all worlds both.

I was in my late twenties or early thirties when two contrasting poetic forms, the poetry of Dylan Thomas and Japanese unrhymed verse, inspired me to write haiku-like poems. It was part of a summer my friends and I spent toasting ourselves on the warm beaches of Kennebunk, Maine, then jumping into the frigid water, listening to the delighted squeals of our lady companions.

I like the feel
of a sea worn stone
smooth edge and flowing.
Warm from the sun
I place you flat
On my cheek.

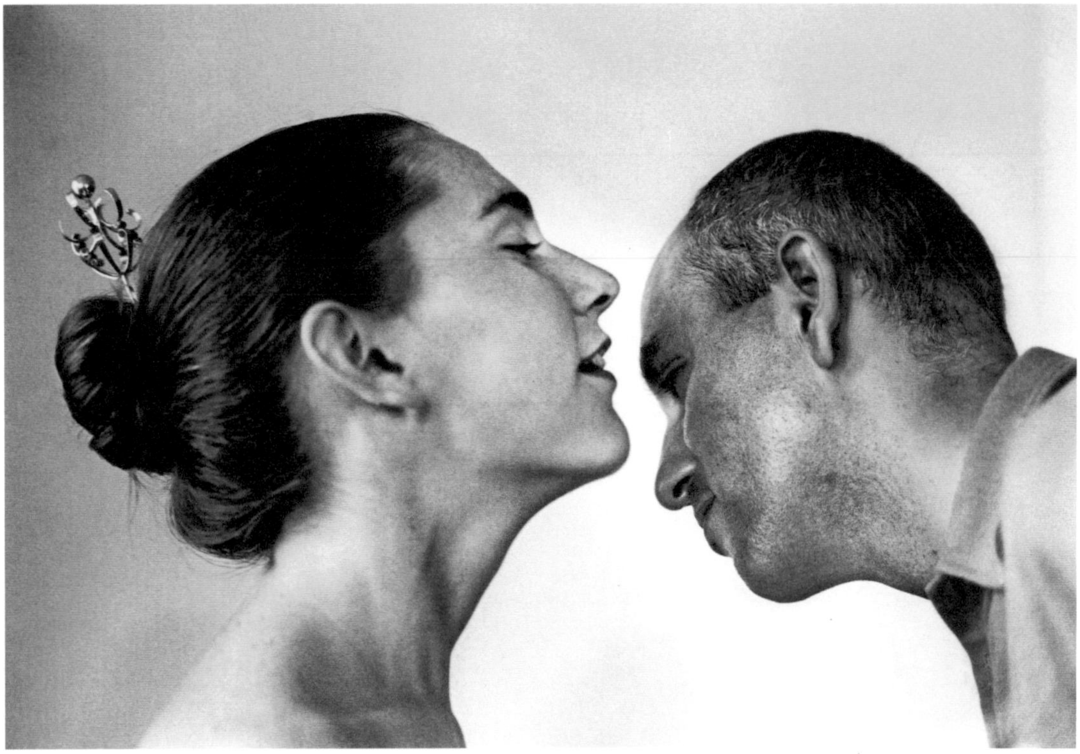

HENRY WITH MODEL, FOR "CRAFT HORIZONS," 1954–55

I am not a scholar, and I envy those who recall the date and the place where things happened. I remember the sensations and only the approximate time. I recall feelings and my own reactions easily. It seems as though the recall of these experiences is on my skin, and one look or even a touch brings it all back: fishing with my father, the fear of drowning in the war, my first arrival in some February at Heathrow Airport, waking at Espiritu Santo in the South Pacific and not quite believing in the reality of home.

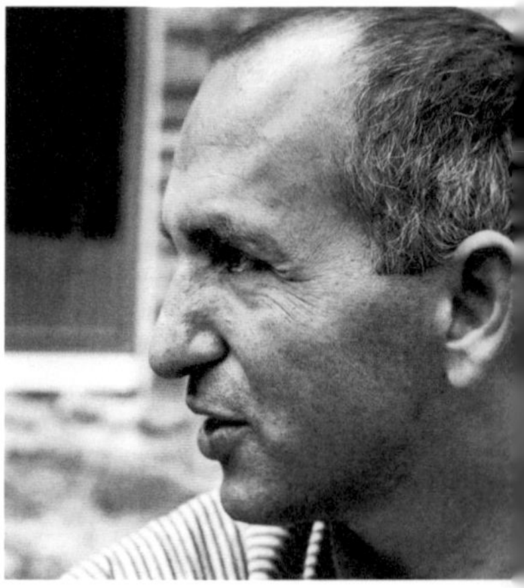

PORTRAIT FOR "CRAFT HORIZONS"

I can easily recall the blaring of the brasses in a parade and the crashing sound of the drums, the terror and exaltation as the frightening prance of horses' hooves gets closer and closer, pounding in my heart, scaring me, scaring me. I want more, and I want to run away. It's like the tango. Performing for your partner, sending messages, feeling the response, arousing an ecstasy that makes you sure you will faint, so instead you think of running away. In art, as in all things, are pluses and minuses, and they hang waiting for one or the other to prevail or let go, to fly high or come crashing to the ground. The crashing or not crashing is the small part. It's the tension of *yes!* dancing with *no!* that holds us enthralled and gasping for breath, like the beginning of an orgasm.

DICK WILLIAMS

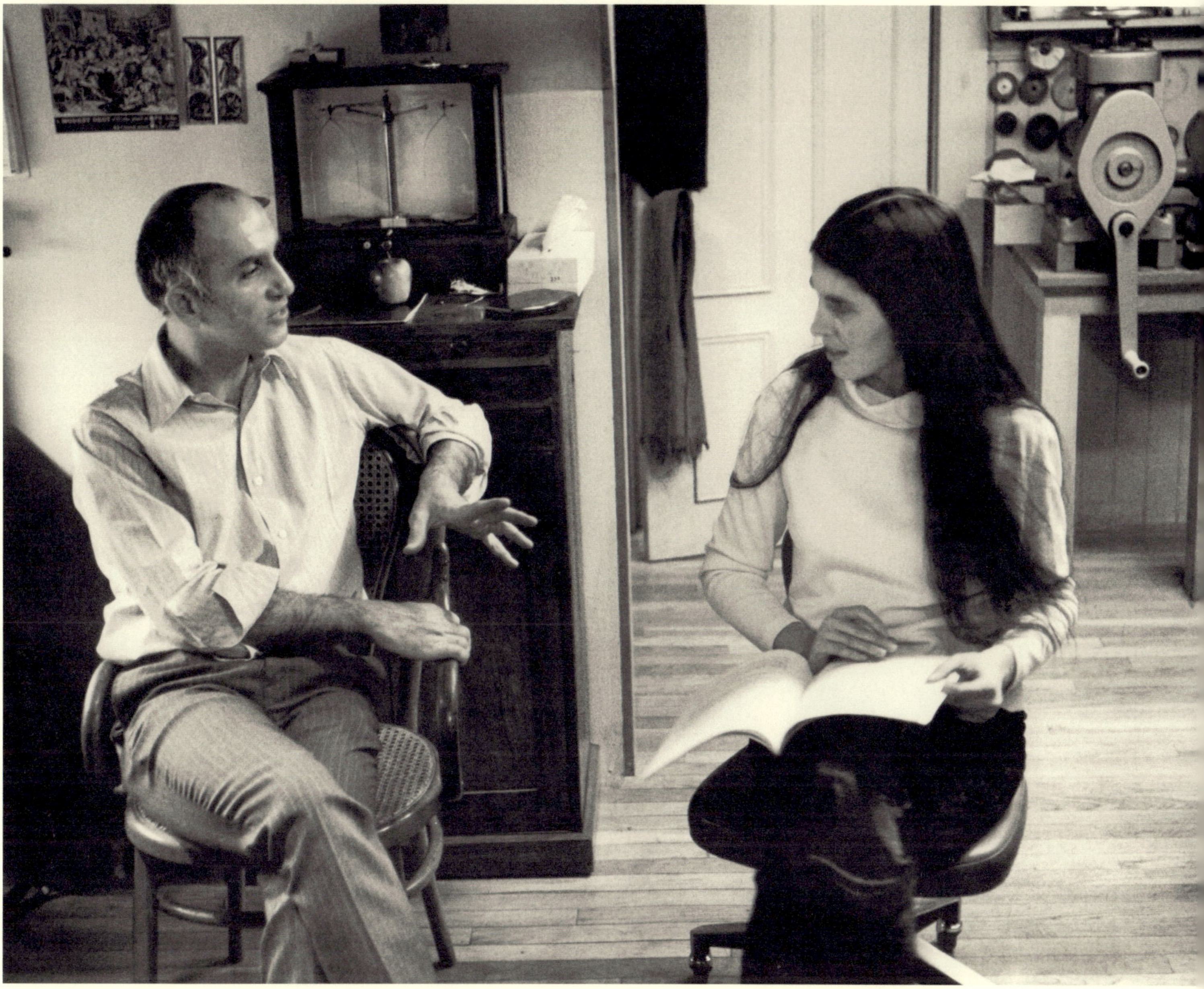

CONSULTING WITH A CLIENT

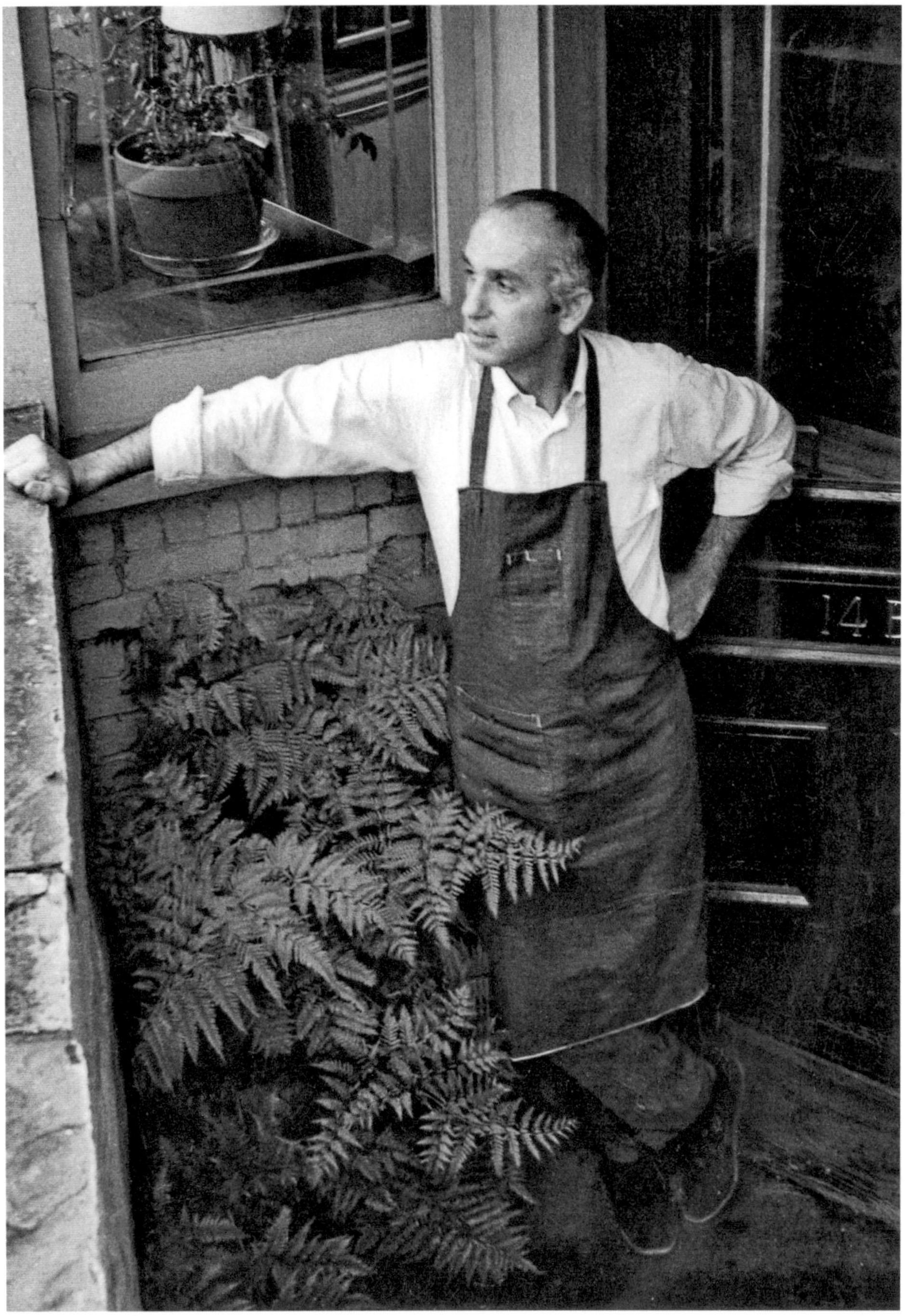

HENRY IN ENTRYWAY AT HARVARD SQUARE SHOP, 1961

HARVARD SQUARE TIMES

Joan Baez was drawing overflow crowds down the block at the Mount Auburn Club coffeehouse in Harvard Square, Cambridge. It was the early days of the coffeehouse craze, and it seemed everyone could play the guitar and sing. I'd sit in my shop forcing strangled sounds from my guitar. However, if loud enough, my tolerable singing could overcome the guitar's agony. My basement shop on Eliot Street was initially discovered by my friend and companion Ruth Leonard, who summoned me to come from New York, where I had gone for my graduate degree at Columbia, to look at the soon-to-be-vacant shop in Harvard Square. We checked out the shop and discovered there was enough room for a small studio-shop plus enough space for a cot and bureau in the back. Total rent: $60 a month. Ruth and I gathered all our friends and reclaimed the basement in a few weeks, cleaning and painting and decorating the place. My training in interior design at Pratt came in handy, and for very little cash 14B Eliot Street became what the cognoscenti called Henry Shawah's atelier. On money borrowed from the local bank, I had an opening and show in November 1960.

An addition to the décor was my black cat, Haroon al-Rashid, who would sit in the shop window enjoying the sun and all but pointing at the objects on display. In those wonderful days the shop door was never locked during the day. Objects were exhibited unattended while I worked in the back making pins, rings, and earrings—priced from $18.

On Saturdays people came to Harvard Square for lunch and browsing. Cambridge drew a much more sedate and somewhat less bohemian crowd than the "Village" in downtown Manhattan. My customers included a wonderful

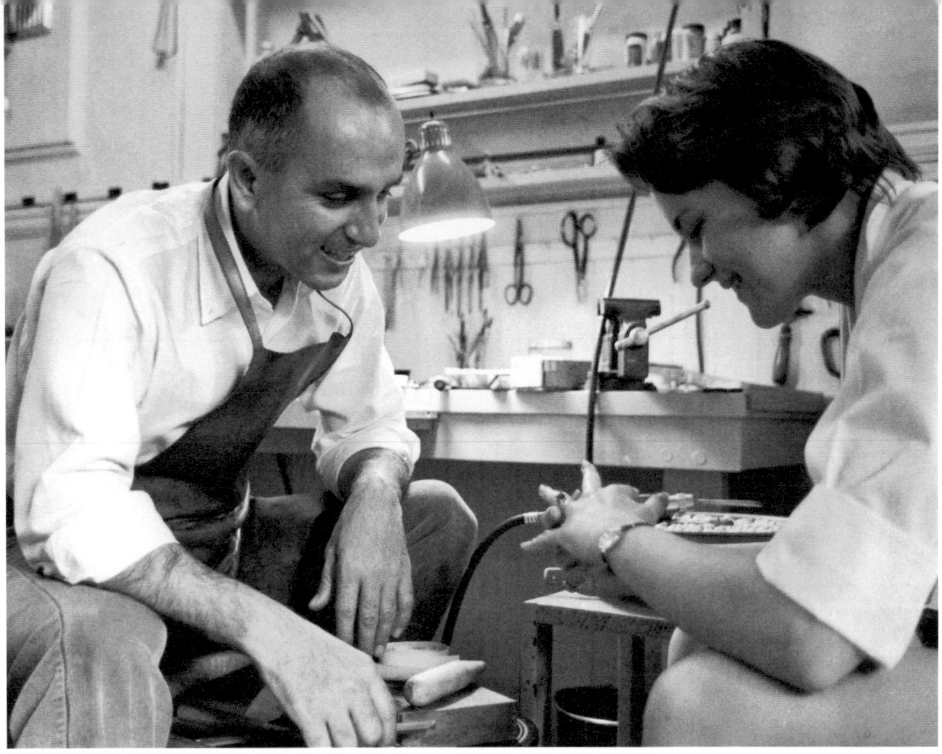

HENRY WITH RING CLIENT IN HARVARD SQUARE SHOP

group of people. Dr. Killian, president of MIT and his wife Harriet Olds, sister to the then Queen of Sikkim. Honchos at Harvard and many noted scholars and some who descended on Harvard Square, including visitors from the Worshipful Goldsmiths of London, as well as young people like Rebecca Harvey and Henry Corning, who dragged their parents into the studio for their shopping. I finally was able to move out of the back room of the studio to a great apartment and then to my current place in an 1882 building with high ceilings and plenty of room for a studio and living quarters.

Harvard Square of the sixties and early seventies was truly a great place. Lots of shops, great restaurants, and happenings all over the place. My career really took off when I had my studio-shop in Harvard Square. I was in the flyway to Harvard Business School, and to this day I still have supporters from the business school. They must have thought I was from Mars—an elegant shop on a side street and a window showing just one or two pieces of work. What I didn't like was having to be there on Saturdays. Somehow Saturday was a "me" day. I didn't mind working extended hours as long as I could keep Saturday for myself, but to survive you had to be available to the Saturday shoppers. Fortunately, I had people helping me run the shop.

My first big commission came from the Smithsonian Astrophysical Laboratories in Cambridge. The laboratory had got hold of a small fragment of the first Russian Sputnik and wanted me to include it in a piece for the retiring head of the institute. It was then I started working with Professor

Heather Lechtman of MIT researching ancient Peruvian metals. As the working goldsmith in this research, I loved trying to figure out how the Peruvians managed to construct their creations.

During this time I was asked by the Polaroid Corporation to teach a course in basic design to their engineering department. Polaroid's cameras were designed by Dryfus in New York, and to build better communication between Dryfus and the Polaroid Company engineers, management wanted their engineers to understand the language of design. It was great fun and really exciting, especially when we were talking pay. Polaroid wanted to pay me much less than their science teachers. I said, "Sorry, I have as much or even more formal education than the scientist." " But, you're only an artist." "Too bad, guys, pay me an equal amount or forget it." They were appalled at the thought. So they brought in higher level honchos, me still at the "no" stage. Finally they relented. The course went so well, they asked me to do it again.

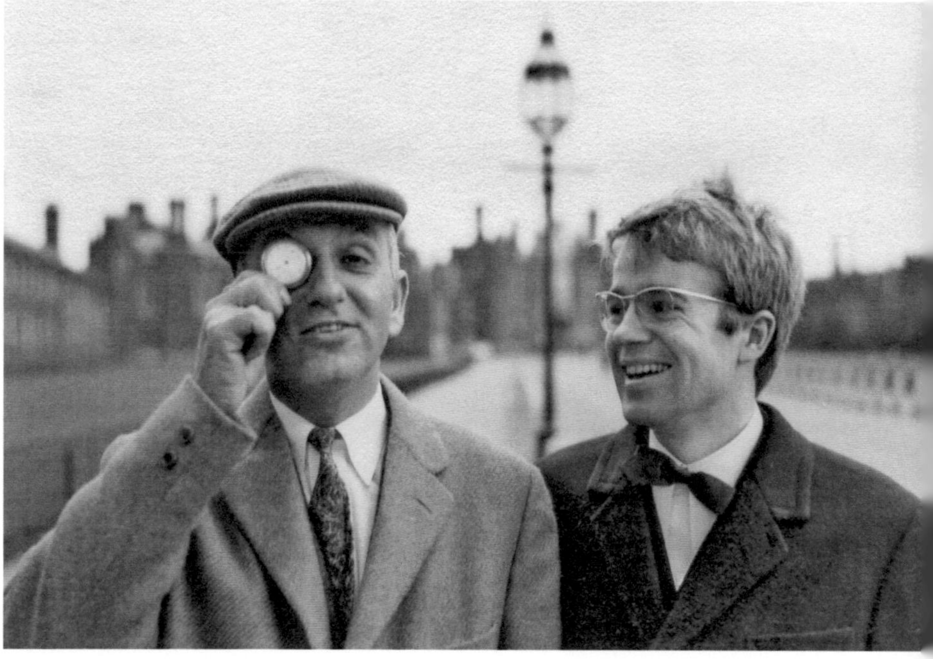

SIR HENRY IN LONDON, 1970S

Although I kept goldsmithing and sculpting, any work that came my way not directly connected with fabricating my work was greatly appreciated—money was a great need. I taught a course at Boston University and lectured at several places, and finally began to make some money. Joy of joys. Soon I was going to London to buy a car, a Rover 2000, their new sports model. That first trip to London was also my first awareness of Goldsmiths' Hall. I made my plane reservation for the minimum time allowed by BOAC, which was two weeks. However, one day in London and I scurried to BOAC and begged to stay the full four weeks. I booked myself at a wonderful hotel called the Royal Court in Sloane Square, at a rate of 40 or so pounds a day, which included full breakfast. Nearly had a seizure my first day at breakfast. Sitting across from me was a very distinguished gentleman reading his morning paper with a monocle. It was the glamorous days of the early sixties and the super exchange rate. The dollar was flying high. I did go to museums and spend time with my new friends

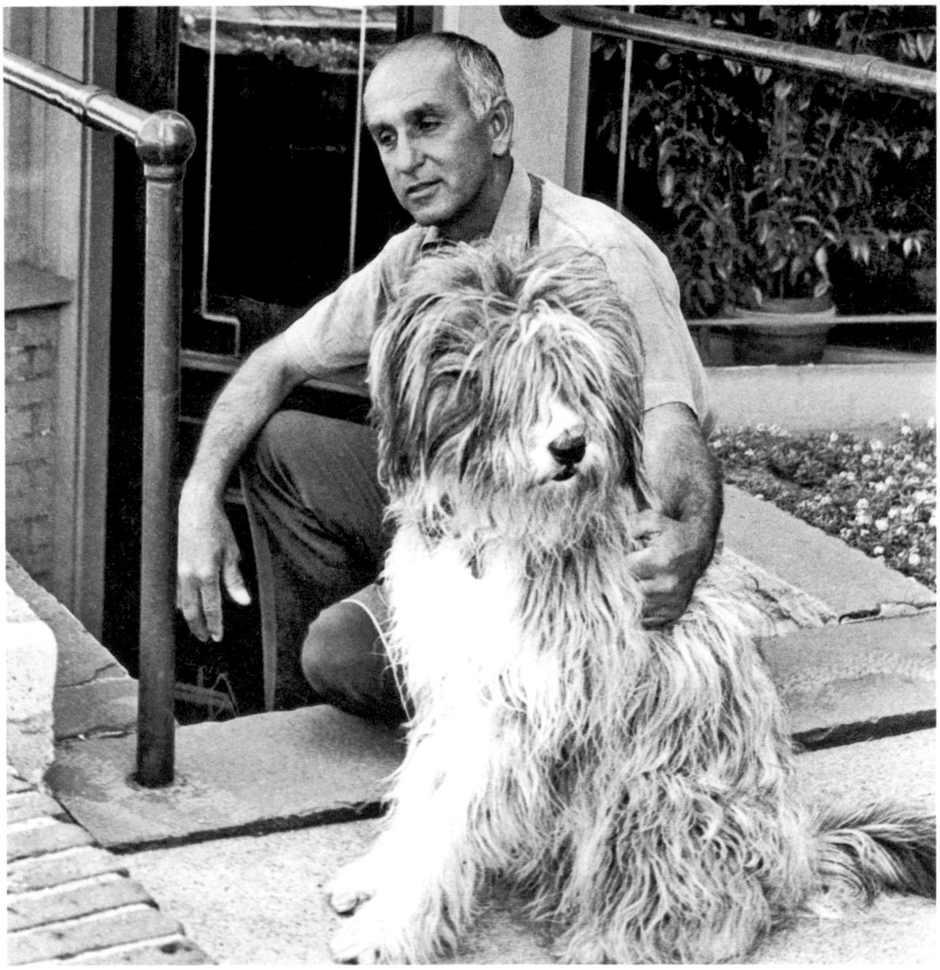

HENRY AND POO BAA IN FRONT OF HARVARD SQUARE SHOP, 1970

in London, but honestly the food court a Harrods was a special place to be. Couldn't believe it—almost twelve different types of butter alone, beautiful fish arrayed in marble stands surrounded by ice, and always a very large salmon perched on top with a lemon in its mouth. Am I dead and in some kind of epicurean heaven?

Then back to Cambridge and a great part of my life—Poo Baa, a large Tibetan terrier. Since I walked to and from work daily and always wanted a dog, Poo Baa was the answer. He was still a puppy, about twelve weeks old, and had more pee in him than a Russian wolfhound. We'd walk slowly to the shop and the minute we got inside, Poo Baa would turn on the waterworks. Well, we got over the puppy stages and Poo Baa proved to be a great companion. Bigger than the kennel club standard, he weighed fifty-five pounds and had a gorgeous coat of black, white, and silver. His favorite trick was this: Give Poo Baa a grape, he'd put it into his mouth, lie on his back, and gently roll it around with his tongue.

The minute it broke, the game was over, and he'd leave the squashed grape behind. Retrieving! Are you kidding? Do you expect me to return that ball to you? If you want it, catch me if you can. Sometimes, he'd let me catch him to get the ball back, and we'd both roll over in the grass, laughing hysterically.

THE END OF HARVARD SQUARE

The Vietnam War was raging and there were almost daily protest marches in the square—the final explosions of the student unrest. Buildings were torched, people were hurt; life as we once knew it in the square was almost nonexistent. Barricades of state and local police tried to bring order out of chaos, and I think at one point we even had the National Guard trying to keep order. We left our shops for fear of being torched and hurt. One day Rebecca Harvey and her husband called to say, in effect, we shop owners couldn't hide; we all had to go back to the square, see what the damage was, and if possible save our shops. Rebecca was the leader of the movement. I finally got to the square and found my shop intact, but other places were not so lucky. A small bank in my area owned by locals was totally destroyed. They never reopened. The students, out to punish big business and corporate America, destroyed many of the small shops and locally owned restaurants, and the old square was gone.

It was time to leave Harvard Square. Staying in my studio after dark became a spooky affair. The door had to be locked at all times. The insurance company asked me to remove the word "goldsmith" from under my name at the entrance. New buildings began to appear in the square, and rents skyrocketed. No place for small shops anymore.

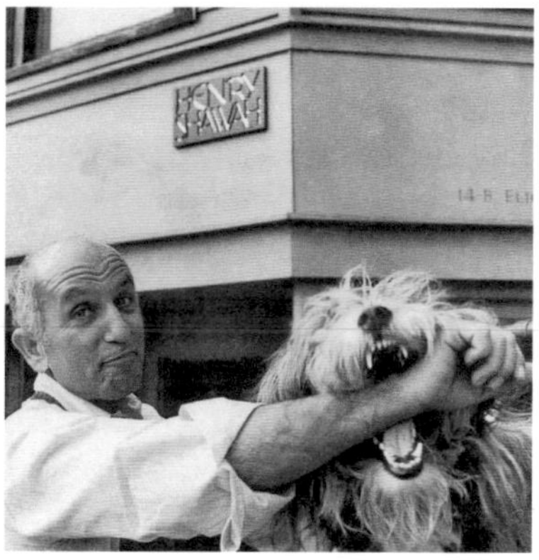

HENRY AND POO BAA PLAYING "JAWS"

So off to my current place—studio and living quarters in one place. Great sadness at leaving Harvard Square and its stimulation and many friendships.

I got used to my new digs in an 1882 building on Massachusetts Avenue, high ceilings and skylights, and only a thirty-foot commute to my great studio. I could work until all hours of the morning, peace and quiet. Poo Baa was confused but happy. Our morning walks were no longer to Harvard Square. Instead we toured our local neighborhood. And, when it snowed, we romped in the big snowdrifts in the parking lot across the street.

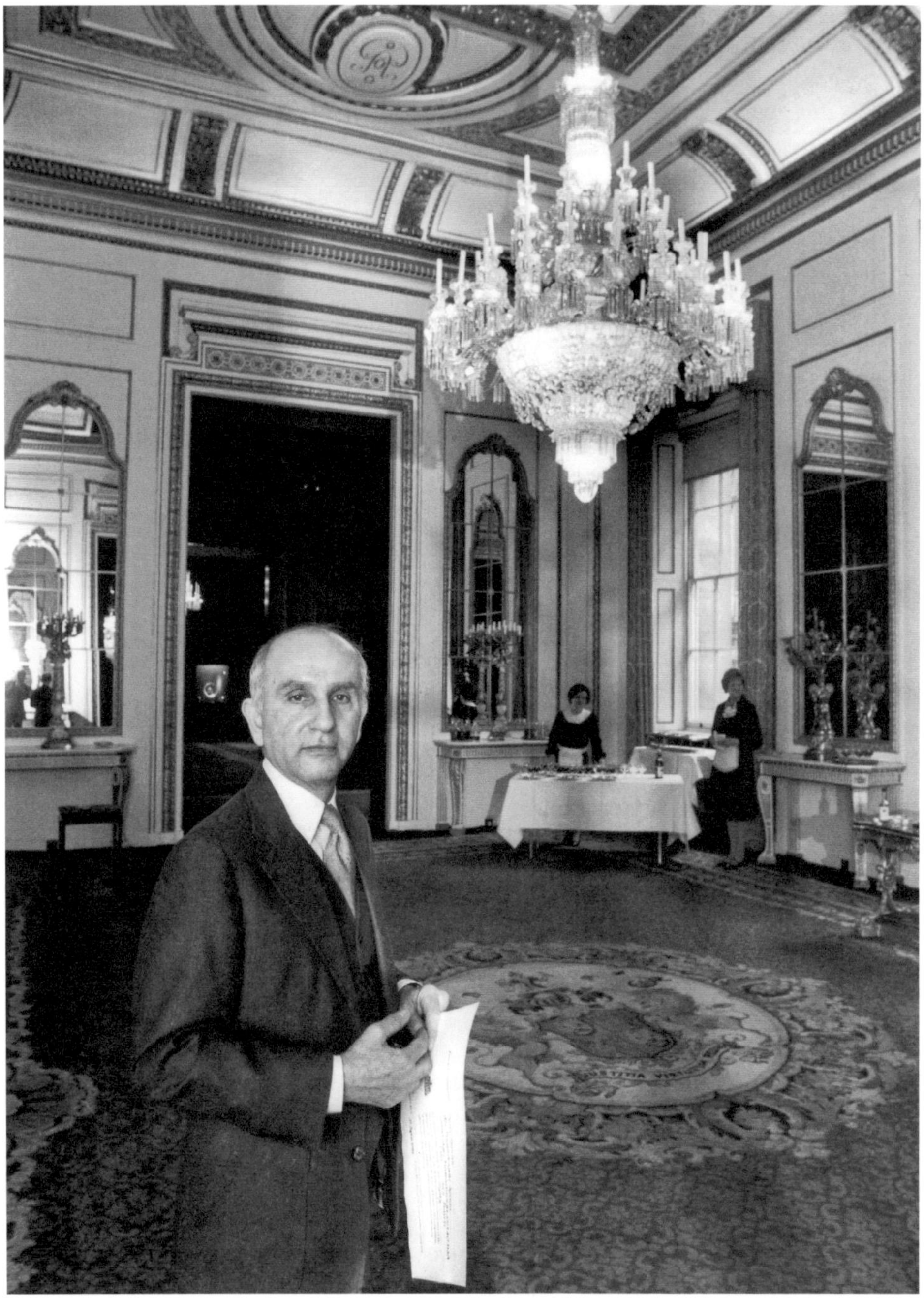

KEYSTONE PRESS AG. LONDON, ENGLAND

HENRY IN DRAWING ROOM
AT GOLDSMITHS' HALL, LONDON

THE LONDON CONNECTION

In the early sixties I received a request from London's Worshipful Company of Goldsmiths to send several pieces of my work for what was to be their first-ever exhibition of modern jewelry, covering the period 1890 to 1961. The show was to include work by Picasso and other artists of his caliber. Needless to say I was floored and very naive about sending work to London or any other foreign country. I packed up four pieces of my work, addressed the parcel to the Worshipful Company of Goldsmiths, and to insure delivery, sent it by registered air mail. Never realizing I should have hired a broker to clear the packages through British customs, I had the disappointment of learning that my work arrived at Goldsmiths' Hall the opening day of the show and definitely too late to be listed in the show's catalogue. In a telephone call to Graham Hughes, art director of Goldsmiths' Hall and organizer of the exhibition, I received the sad news about my work. But Graham Hughes, I'm sure to soften the blow, said the work was exhibited in the Company's vaults. I could at least dream that the Queen Mother, who had opened the show, was escorted to the vaults and had looked upon and admired my work.

Graham Hughes then said, "Henry Shawah, I know how disappointed you must feel. However, we will give you a one-man show at the Hall." I jumped at the chance. Frank Foults, a great friend and former owner of an advertising agency in Boston and New York, gave me great advice about working with a public relations agency and hiring a customs broker to handle shipping and clearance when the work reached London.

Well, my show made the newspapers and magazines, but even with a special customs agent, British customs held up the work until the Company of Goldsmiths could vouch that the work was for exhibition only and not for sale. Me, exhausted. The work, finally released. The show opened late to this notice on the front page of the *London Times:* "The most disappointed man in London is American goldsmith Henry Shawah, whose show at Goldsmiths' Hall was to open today, but due to the action of British customs, the work was held up for clearance."

In the end the exhibition, even though on a modest scale, was wonderfully successful. Special envoys from the American Embassy came to sing my praises and said they would bring Mrs. Annenberg, wife of the U.S. ambassador to Great Britain, the next day to see the show being held in the grandeur of Goldsmiths' Hall. Late again, the envoys arrived the day the show was closing. So that was that. I was through crying, and with my new-found London friends, especially Graham Hughes and his beautiful wife Serena, enjoyed dinners, wine, and genteel carousing. Not bad to be able to say that I am the first American to have had a one-man show at Goldsmiths' Hall, home of the Worshipful Company of Goldsmiths' Livery to Her Majesty Queen Elizabeth. Goldsmiths founded the company in the thirteenth century and have since been serious benefactors to numerous charities, schools, and causes. Its members include Crown Prince Charles, the Duke of Windsor, and other notables of the realm.

INSTALLATION SHOT OF HENRY'S 1970 EXHIBITION AT GOLDSMITHS' HALL.

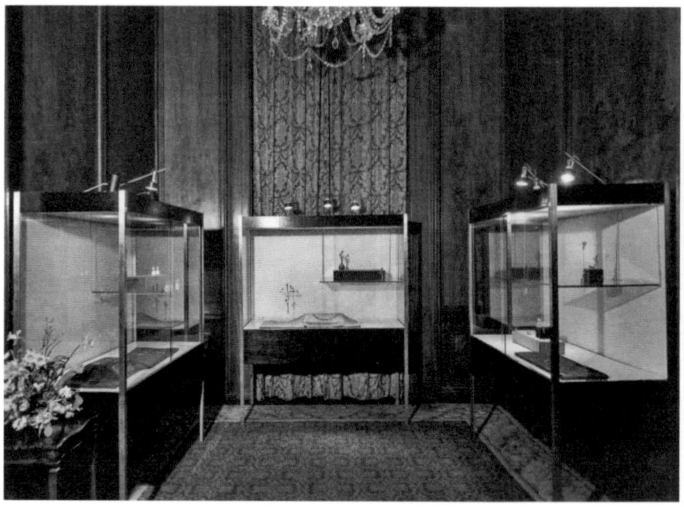

Back to New York and a planned show at Georg Jensen's. Unfortunately Jensen's had serious financial problems and had given up their famous Fifth Avenue store. Having moved to much smaller quarters on Madison Avenue, they had to put off my show. Tears but not a disaster. Instead I hired a suite at the Plaza and invited my friends and patrons to see the work exhibited at Goldsmiths' Hall in London. We had a great time, drank wine, and made expenses; a dear friend and weaver, Margarata Grundine (now Margarata Grundine Nettles) acted as hostess.

It was back to austere Cambridge and Boston, but I was cheered by the prospect of many more trips to London and Goldsmiths' Hall and visits to Cambridge by my new friends from the Hall.

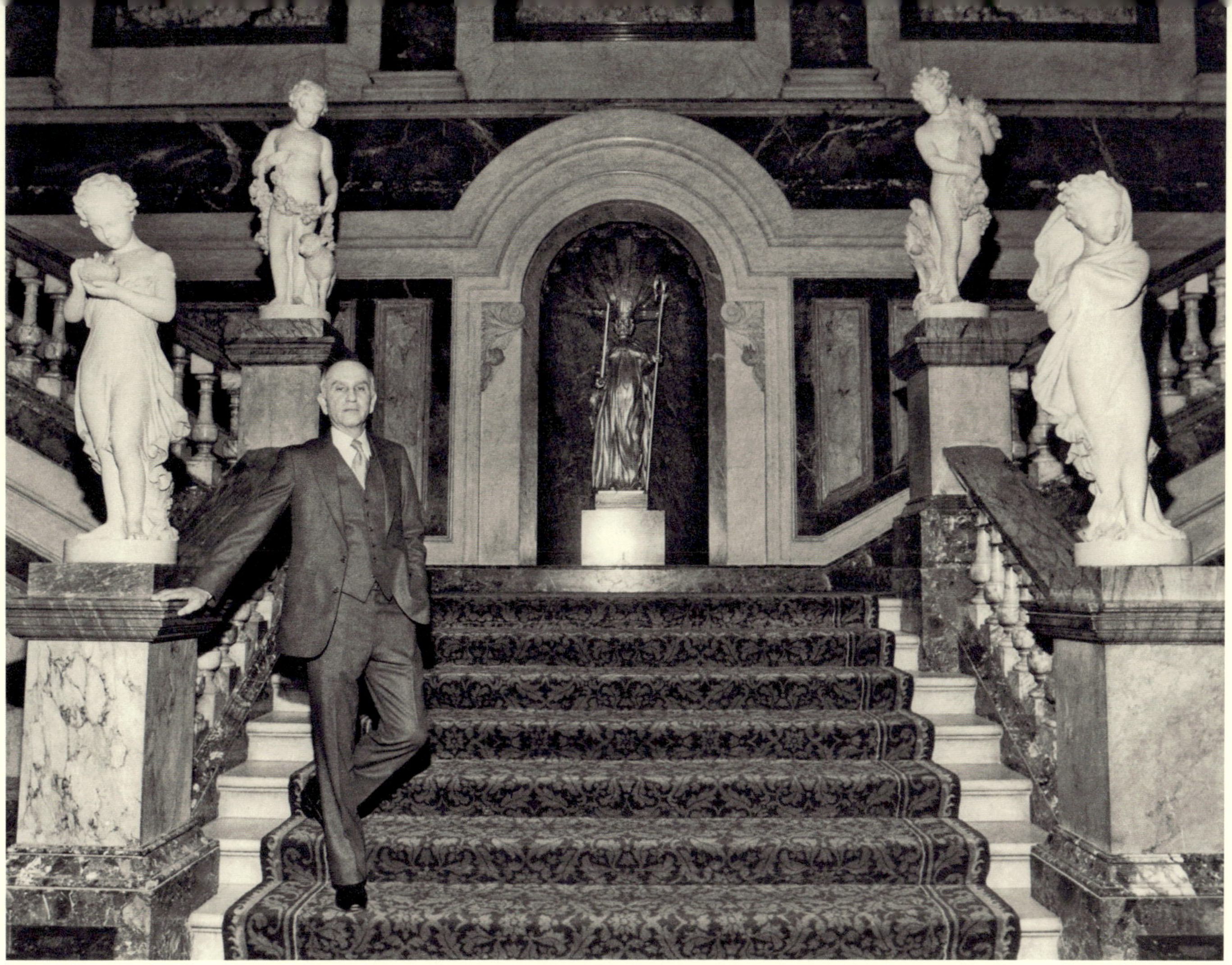

KEYSTONE PRESS AG. LONDON, ENGLAND

AMONG THE STATUARY IN GOLDSMITHS' HALL

In 1981 I was made an Associate of the Worshipful Company of Goldsmiths. As an American, I could not swear fealty to the Queen, so instead of being named a Liveryman, I was given the honorary title of Associate. At that time there were only forty Associates in the world, and I was the only American. I also was given the "freedom of the Hall," which meant I could visit as I wished. Very heady stuff for Henry Shawah, goldsmith from Cambridge, Massachusetts.

Before I finish with the British experience, I must describe the famous fiftieth anniversary of the London Home Show. The Company of Goldsmiths was chosen to celebrate the Golden Jubilee of the show by exhibiting the work of European goldsmiths. The exhibition was to be opened by the Queen. It was a day or two after the first London bombing by the IRA in July 1982. The show opened on time, but there was great tension in the air regarding public safety during the Home Show and the Queen's first major public appearance since the bombing.

In order to experience the Home Show, see the Queen, and view the work of some fabulous European goldsmiths, I asked Graham if I might help at the

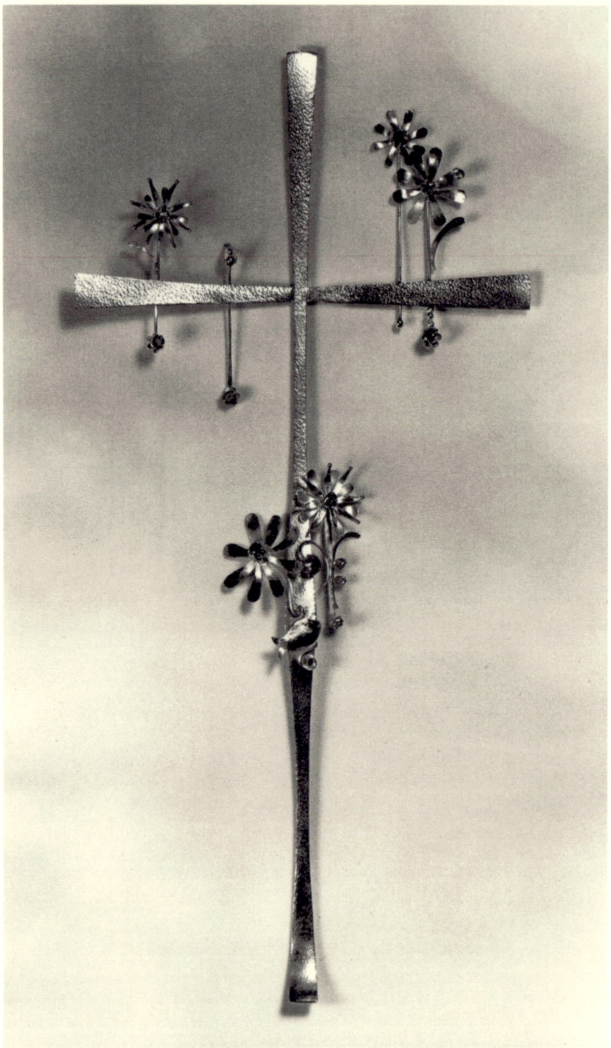

HENRY SHAWAH WAS HONORED BY THE WORSHIPFUL COMPANY OF GOLDSMITHS WITH THE FIRST ONE-MAN SHOW BY AN AMERICAN AT GOLDSMITH'S HALL, FOSTER LANE, LONDON, ON MARCH 9–16, 1970. SEVERAL OF THE PIECES IN THE EXHIBITION ARE SHOWN HERE.

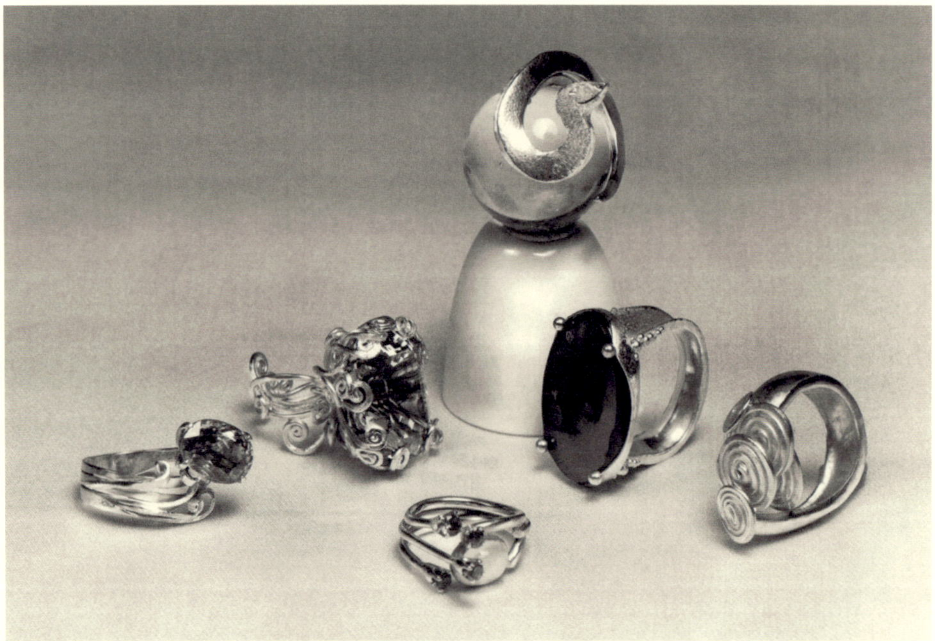

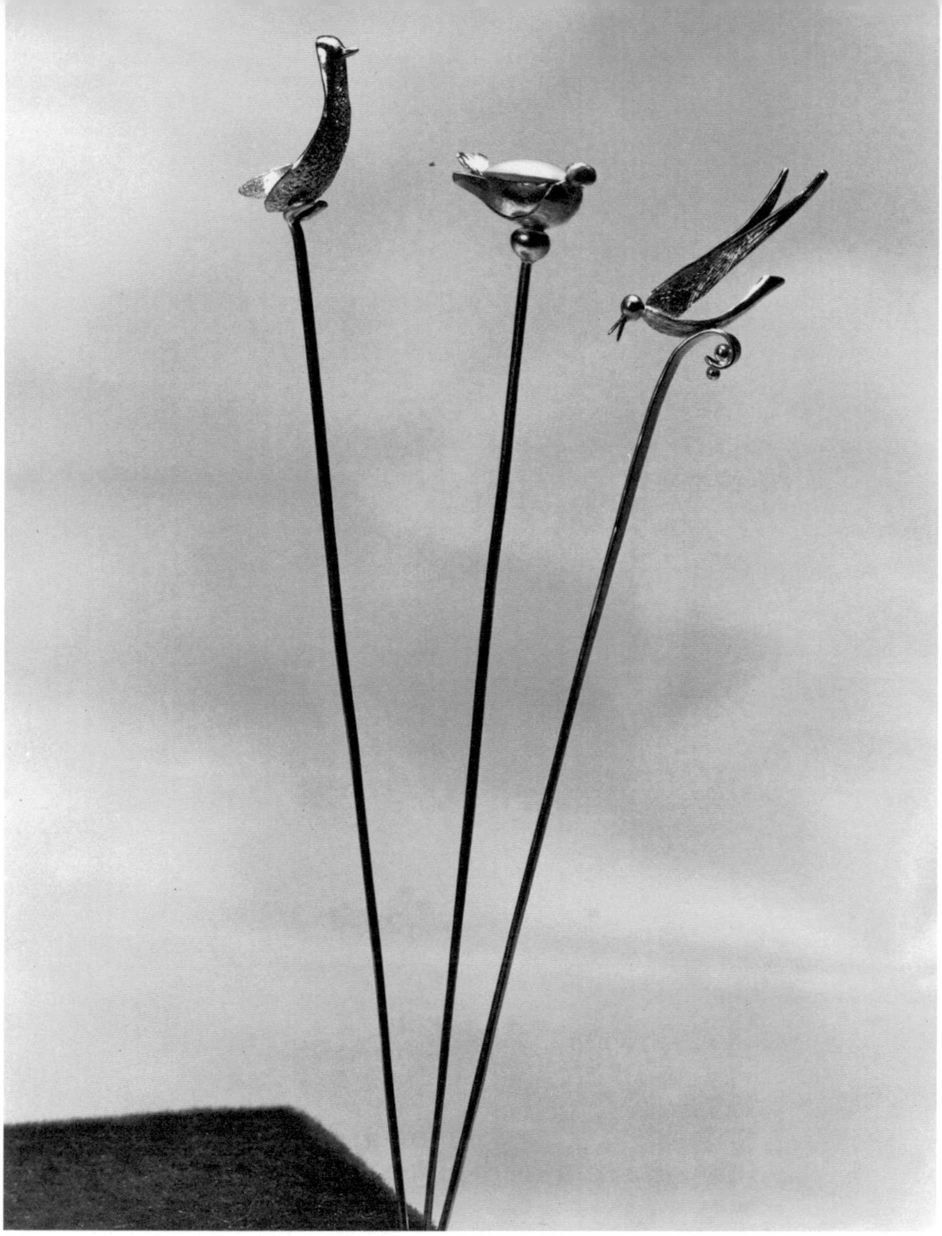

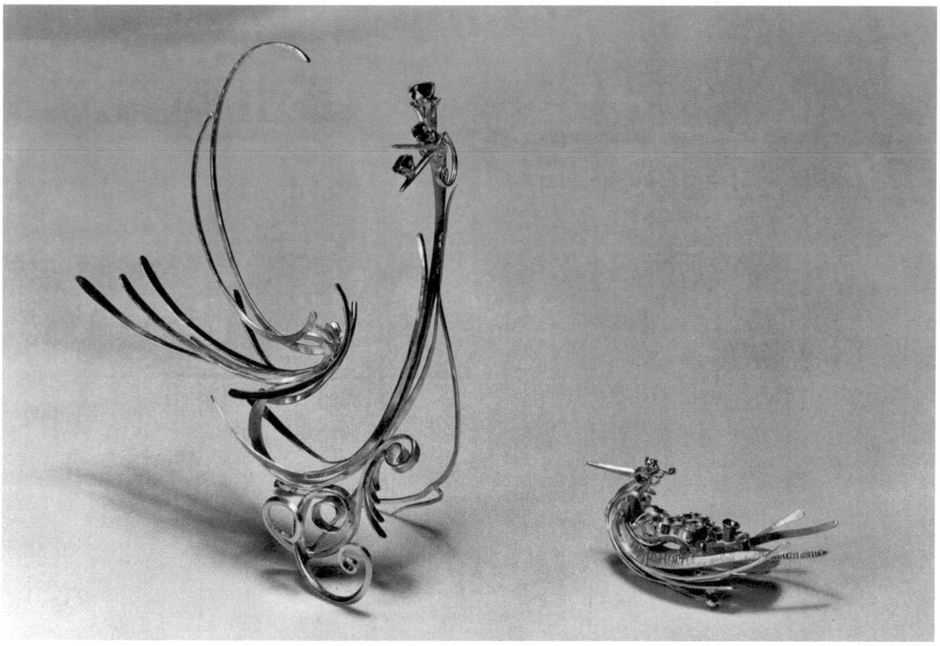

opening. He obliged, and Nevin Holmes, an exhibiting goldsmith and friend, and I were assigned to open the boxes of champagne glasses and arrange them on a highly decorated table. Horror of horrors! When we opened the boxes, every glass was covered with a thick layer of dust. No cloth. No water. And the Queen's arrival was imminent. God bless my mother, whose last admonition whenever I left the house was, "Do you have a clean handkerchief?" On this very important occasion I did. I tore my handkerchief in two—half for Nevin and half for me. Like demons we cleaned the dust off what seemed to be dozens of glasses. Graham Hughes was greeting the courtiers waiting on the Queen's

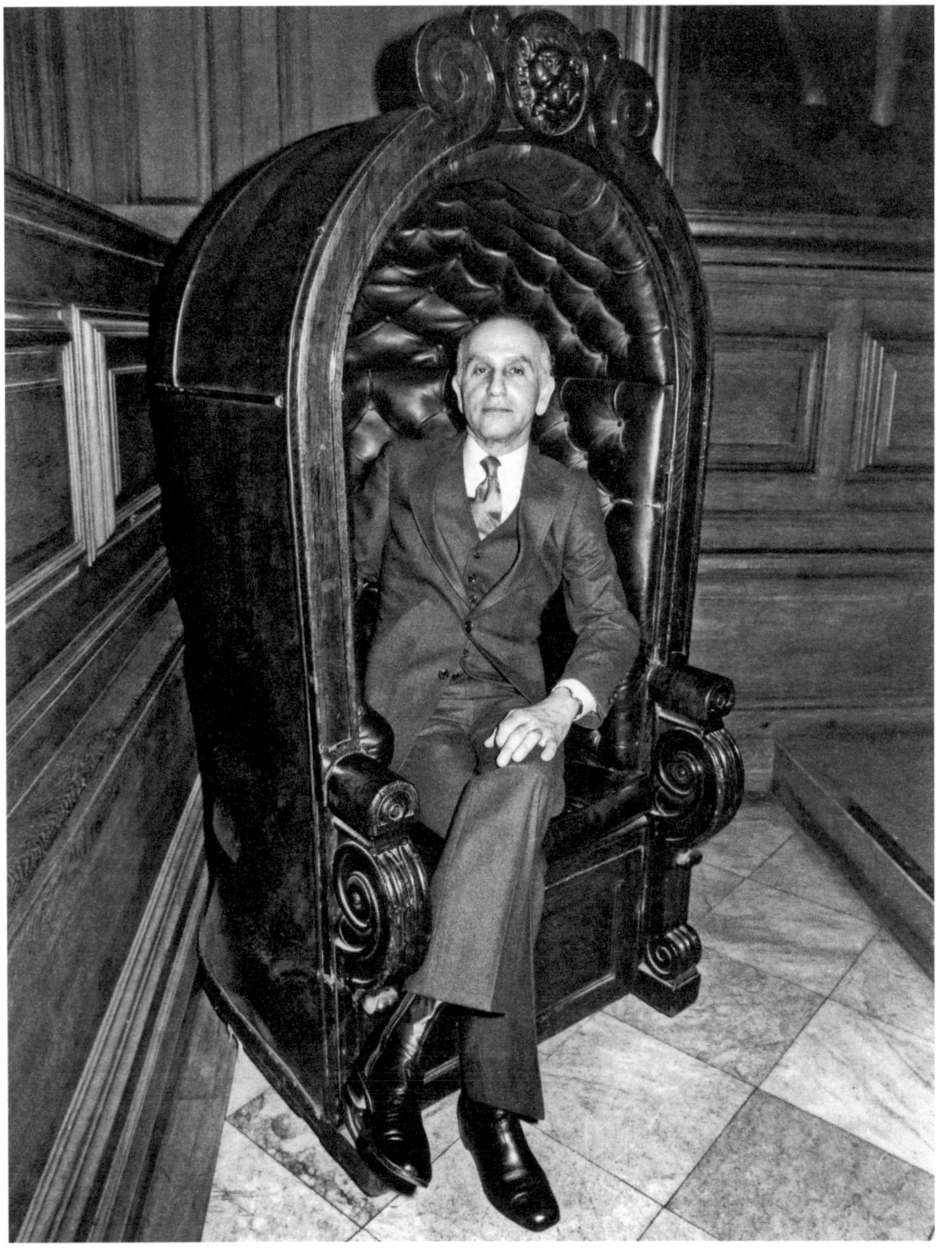
KEYSTONE PRESS AG. LONDON, ENGLAND

HENRY IN BEADLE'S CHAIR AT GOLDSMITHS' HALL

arrival. Okay, we had clean glasses, but we needed champagne to fill them. I remembered Graham's frantic instructions, "Henry, will you open the champagne?" Glad to show off that Americans could easily open champagne, I had one hand to the cork, the other hand starting to twist the bottle—and suddenly we hear the blare of trumpets announcing the entrance of Queen Elizabeth, with her entourage and security men all over the place. Dear God, dear God, the cork starting to free itself from the bottle. Please don't let there be a loud pop. Tension was so high that any loud noise would definitely put the popper in jeopardy. God was on my side. A genteel wisp of air escaped from the bottle and the cork was free. I was saved.

The exhibition was on a balcony overlooking the Hall. As the Queen arrived, I heard a strangled voice at the approach to the balcony: "Stop the damn Hoovering, the Queen is here!" The elegant group gathering at the Goldsmiths' table is daintily sipping champagne and acting the way one does in the company of nobility. Champagne is offered to the Queen. Thank God, thank God, she graciously refuses. I hated to think of the outcome: stray dust causing paroxysms of coughing by the monarch.

The gracious Queen stopped at each display case and listened to each goldsmith describe the work as the security men stood by in a state of anxiety. The Queen was an easy target, and she needed to move along as fast as discretion would allow. I was in line hoping to be presented to the Queen as a helpful foreigner. However my friend Nevin Holmes went into great detail in the explanation of her work. Standing just three feet from the Queen, I was nevertheless bypassed. Nevin and the seriousness of the security kept Her Majesty in the fast lane. If only she had at least stepped on my foot. So, no story. Except for the wonderful attentiveness of the Queen as she listened to each explanation, knowing full well most of the goldsmiths were doing their best to remain upright and not faint in her presence.

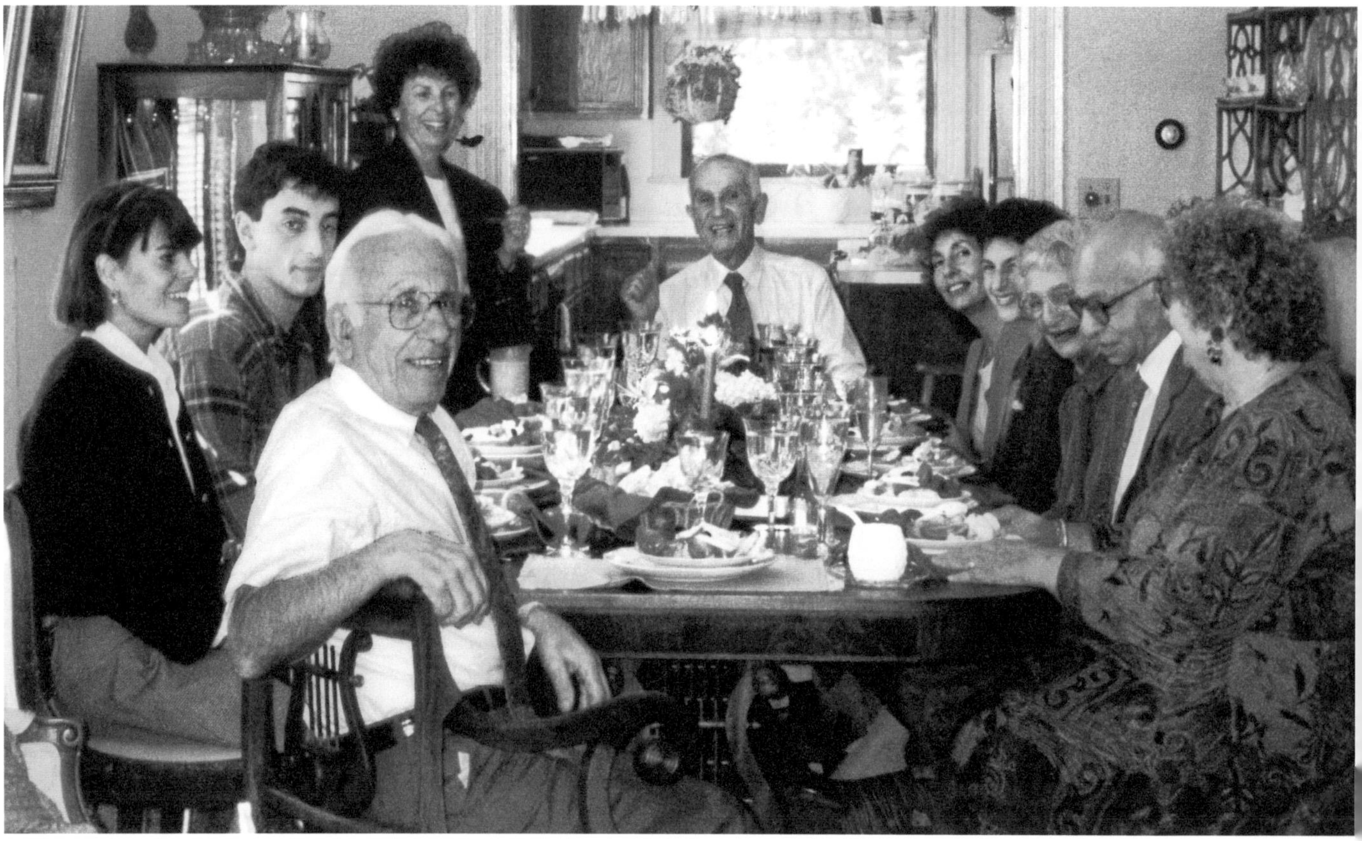

FAMILY DINNER AT JOAN'S

FAMILY TIES

WE ALL COOK, WE ALL EAT

What did you bring, Judy? Is that the recipe Renee gave you? Did Heather make her killer cookies again? Beer and wine, sip and slurp. Harold, you've really got your grandmother's kibbee recipe down to perfection. Oh God, here comes Uncle. First class show-off. It's really nothing, guys. Just a pear Bavarian cream in a fancy mold with raspberry coulis and fresh raspberry decorations.

Discussion, at least four or five family members. Are you sure the turkey's done? Remember last year it took forever. John senior—dad, grandfather, great grandfather—picks up the carving knife. His wife Ann daintily sips her wine, the sage of all cooking, ready to answer questions.

Joan: "Mom, are these cups okay for making the popovers?" Mom-Ann: "How can you make popovers, hon? There's no more oven space, and besides they're so hard to make." Uncle, sundry cousins, siblings, and other observers: "No, no, Joan." Joan, unconcerned, continues with the popover batter. She finds a clear oven space and out come unbelievable popovers. There is a hush. Then: "We want real gravy and mashed potatoes," even if Big Sito Shawah (my mother) decreed many years ago that rice with pine nuts is standard accompaniment to the turkey.

There are more than twenty of us. We line up at the buffet to serve ourselves. Older family go to the dining-room table, which has been opened to its creaky length. Young folk head for the other end of the dining room, where Joan has pushed two tables together. We say a hasty grace and start our wonderful dinner.

Then come the desserts: cakes, pies, tarts, molds, fruit, and ornamental cookies. Now the real salivating begins. It's story time, and we talk and laugh and are slightly appalled to realize we're now talking about future feasts or memorable ones long past when all our dear ones were here at our table.

Now my sister Ann, matriarch of this large group, tells how John junior woke up one night and was shocked when he looked in the mirror and saw he resembled a bullfrog. Neck swollen to twice its normal size. He quietly ran downstairs to check the family medical book. His diagnosis: elephantiasis. In the morning nine-year-old John says to his mother, "I know I'm going to die soon. I have this bad tropical disease." His mother: "No, no, sweetheart, you have the mumps." John takes this in. "Well, do I have to go to school?" "No, sweetheart, you don't have to go to school, but you'll have to stay quietly in bed, or when you grow up you won't be able to make babies."

We all laugh and laugh, then look at one another and stop. John junior is no longer here. He died last year. Ann looks at her daughter. "Is there anymore coffee, Joan?"

CARNEGIE HALL

It's a mid-December evening in 1987, intermission at the Carnegie Hall performance of Handel's *Messiah.* The delicious smell of lamb, parsley, toasted pine nuts, and onions inside tiny bulgur dumplings breaks loose from a group of mezzanine boxes . . .

It was the year I had completed several successful commissions. The jingle of money in my pocket. I decided to hire a bus and take the whole family and some close friends, about twenty-two of us, for an evening performance at Carnegie Hall. We had elegant box dinners and wine on the bus, which we decorated with Christmas greens, and took off to New York from Joan's house in Fairfield, Connecticut. And because I knew it was something my parents would have loved doing, I asked my sister Ann to make little bulgur dumplings, "kibbee footballs" as we called them, so we could eat them during intermission in memory of our

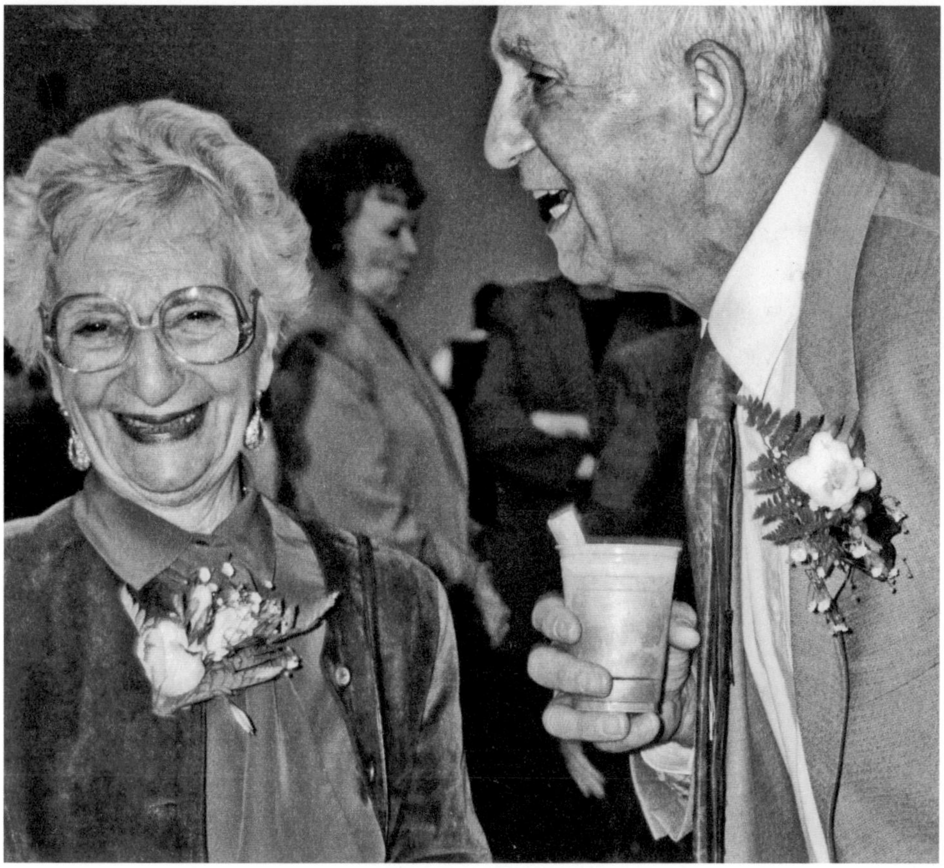

HENRY AND HIS SISTER ANN, CELEBRATING THEIR BIRTHDAY IN COMMON, SEPTEMBER 20, 1995

parents. I had reserved three boxes where we could sit resplendently. The girls in their party dresses, everyone dressed to the nines.

Intermission came, and as we toasted MaMa and PaPa, all eyes turned toward our boxes, and the aroma of parsley and lamb floated over the famous concert hall.

We learned later, of course, that all food was forbidden in Carnegie Hall. Woops, too late. We had devoured everything before the intermission was over. I was too embarrassed to write to Isaac Stern, who had saved Carnegie Hall from the wrecking ball in the 1960s: how beautiful the renovation was, and I'm sorry we broke the food rule.

Our bus driver showed us all the most brilliant Christmas decorations in Manhattan, and we sang all the way home.

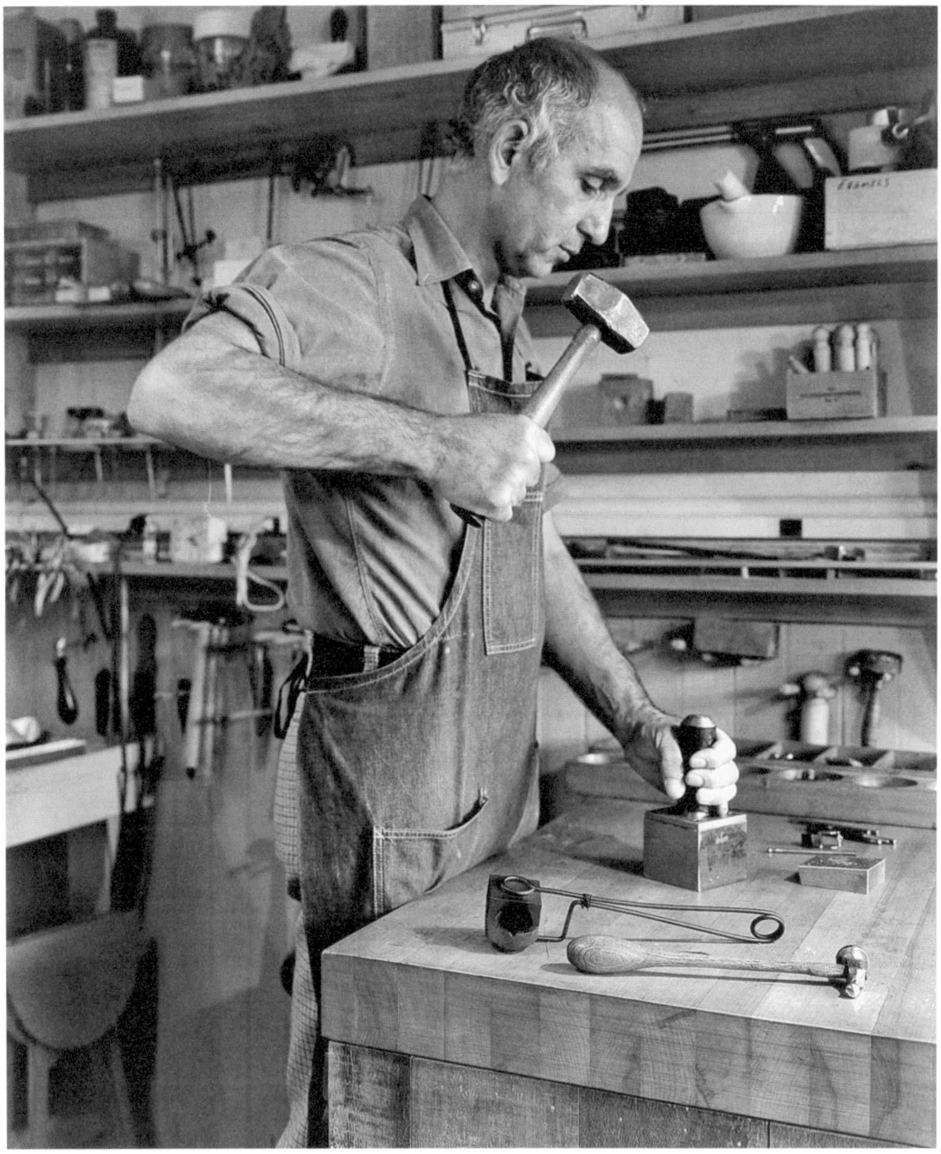

IN CAMBRIDGE STUDIO, 1974 (FOR *New Yorker* MAGAZINE AD)

IN THE STUDIO

MATERIALS

The materials I work with primarily are 24-karat gold—pure gold—and alloys, and the technique I use most often is forging. The addition of an alloy to pure gold is what determines the gold karat. The amount of gold and alloy must create the number 24. For example, 18-karat gold has 18 parts of pure gold and 6 parts of alloy to make the number 24; 14-karat gold has 14 parts of pure gold and 10 parts of alloy. Alloys can be silver or copper in varying quantities. I prefer to use mostly 18 karat; the alloy is usually silver with a smidgen of copper to strengthen the gold. More copper than silver produces a redder gold and more silver a slightly greener gold and, I feel, a richer material.

My 18 karat is perfect for forging; it gives under the hammer yet retains a certain stiffness. Forging is exactly what a blacksmith does, except the blacksmith heats his metal to a bright red and hammers it into shape. Nonferrous metals—gold, silver, copper—are forged cold. I hammer the gold and silver against a stake (or anvil). As the hammering (forging) proceeds, the malleable metal, due to the rearranging of its molecules, becomes stiffer and less malleable. Heating the gold or silver to a dull red and quenching it in water or a mild acidic solution returns the molecules to their original position, making the metal soft again and more workable. The acid is used to remove oxidation from the gold's alloy. This process may be repeated many times before the work is completed.

Sterling silver is a combination of fine silver and a small amount of copper, which gives the sterling more rigidity. I use fine or pure silver, a very soft material

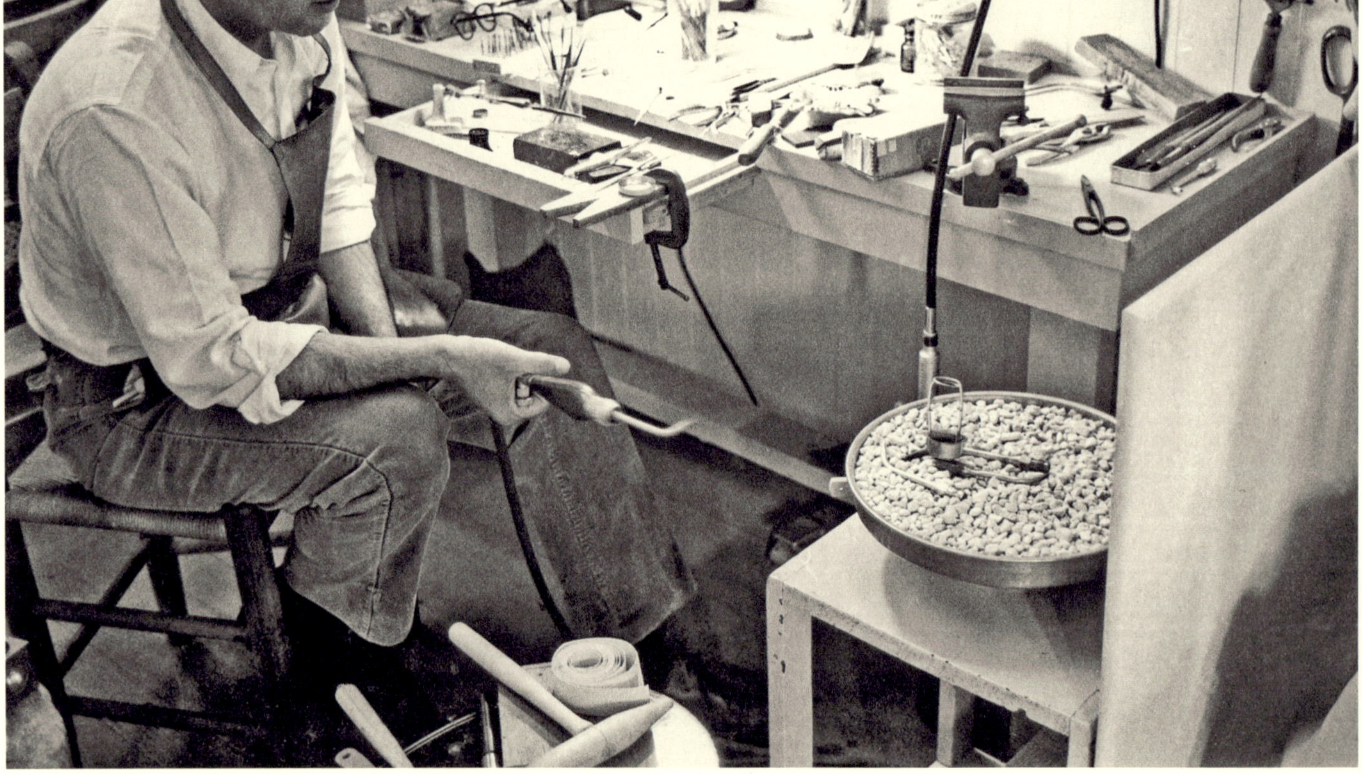

HENRY IN HARVARD SQUARE WORKSHOP, C. 1961

with a beautiful white-silver surface, as compared to sterling, which has a darker, grayer surface. All well and good, but think of a "fine" silver spoon—the handle would easily bend with the slightest pressure. To use fine silver that has softened during the soldering process, I hammer the surface lightly—called planishing—to help stiffen the final work so that it can withstand reasonable use. So soldering or any heating must be done before the final forging.

Most gold and silver works are highly polished with a variety of compounds on buffing wheels made of cloth or bristle. I use the polishing wheel only for highlights. I find that highly polished silver or gold—instead of emphasizing the shape of the object—reflects the object's environment in its mirror-like finish. Therefore, I keep all of my hammers and anvils (called stakes) polished, which gives the metal a duller and softer finish overall. I go so far as to put a polishing agent on my thumb and gently tease a highlight on the work.

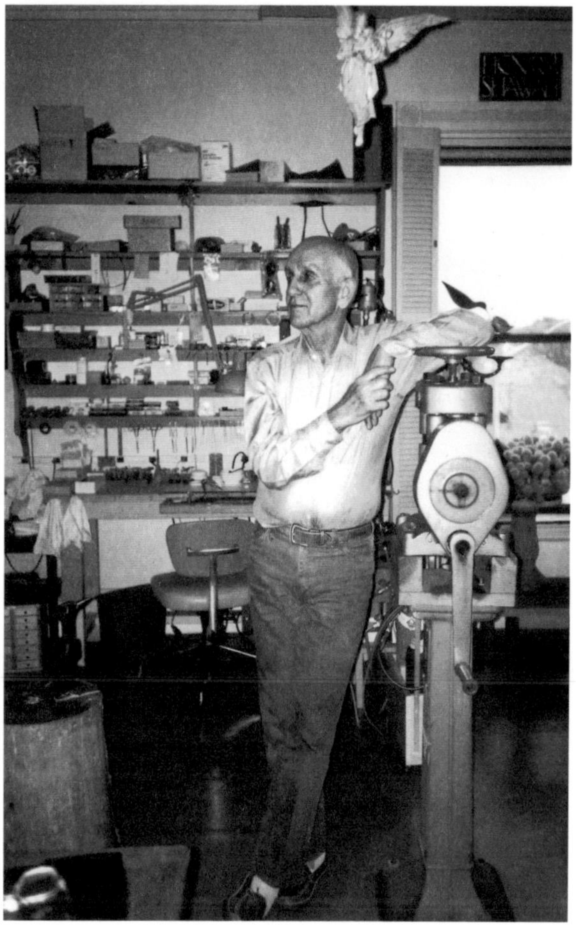

HENRY IN CURRENT WORKSHOP, 2003

There are ways of working with gold and silver other than forging, such as casting or lathe spinning for objects that are to be made in quantity. Most tableware is pressed into form in hydraulic presses, very much as auto-body parts are formed, but of course, on a much smaller scale.

For many years I have worked with Professor Heather Lechtman at MIT, whose specialty is Peruvian gold and silver. How these ancient people worked their gold are the secrets we try to uncover. In a recent publication for Dumbarton Oaks, Professor Lechtman discusses the earlier metalworking techniques and some of our experiments. With the exception of torches and electrical tools, there is a strong correlation between how a good number of metal smiths work today and how the Peruvians worked in the year AD 500. Their hammers were stone instead of steel; their saws were made of string charged with an abrasive instead of the tempered steel blades we use today. Not surprisingly, the steel saws and hammers make our work less labor-intensive. However, hammering is still hammering and sawing is still sawing.

There is something very special about working with gold and silver. I don't know why, but holding a piece of gold or silver is magical, especially if the metals are in their basic form without alloys. I love to give the pure gold a bite and see the impression of my teeth in the metal. The metal accepts the pressure of the teeth; it is amenable to a slight change in its form. I should say that I loved doing it until a medical friend reminded me there is such a thing as gold poisoning. But I still do it once in a while, hoping each bite by some miracle is gradually gilding my interior.

HOW I WORK

Phase one. I start with procrastination—not ordinary procrastination but real serious stuff.

I tell myself I am not starting now because I need to clean up my work area. Then I must do some serious looking out the window, and thank God the phone rings. "Hello, Kitty. What's happening? Your plants are dying? I told you you weren't saving any money when you let that guy talk you into buying cut-rate plants. Oh, they weren't cut rate? That's even worse. Oh, they're not really dying; they're only tired? Why aren't you going to the gem show in Tucson? C'mon, Kitty, it'll be a big break from your shop. Oh, you think you'll over-buy? Are you headed for your shop now? I'm working on a commission for Daniel Shapiro. Aggie's having a birthday soon. No, no. I'm just laying out the materials. Stop by and tell me what you think about the colors. I'll make some coffee."

Phase two. Shit and shinola. These birds are beginning to look like they've been dead for at least a month. I want them to look sprightly. There are three of them, 18 karat, a fresh water pearl, a sapphire, and peacock feathers. They are mounted on a plinth of malachite-azurite and can be removed and worn as pins.

Phase three. Kitty arrives. "What do you think? Nothing to think about? Do you really want three spoons of sugar in your coffee?"

Phase four. Oh, my God, this commission will never be finished in time. It'll be the first time I've missed the deadline. Hammer, bang, solder, saw... frenzy,

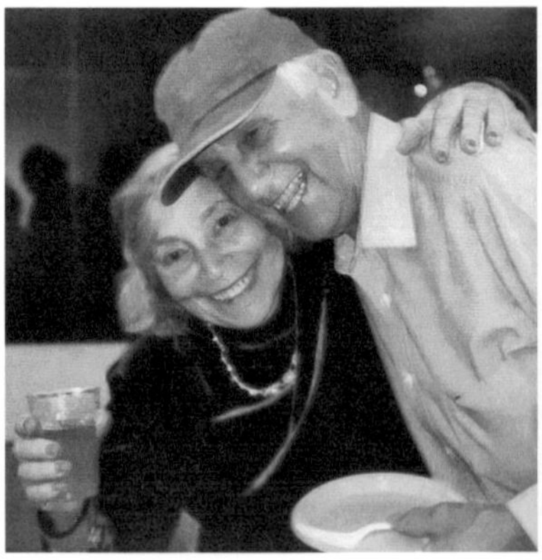

HENRY AND GOOD FRIEND KITTY HAAS

frenzy. Thank you. Thank you. Thank you, whoever's in charge, God, I presume. Now the three birds really look like they're ready to take off. I'll use the great fresh-water pearl from a lake in Mississippi that I've been saving for years. The three water-bird girls—and they are girls—will like that. The swan is really beginning to float majestically. Great. Great. I'll make a little cygnet for each of Aggie's grandchildren and weld them to the back of the swan—a special and personal thing for Aggie. And as soon as I can figure out how to attach the feathers to the peacock, I'll be well on my way. Kitty loves the piece and thinks I should be in New York or Paris because "You're a genius." I do believe her, really, really.

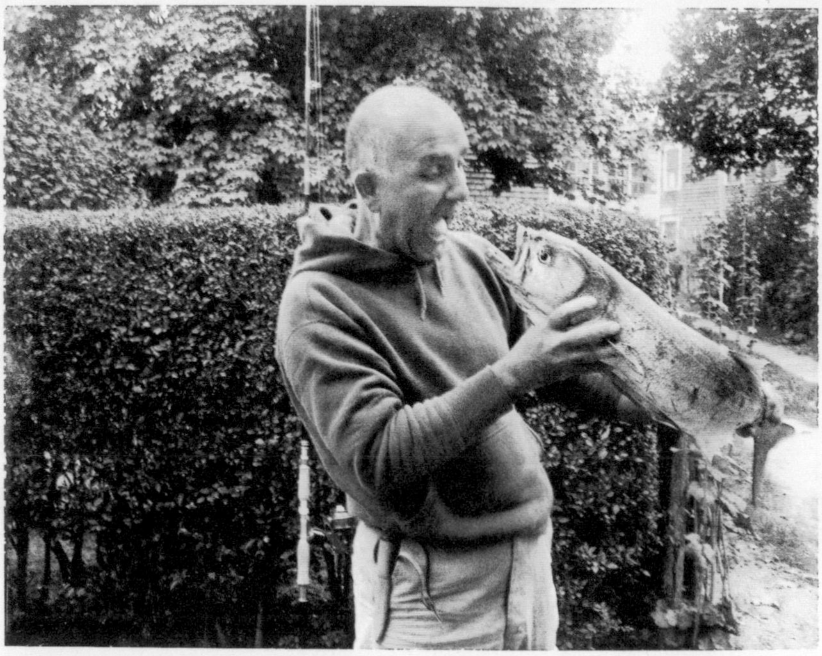

FISH TALK

Phase five. Late night. Time for bed. Lights out. I'll just check out the studio before I hit the sack. Look at that strange piece of gold on my workbench. Turn, bend, shape, sit down, hammer, hammer, hammer. It's a fearsome creature of the deep—wow, it can really bite if it wants to. Give a little smile to its mouth with the saw. Holy, holy, a Mona Lisa fish!

It's 2:30 a.m. You'd better go to bed or you'll be a zombie when Stephen Larch comes over tomorrow to see what you're doing.

The next morning. Is that the same fish I was working on last night? Don't, don't frig with it. Leave it alone. Keep it simple. Put it away. Check it out in a few days. Experience: things that look like wonders at 2:00 a.m. can turn into real dogs the next morning. But then, dogs in the exhausting, frustrating early a.m. can blow you away the next day.

THE
EAGLE FLIGHT

Clouds sweep by
In crashing flights
Flash and flash
Sun's plaited
Light
Wings that split
And torment the air
Eye whose gaze
Commands the earth
Obey, obey, obey

EAGLES

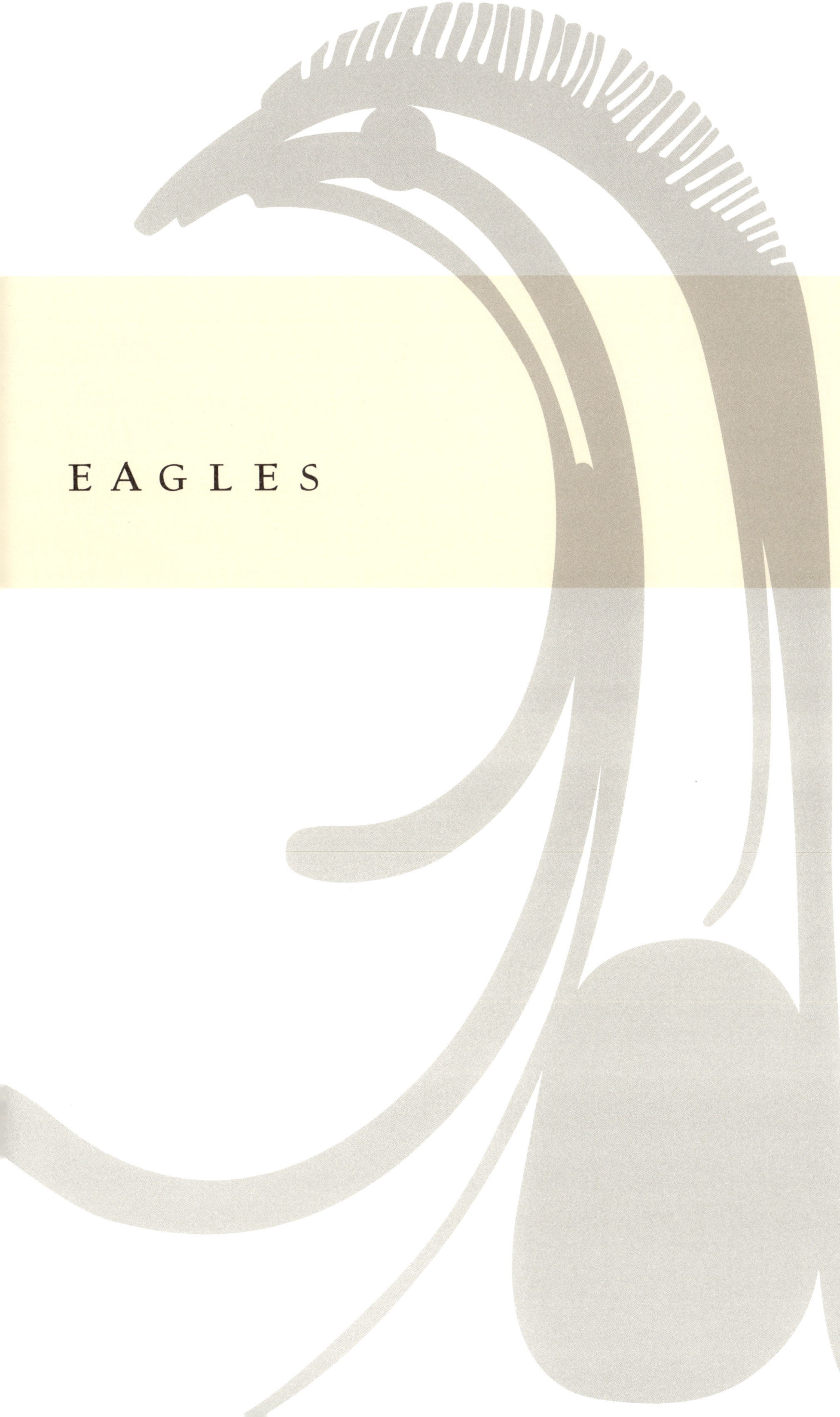

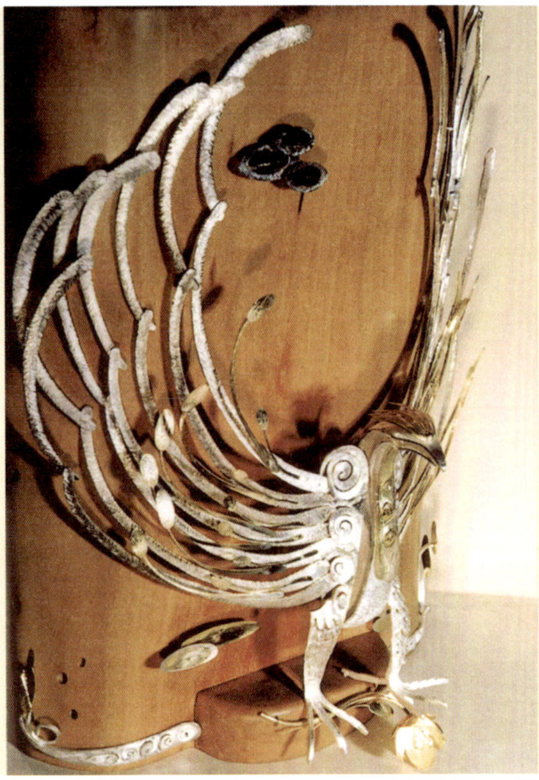

Eagle and the Rose, fine silver, 18-karat gold, and freshwater pearls, mounted on a plinth of aged Belgian pearwood. Rose may be removed from talon and worn as a pin. Approximately 15″ high

This sculpture was exhibited in the White House for the millennium celebration and is currently in the National Archives.

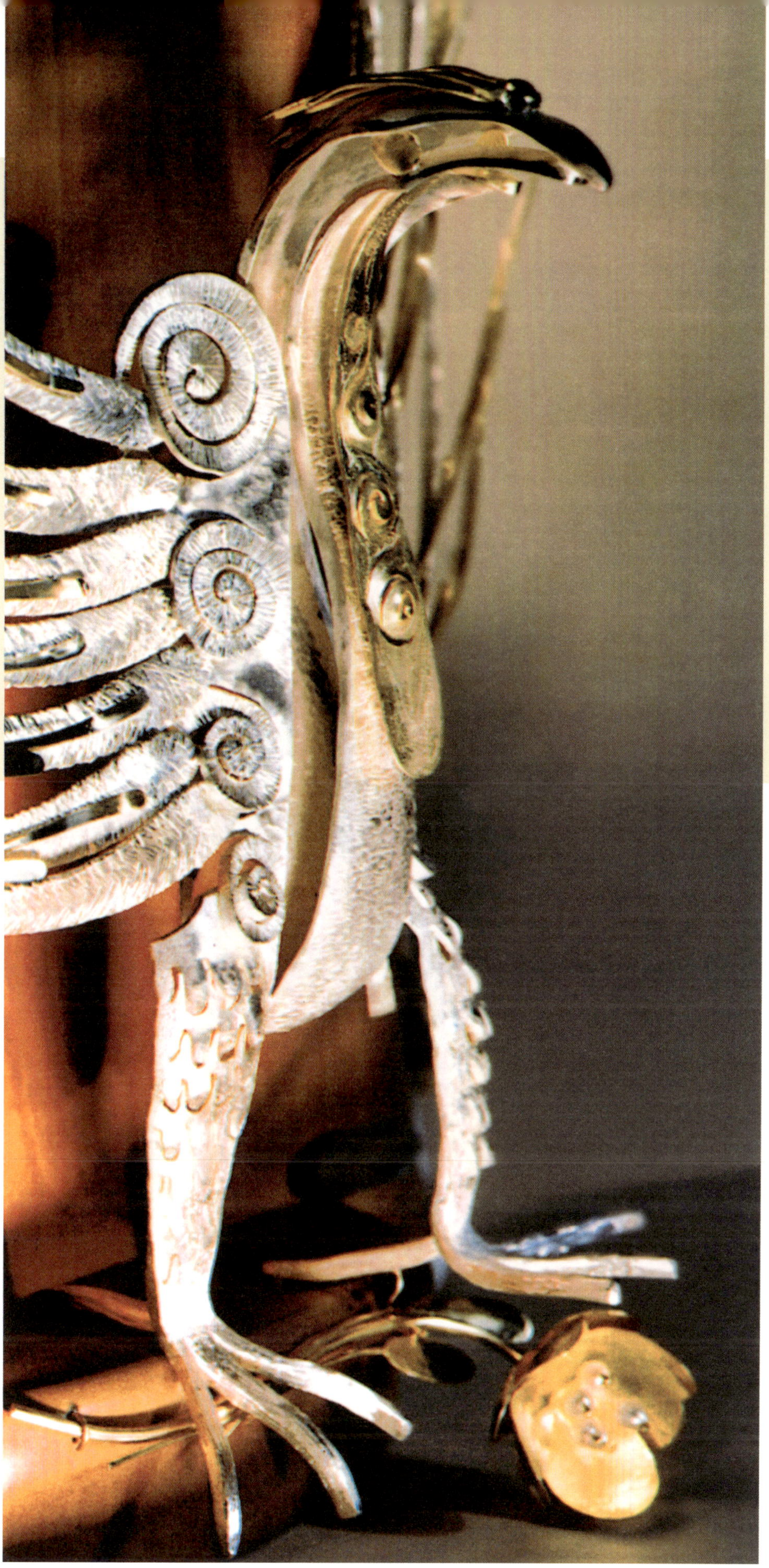

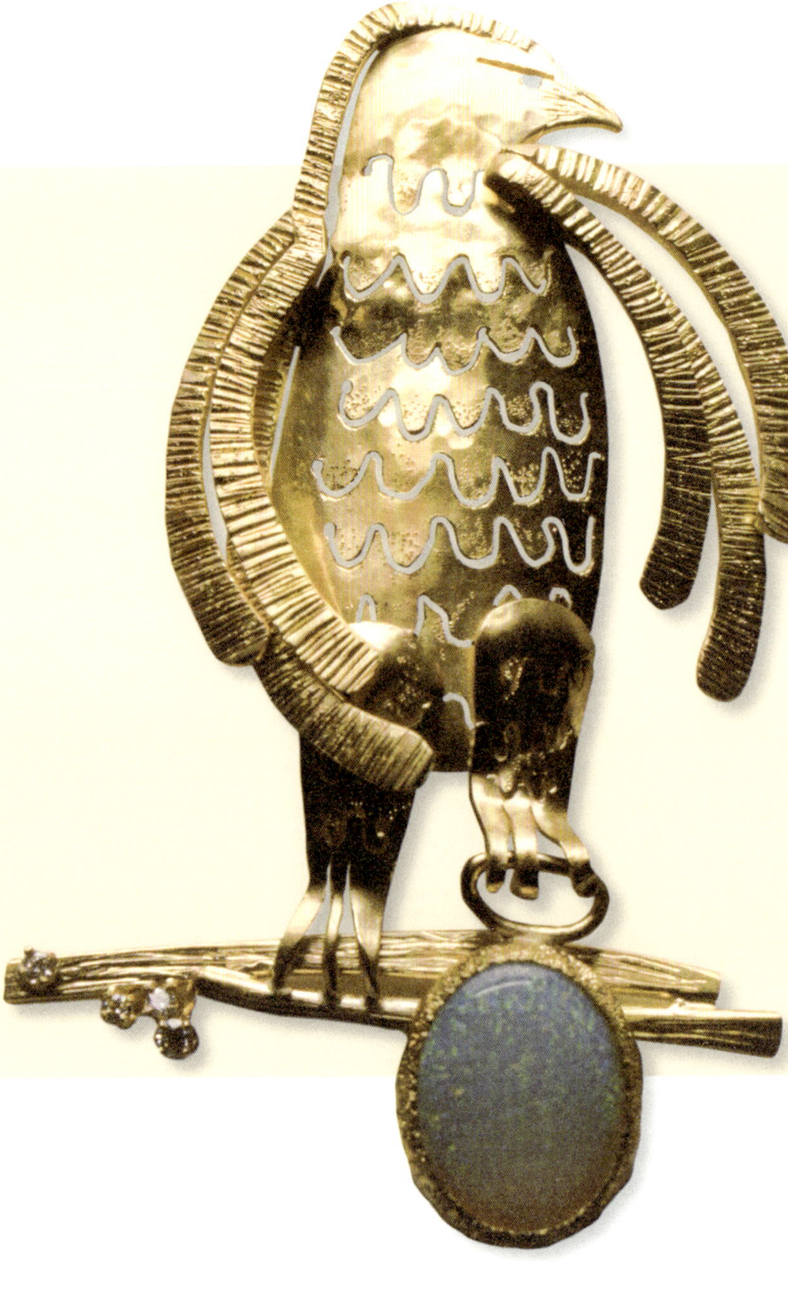

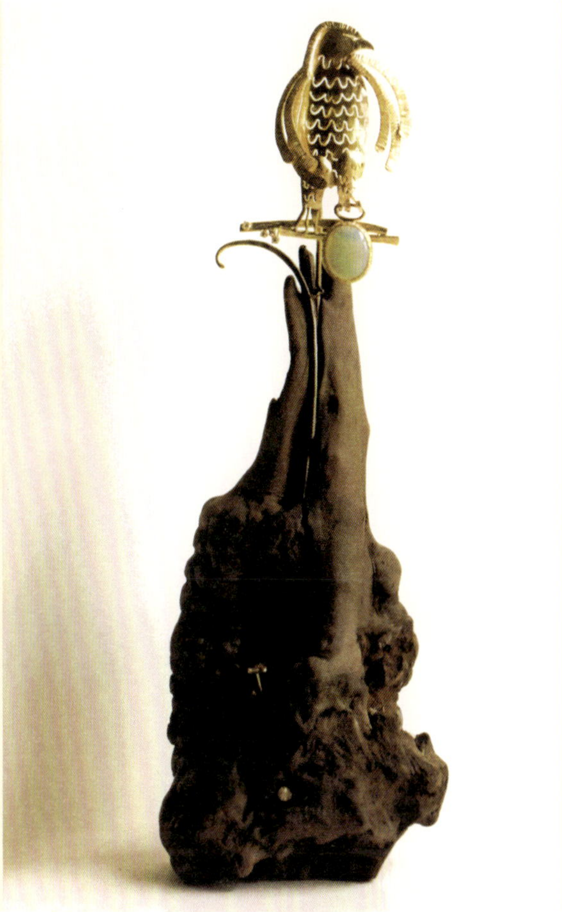

Eagle sculpture and pin, 18-karat gold and boulder opal, mounted on manzanita driftwood. Approximately 14″ high

OPPOSITE: Pin removed from mounting

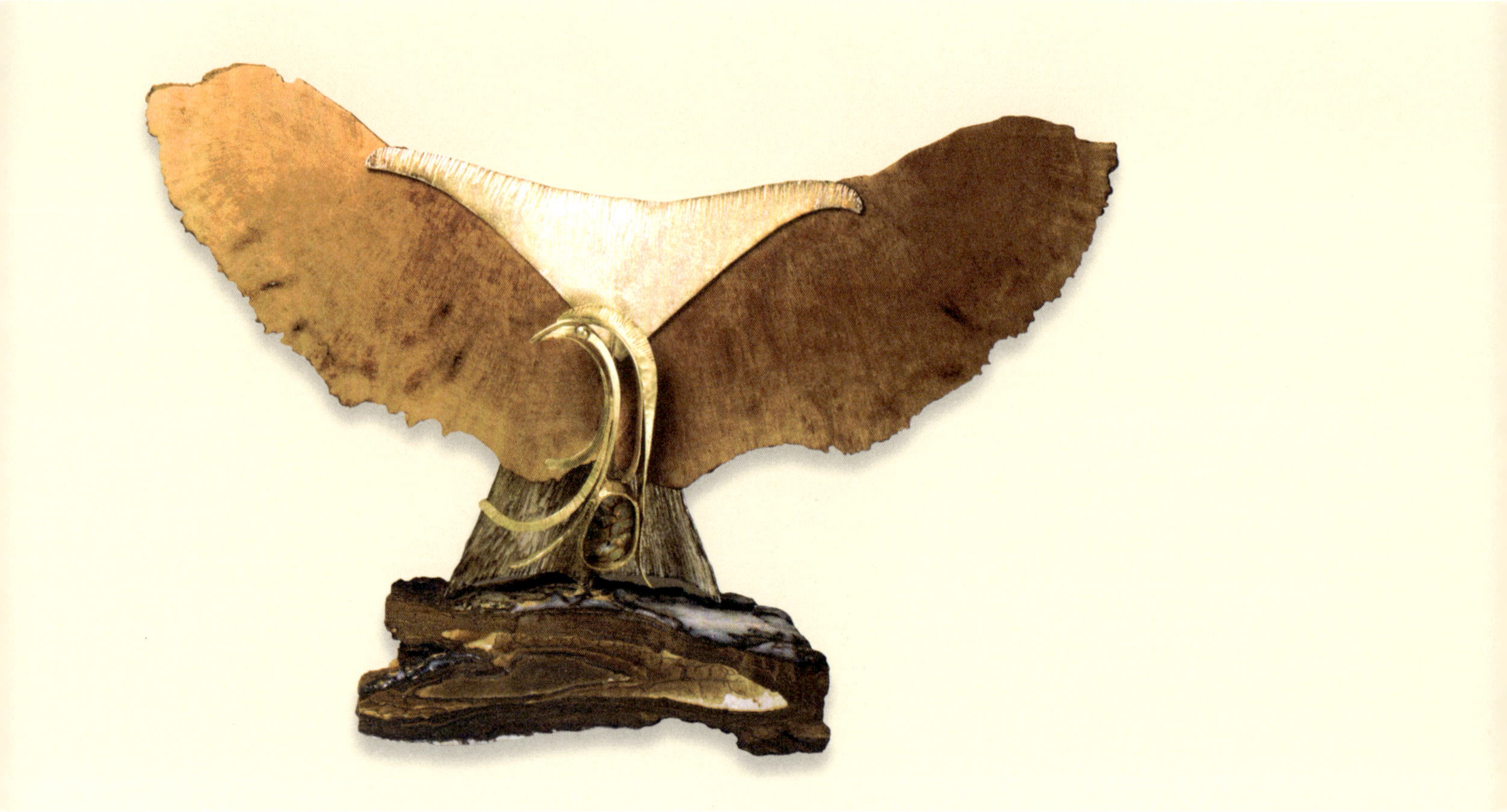

Eagle sculpture and pendant, 18-karat gold, sterling silver, and boulder opal, with wings of thin-sliced brier, mounted on opal in matrix base. Approximately 6″ high, 12″ wide

OPPOSITE: Pendant removed from mounting

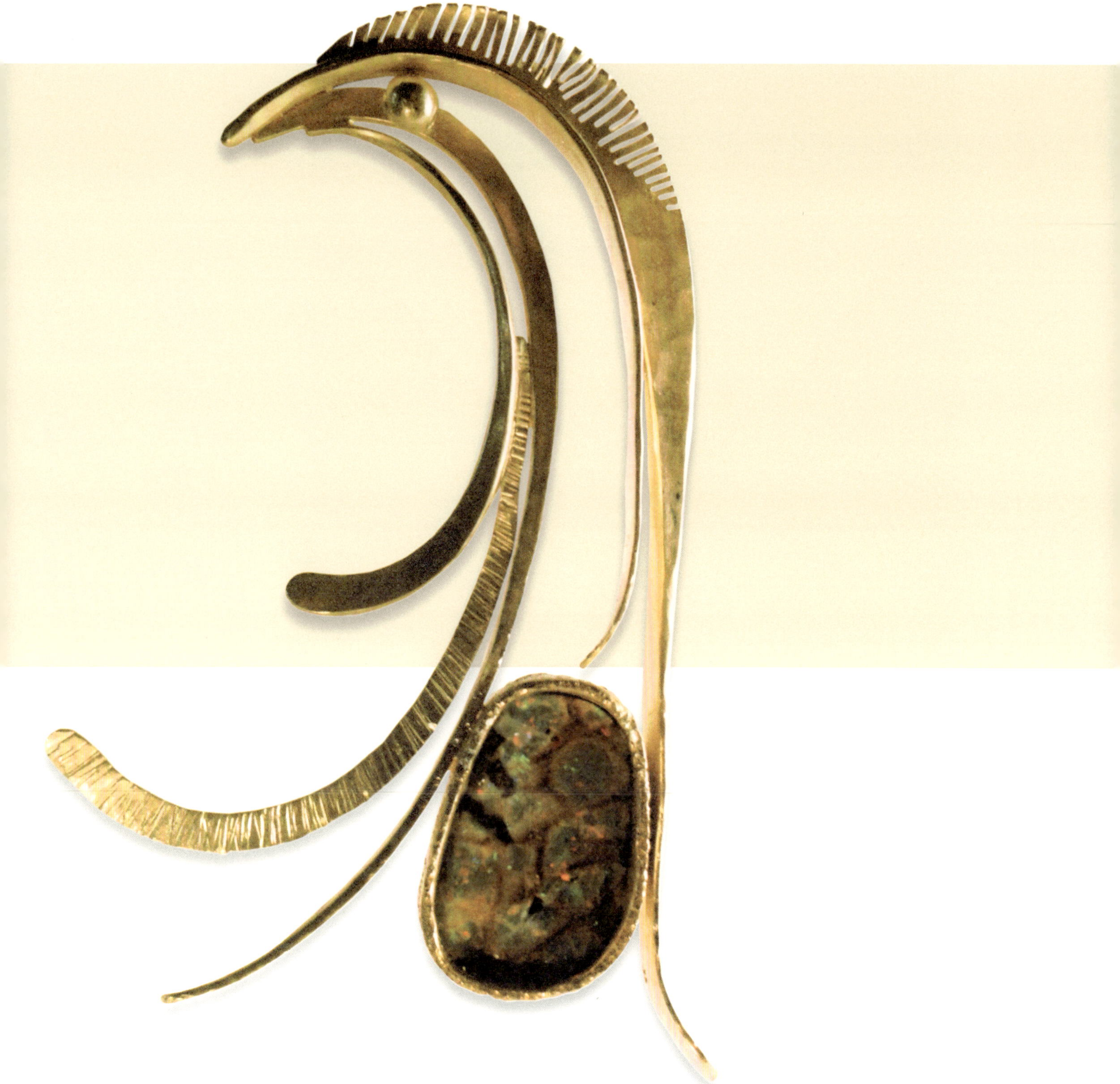

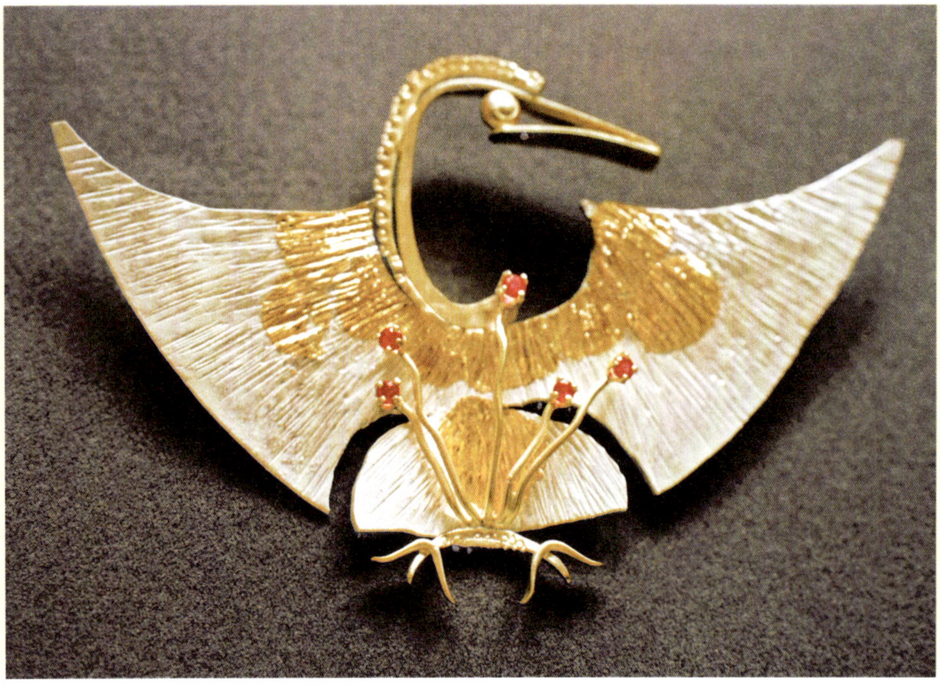

Spread eagle pin, 18- and 24-karat gold,
fine silver, and Burma rubies.
Approximately 2¼″ high, 4″ wide

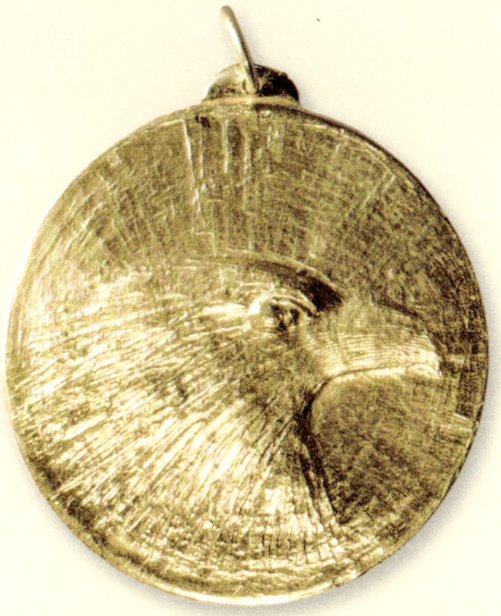

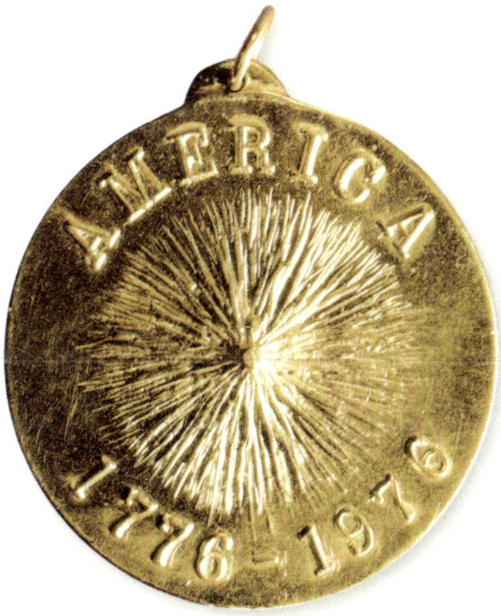

TOP: Bicentennial medallion (obverse), handstruck from a hand-carved steel die, 18-karat gold. Approximately 1″ diameter

BOTTOM: Reverse of Bicentennial medallion

RINGS & EARRINGS

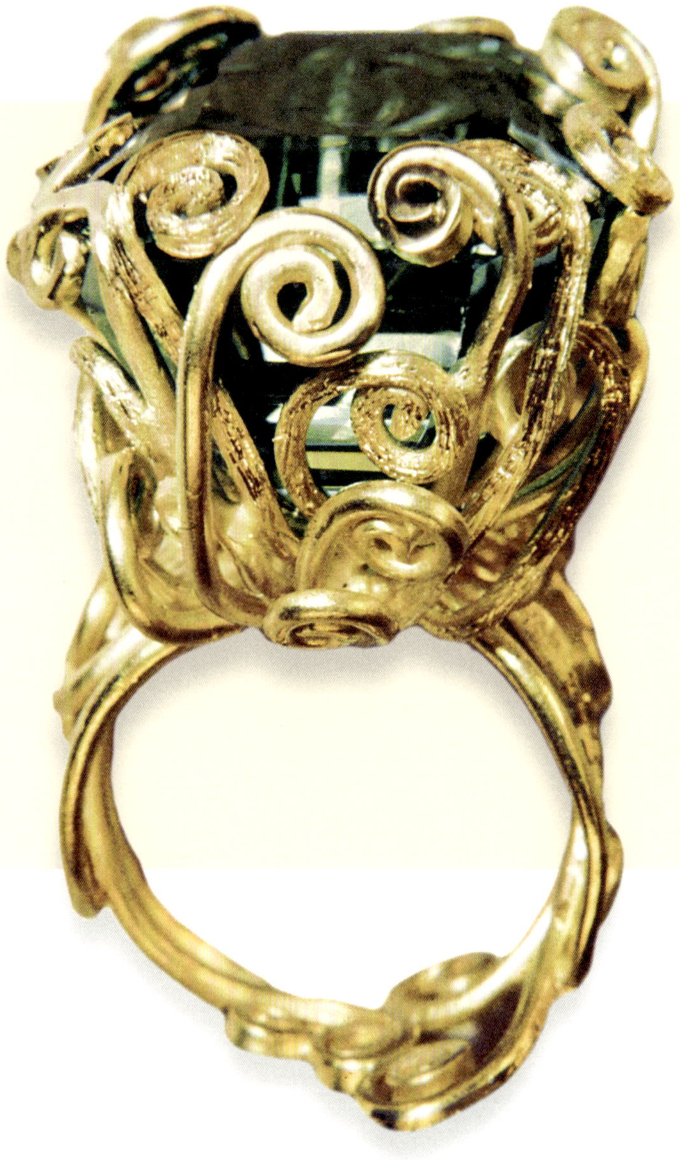

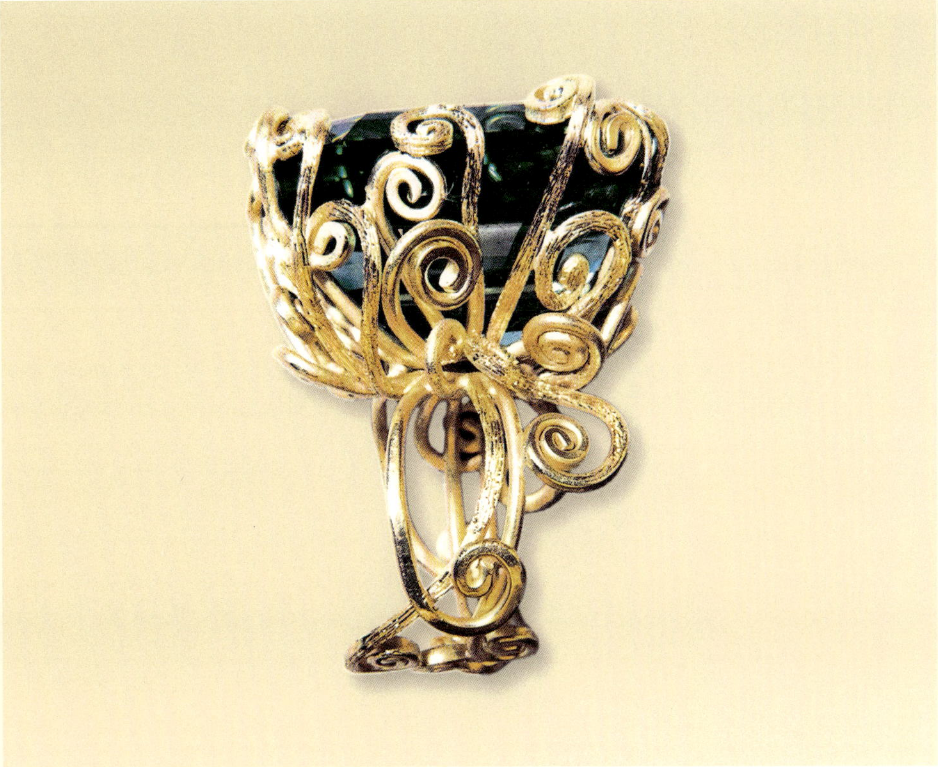

Aquamarine and 18-karat gold ring, c. 1962

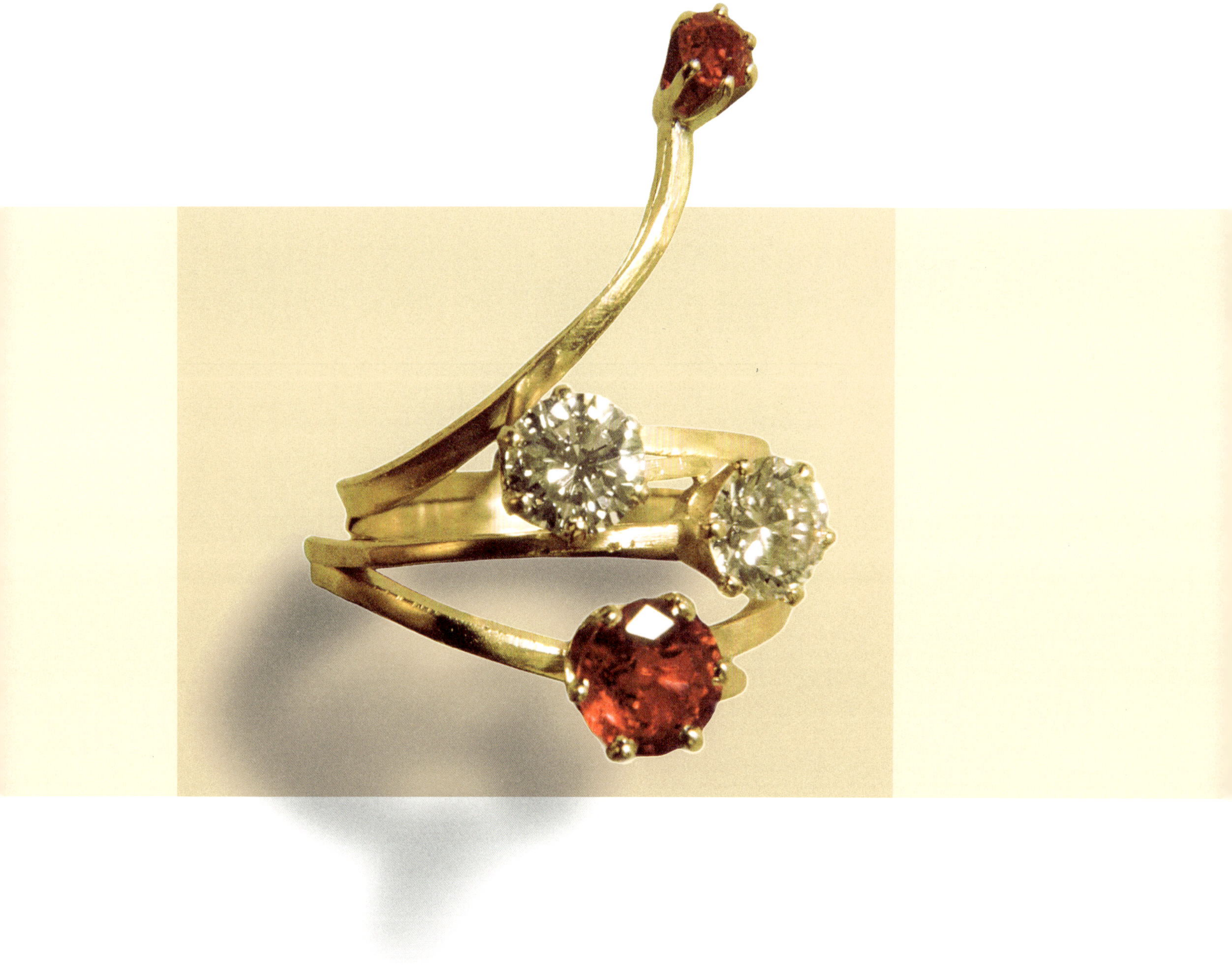

Diamond and Burma ruby ring, 18-karat gold

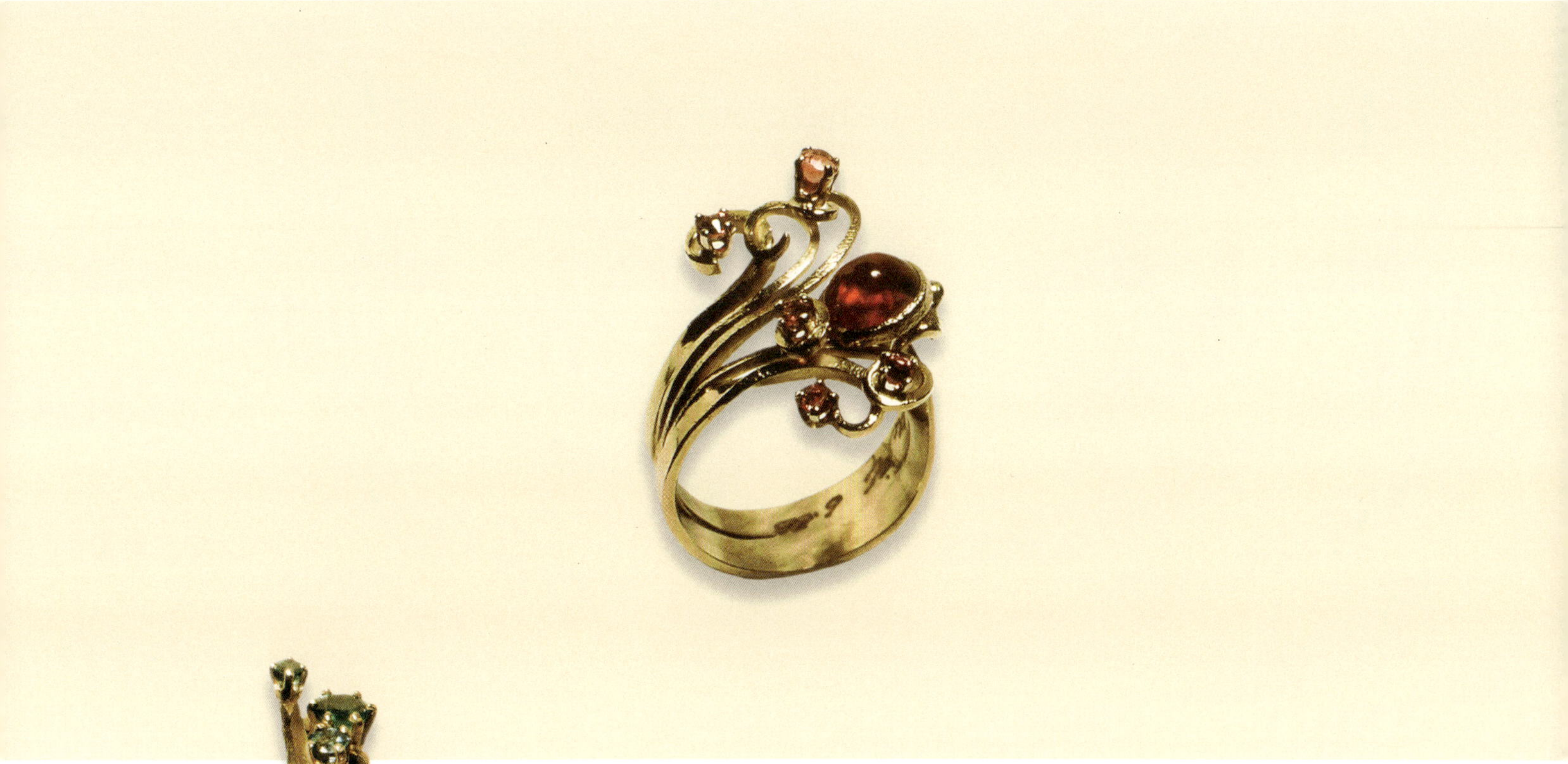

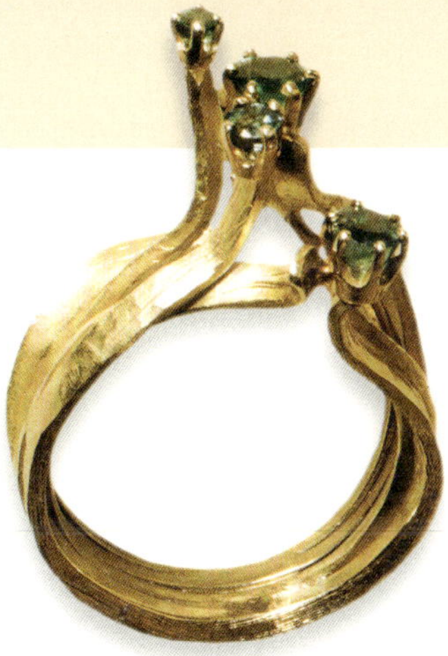

TOP: Cabochon ruby and pink sapphire ring, 18-karat gold

BOTTOM: Emerald and 18-karat gold ring

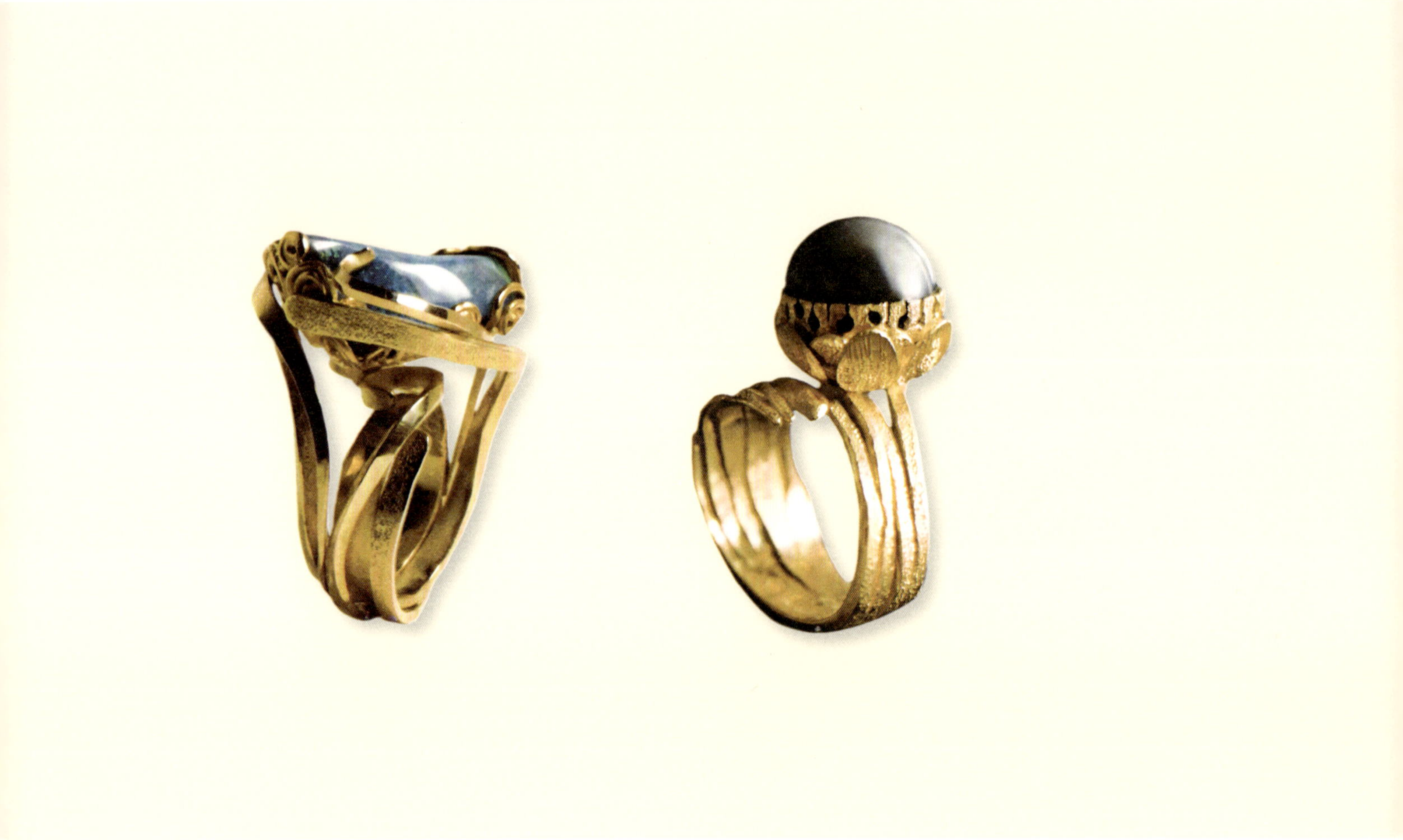

LEFT: Boulder opal and 18-karat gold ring

RIGHT: Black pearl lotus ring, 18-karat gold

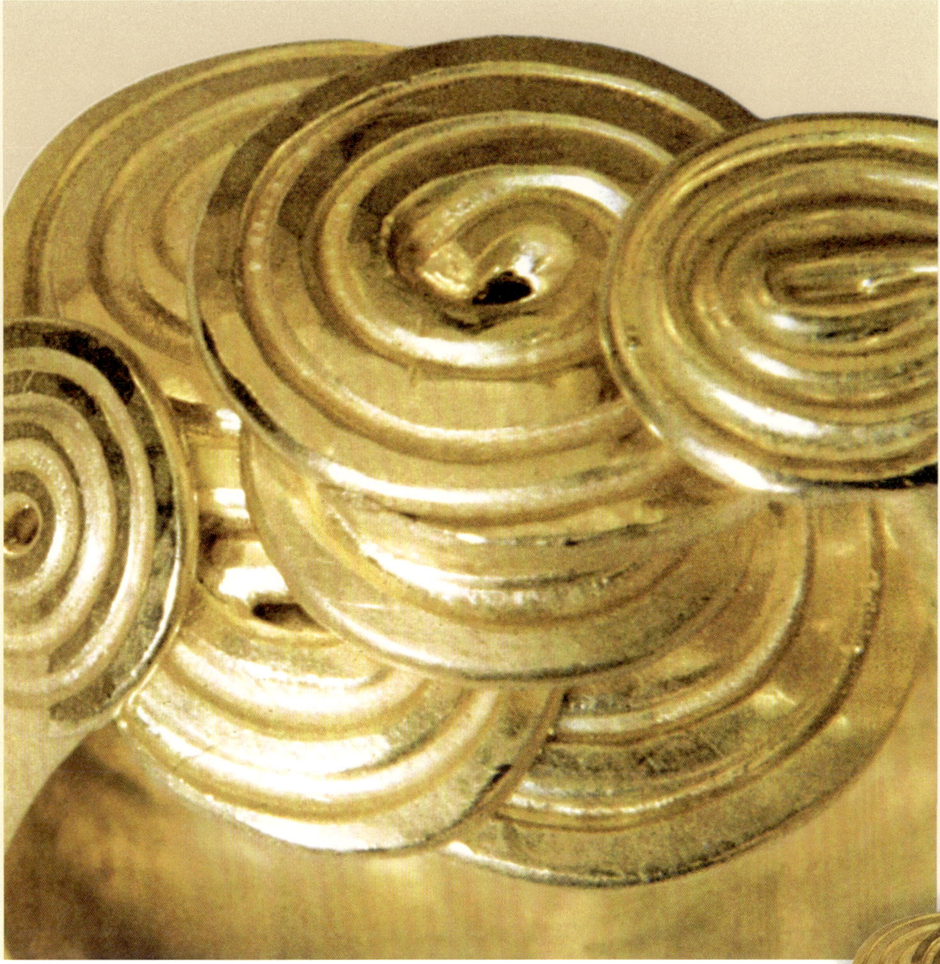

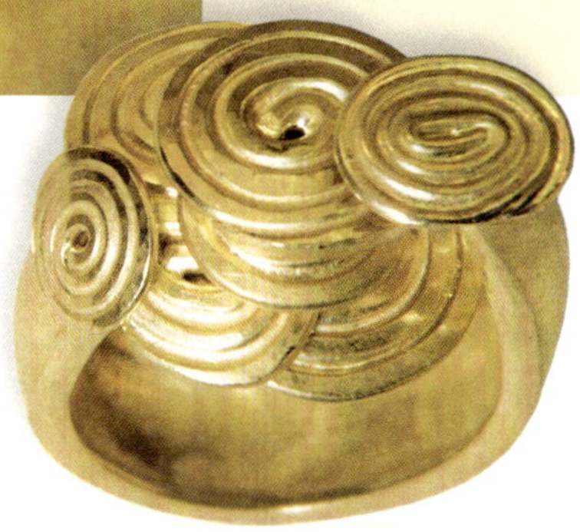

Disk ring, 18-karat gold, c. 1958

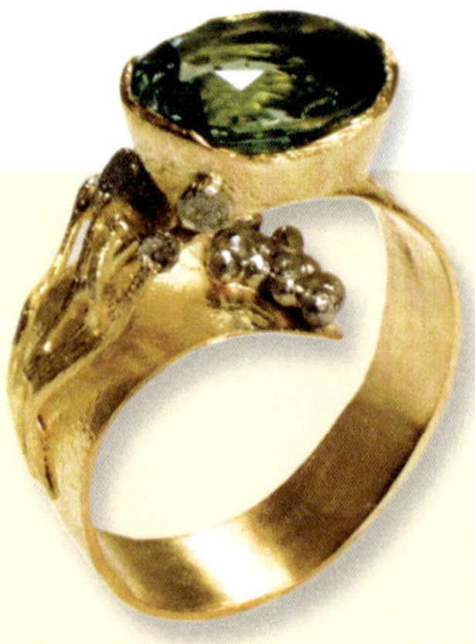

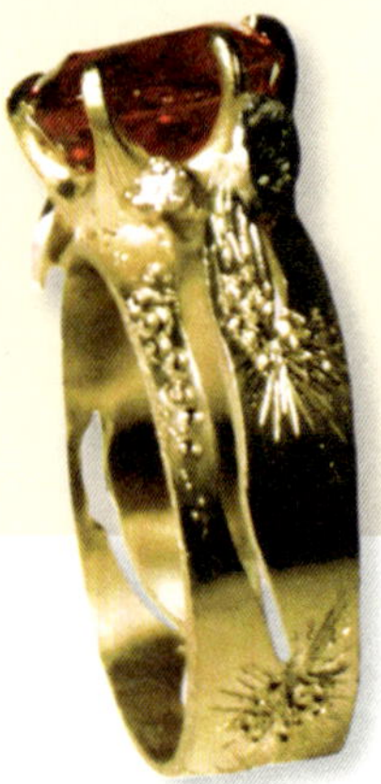

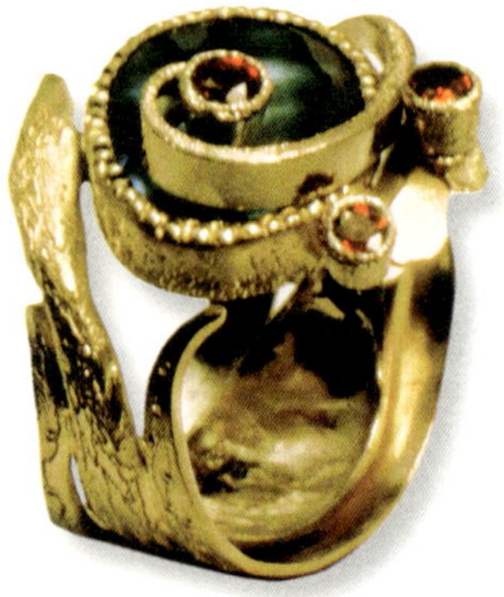

TOP: Green tourmaline and 18-karat gold ring, reflecting light onto white gold beads

MIDDLE: Amber diamond ring, 18-karat gold

BOTTOM: Ring of 18-karat gold, abalone shell, and Burmese rubies

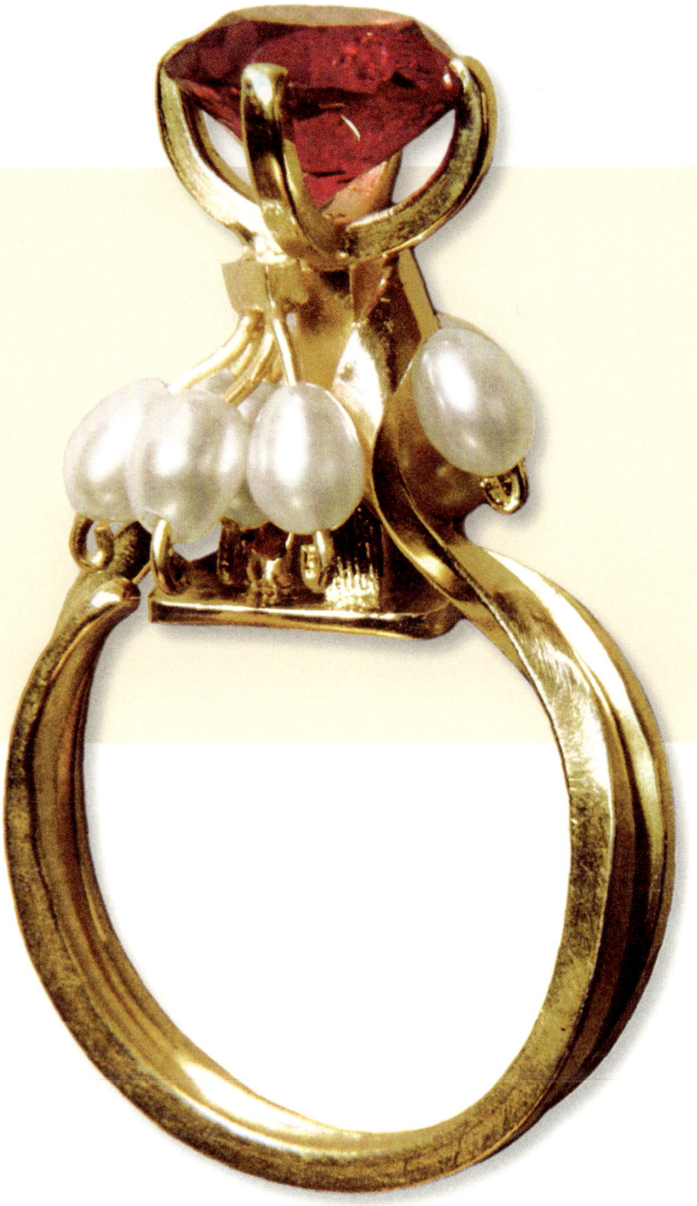

Rhodolite and freshwater
pearl ring, 18-karat gold

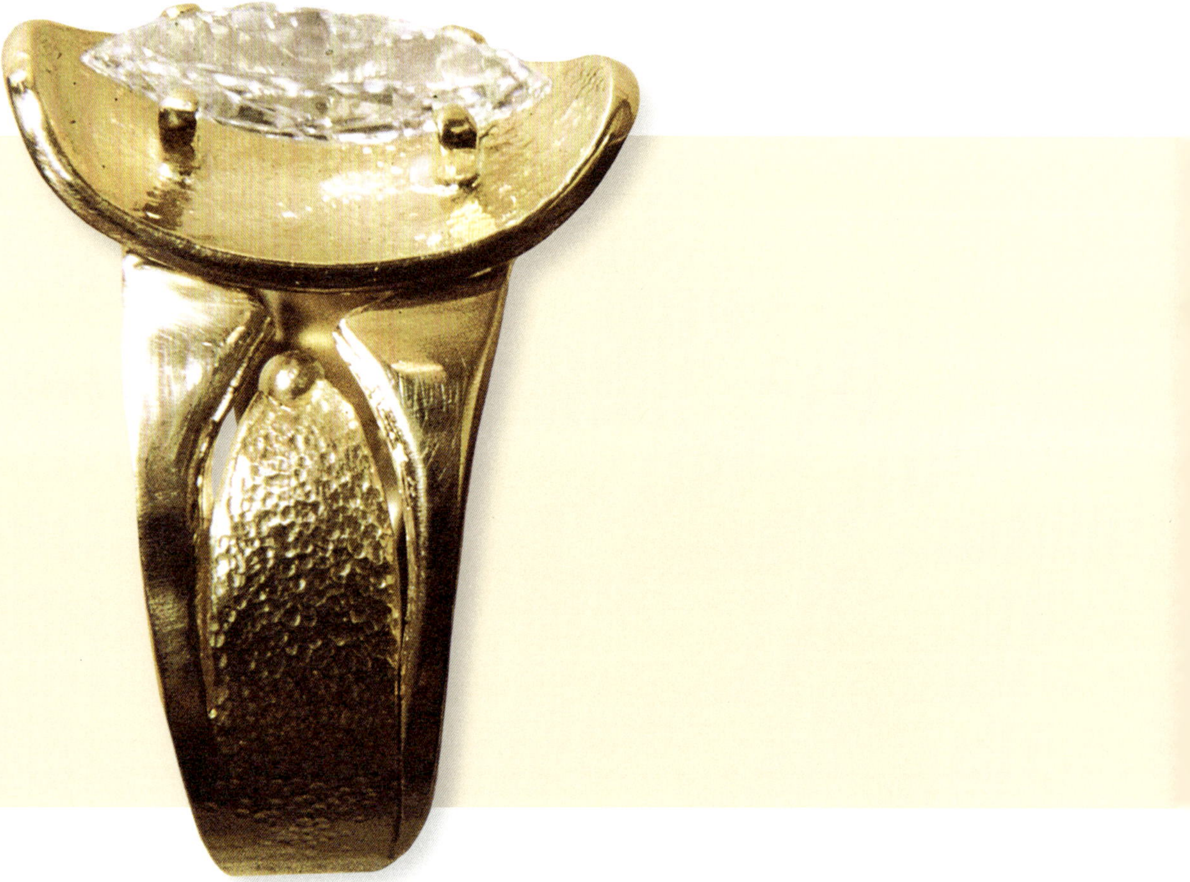

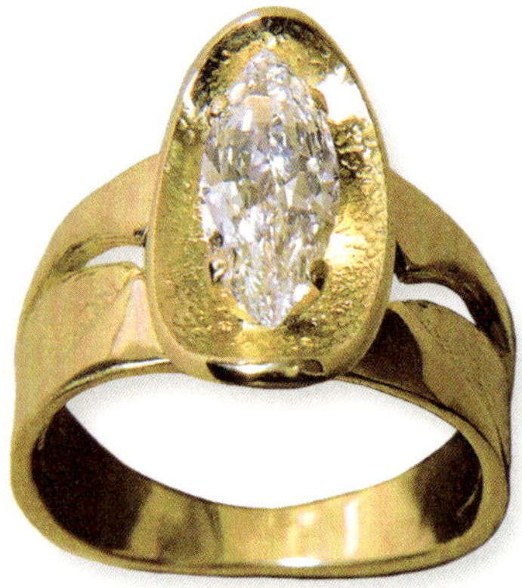

Marquise diamond ring,
18- and 24-karat gold,
c. 1967

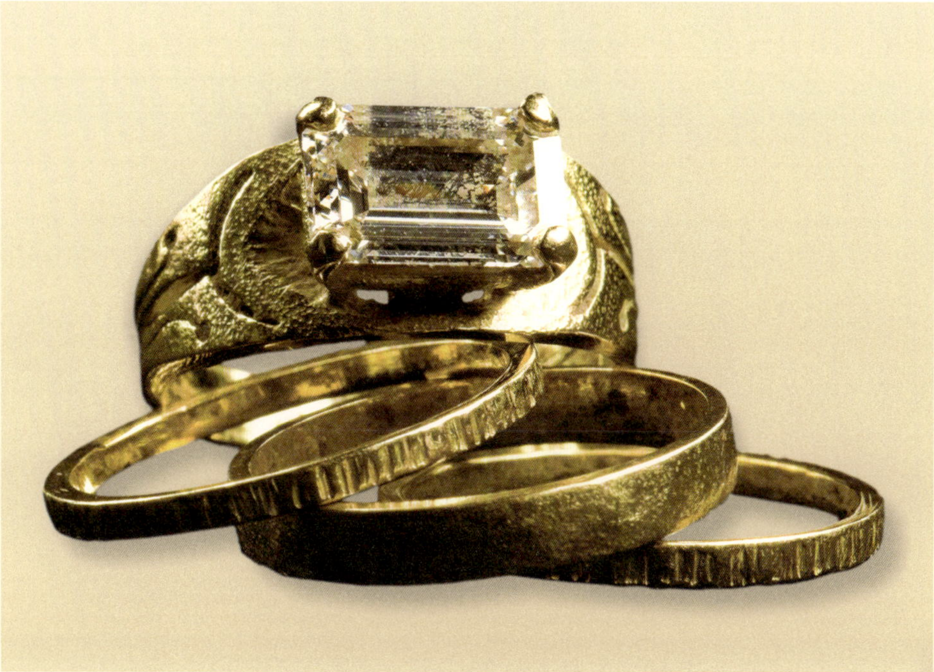

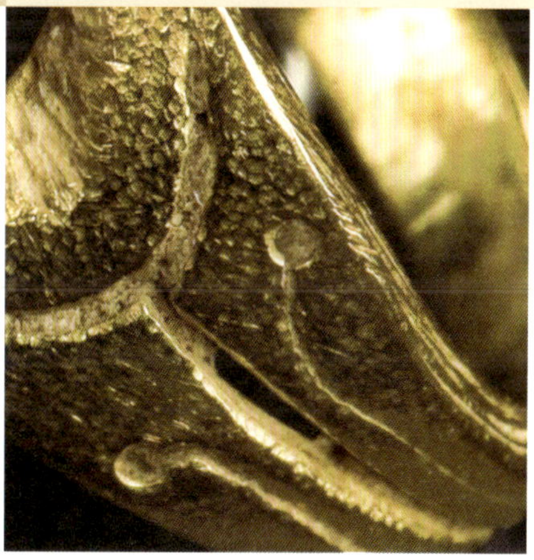

Ann's Ring, emerald-cut diamond, 18-karat gold, with 18-karat gold side mounts (David Gunn Photography)

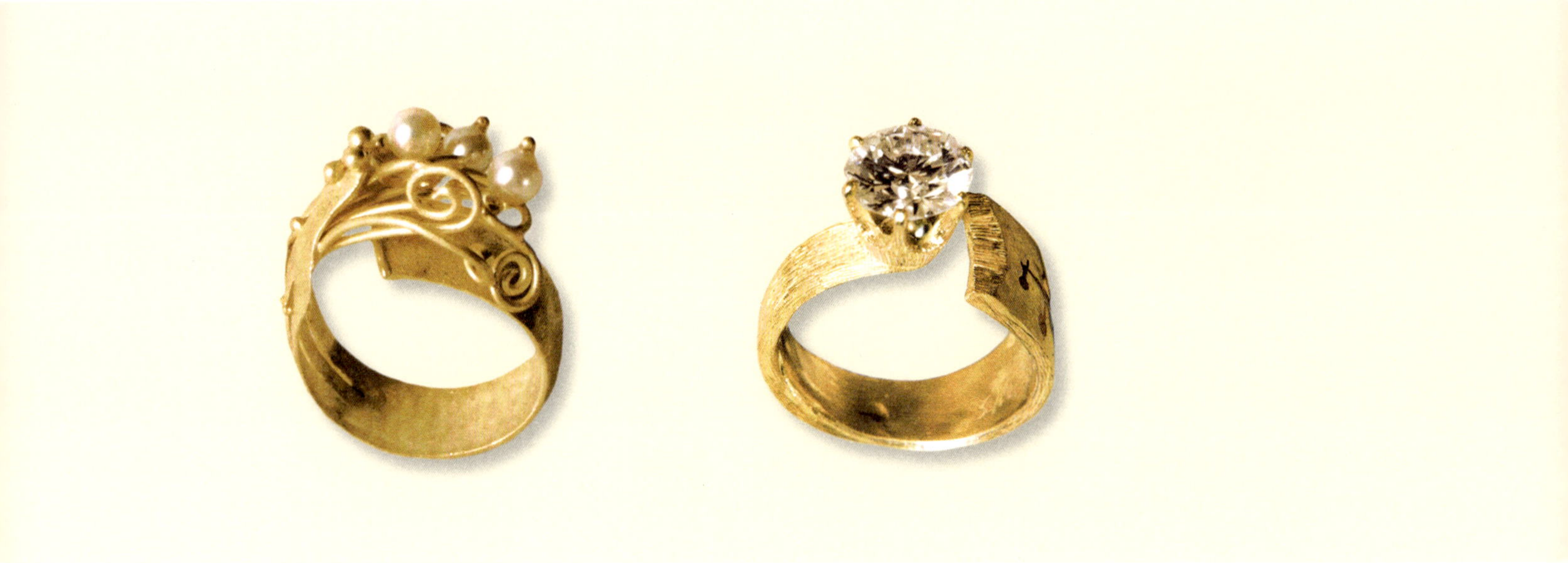

The Nautilus, 18-karat gold ring, South Sea pearls

Open diamond ring, 18-karat gold

RIGHT: Emerald and 18-karat gold earrings, c. 1955

BELOW: *Ring of Many Pearls,* 18-karat gold, pearls

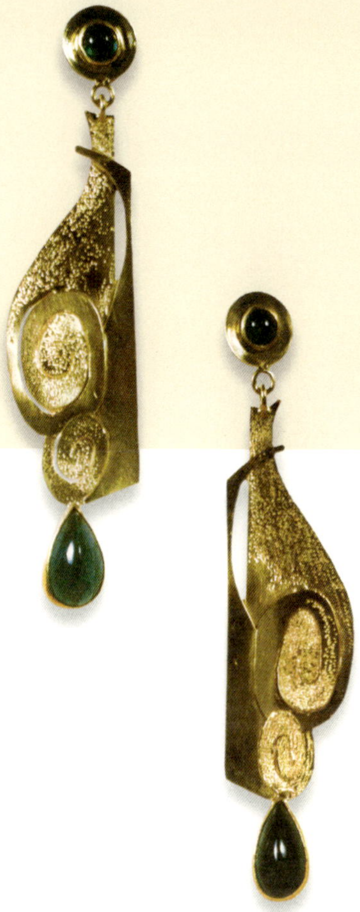

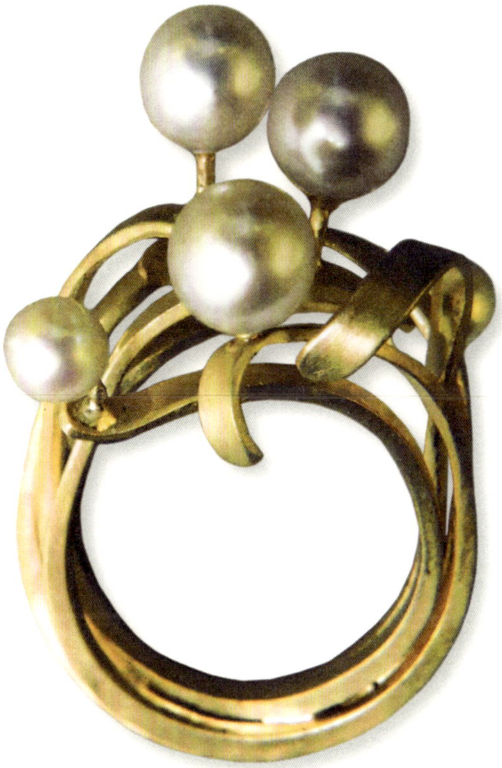

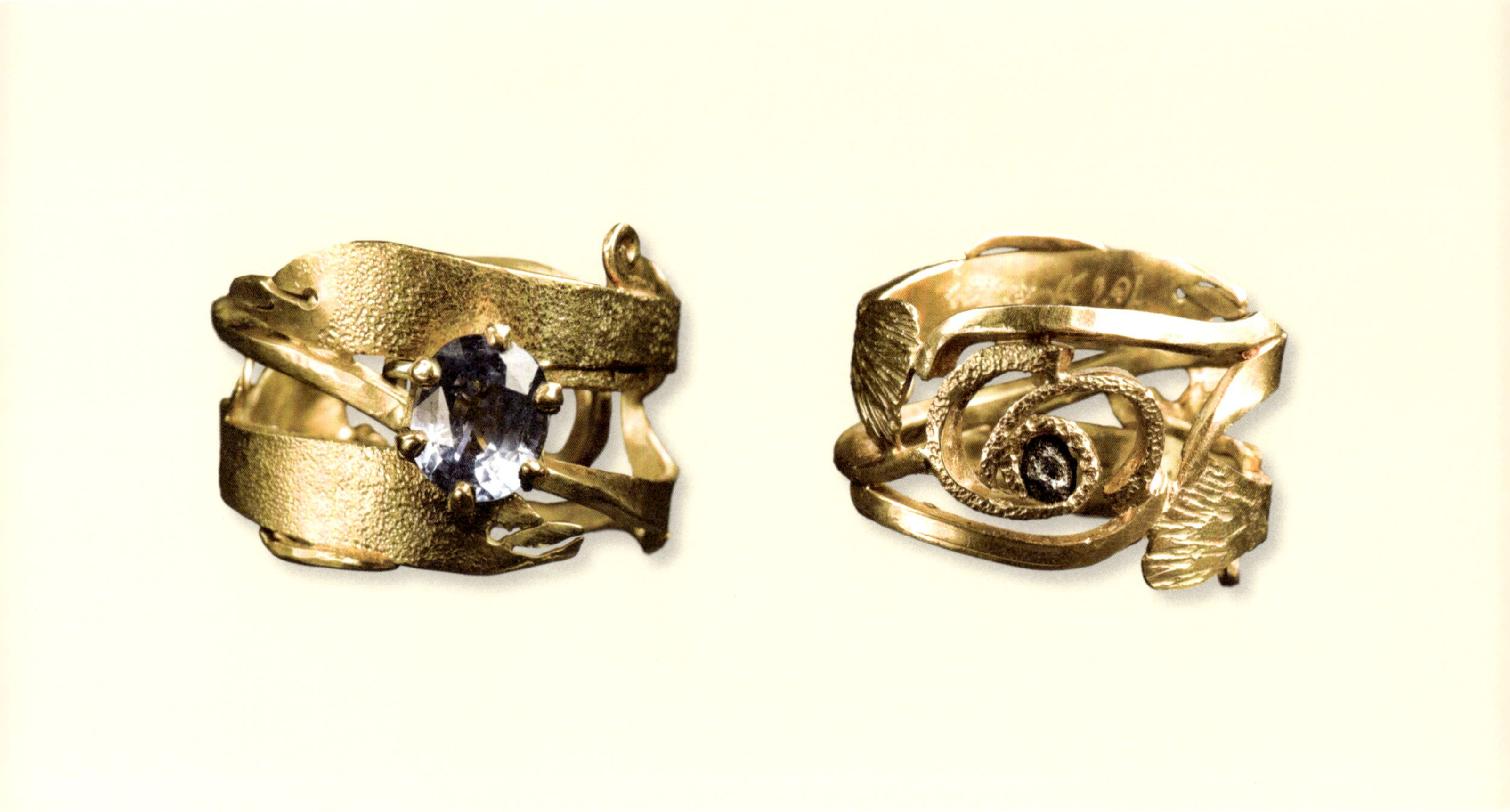

Front and back view of 18-karat gold ring with sapphire, and on the back, a small piece of iron ore. Made for a competitor in the 1994 Ironman race in Hawaii. (David Gunn Photography)

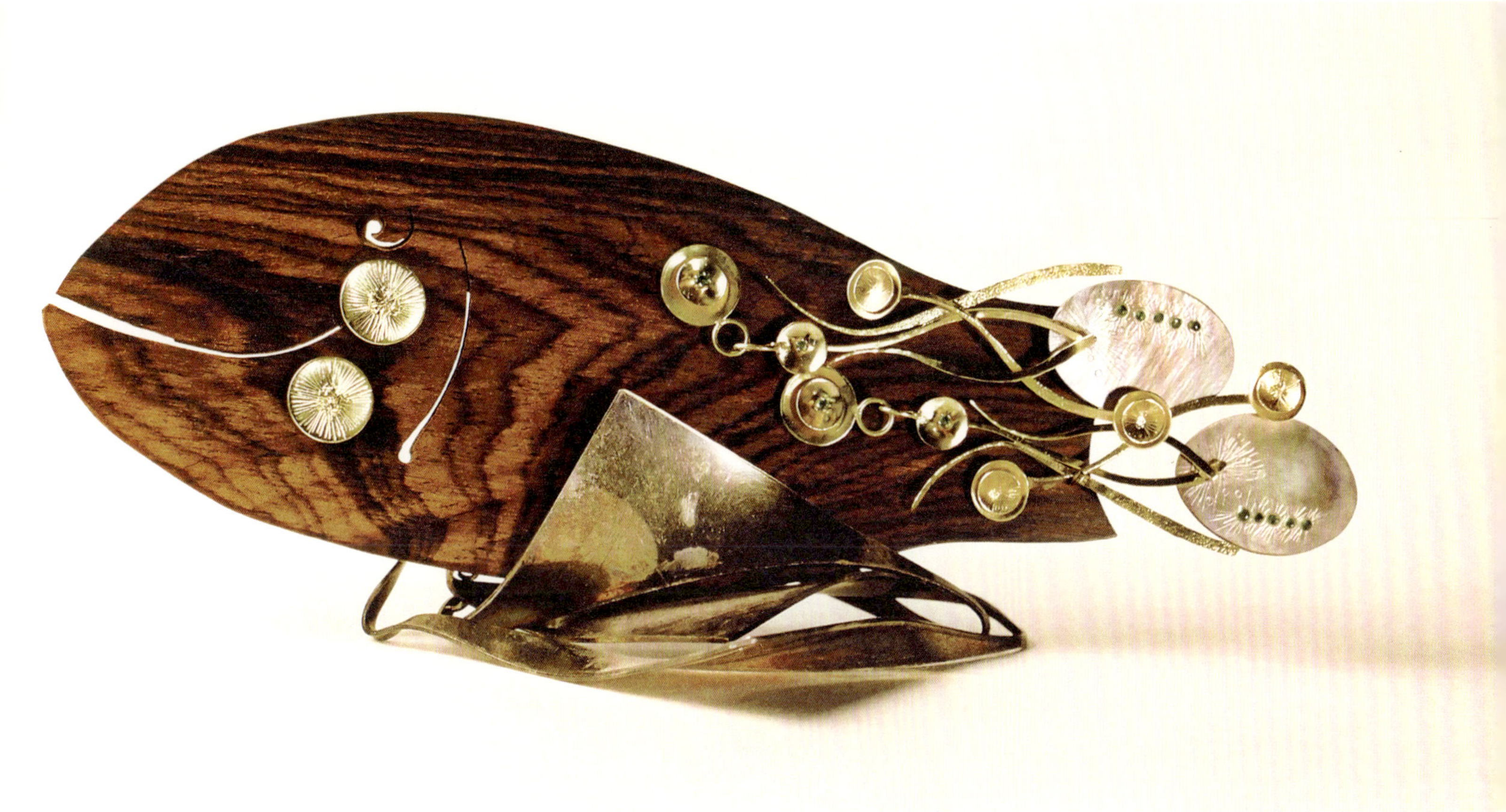

Ornamented ebony fish sculpture with two pairs of earrings, 18- and 24-karat gold, mother-of-pearl, and emerald, mounted on a fine silver base. Approximately 11″ wide

RIGHT: Earrings of 18-karat gold, mother-of-pearl, and emerald, removed from fish sculpture

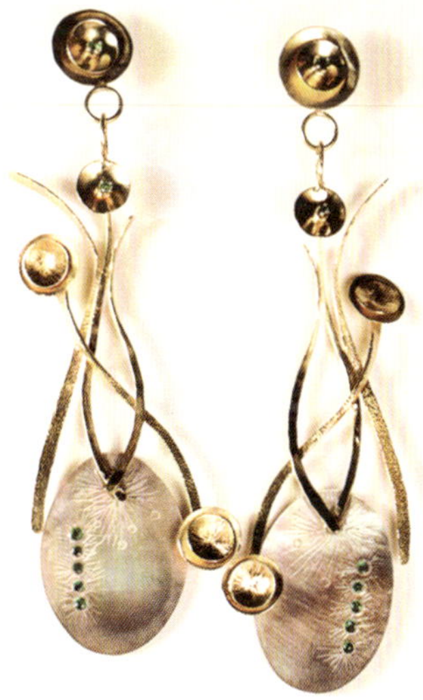

PINS, BRACELETS & NECKLACES

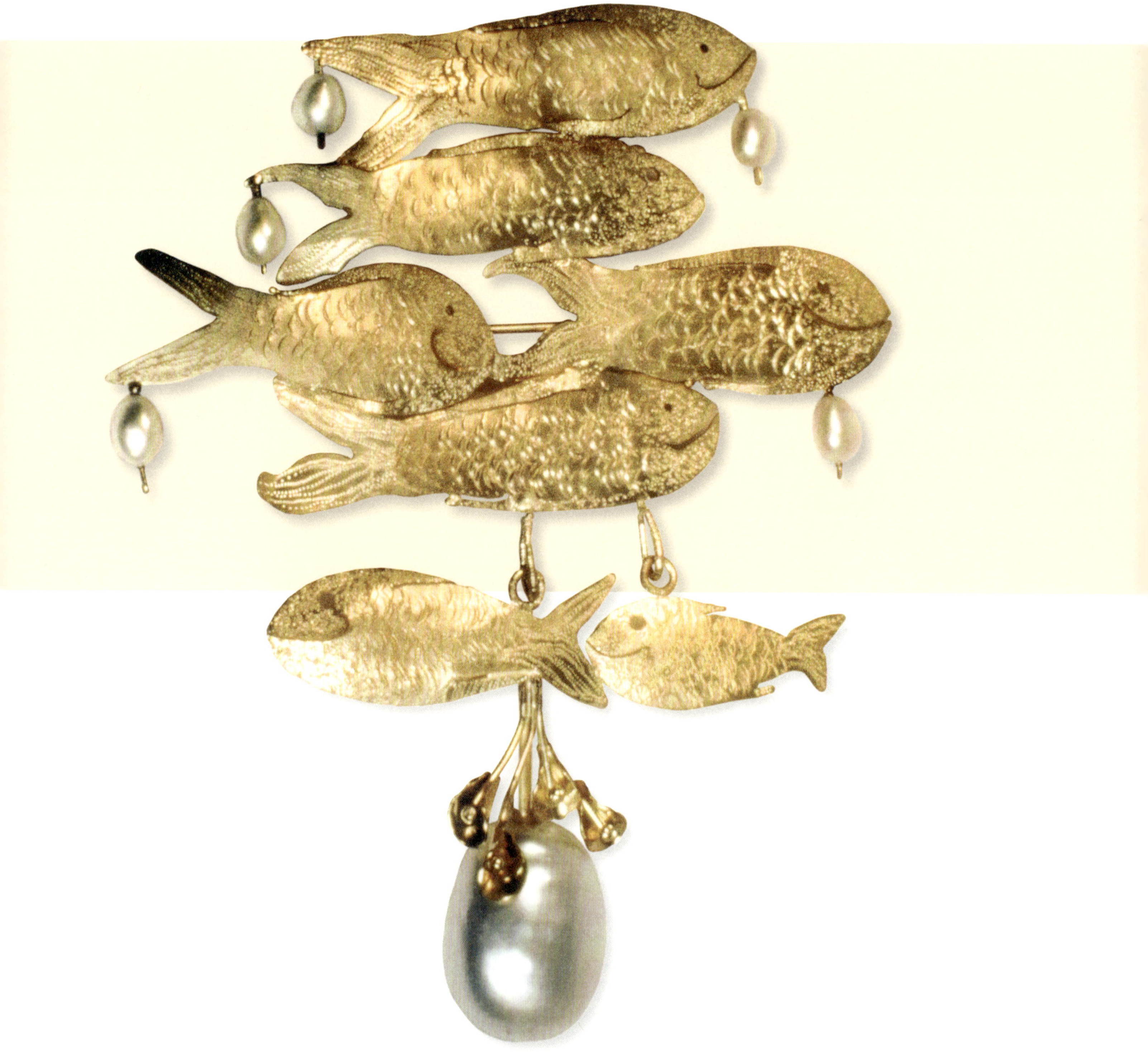

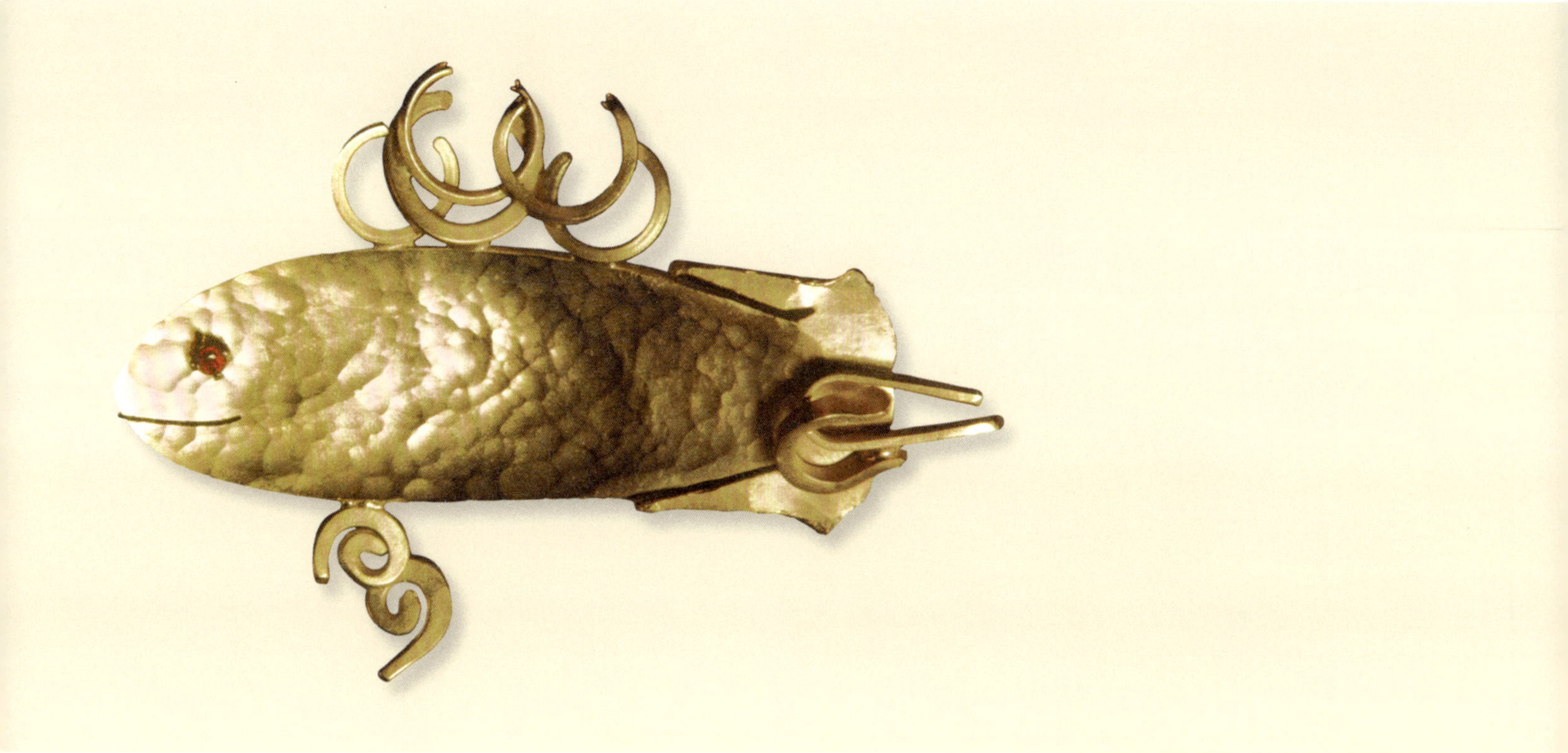

Fish Pin No. 1, 18-karat gold with Burma ruby, c. 1953

OPPOSITE: *Frolicking Fishes,* 18-karat gold, Lake Biwa freshwater pearls, diamonds, and large baroque pearl

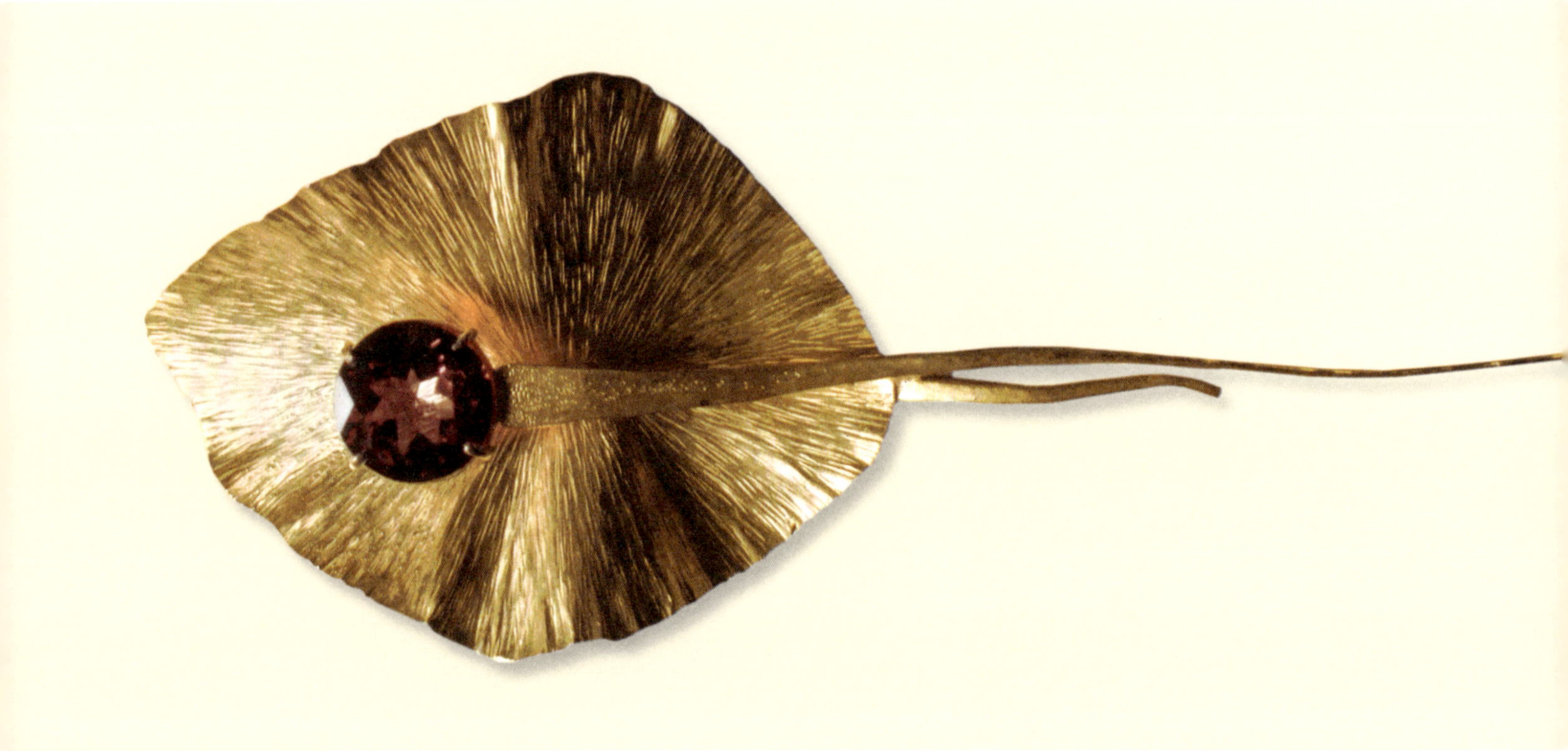

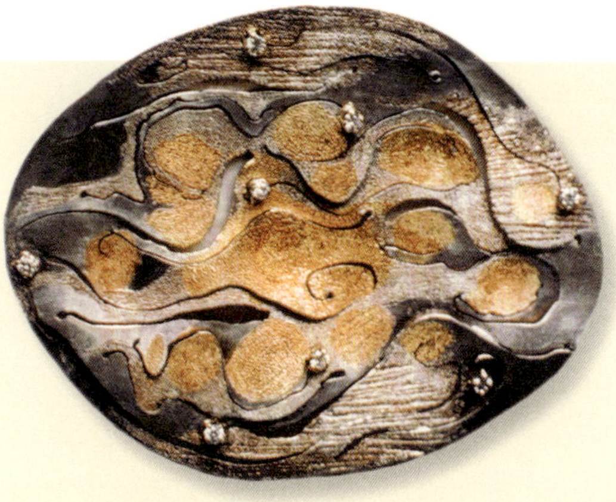

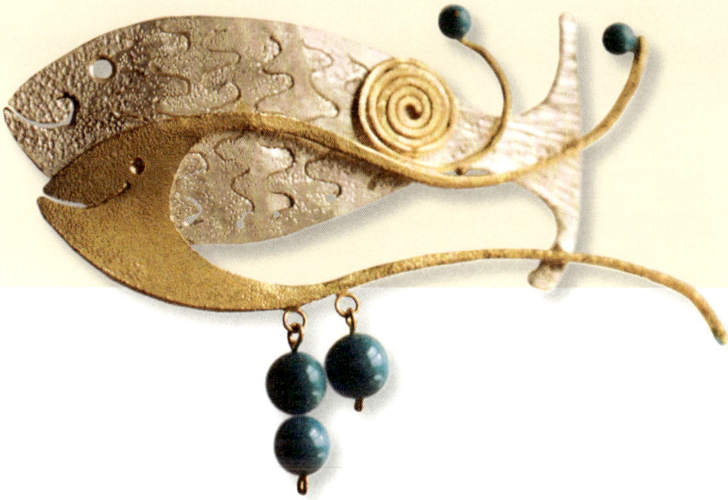

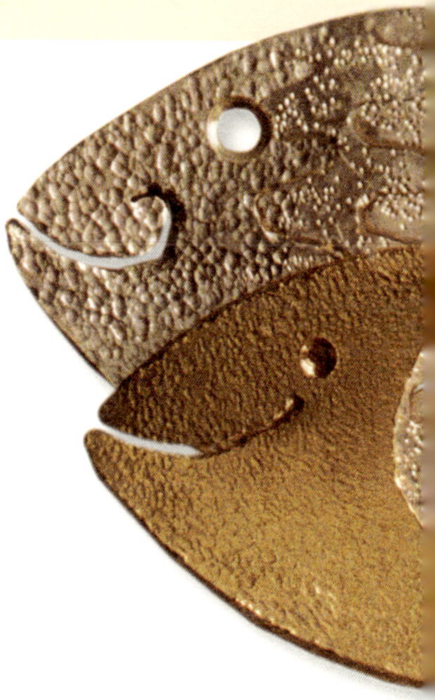

TOP: *Cavorting Whales,* fine silver, 24-karat gold, and diamonds

ABOVE AND RIGHT: *Due Pesce,* fine silver, 18-karat gold, and turquoise beads

OPPOSITE: Sea creature pin, 18-karat gold with rhodolite

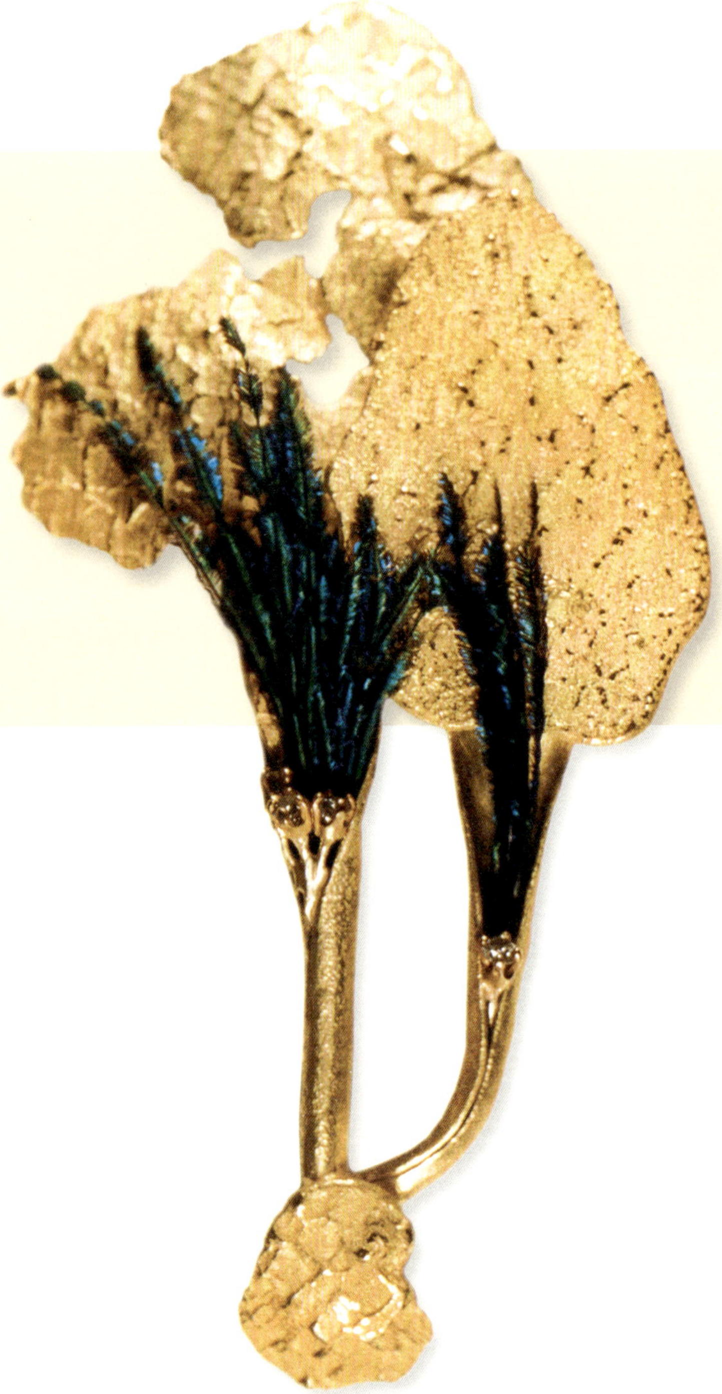

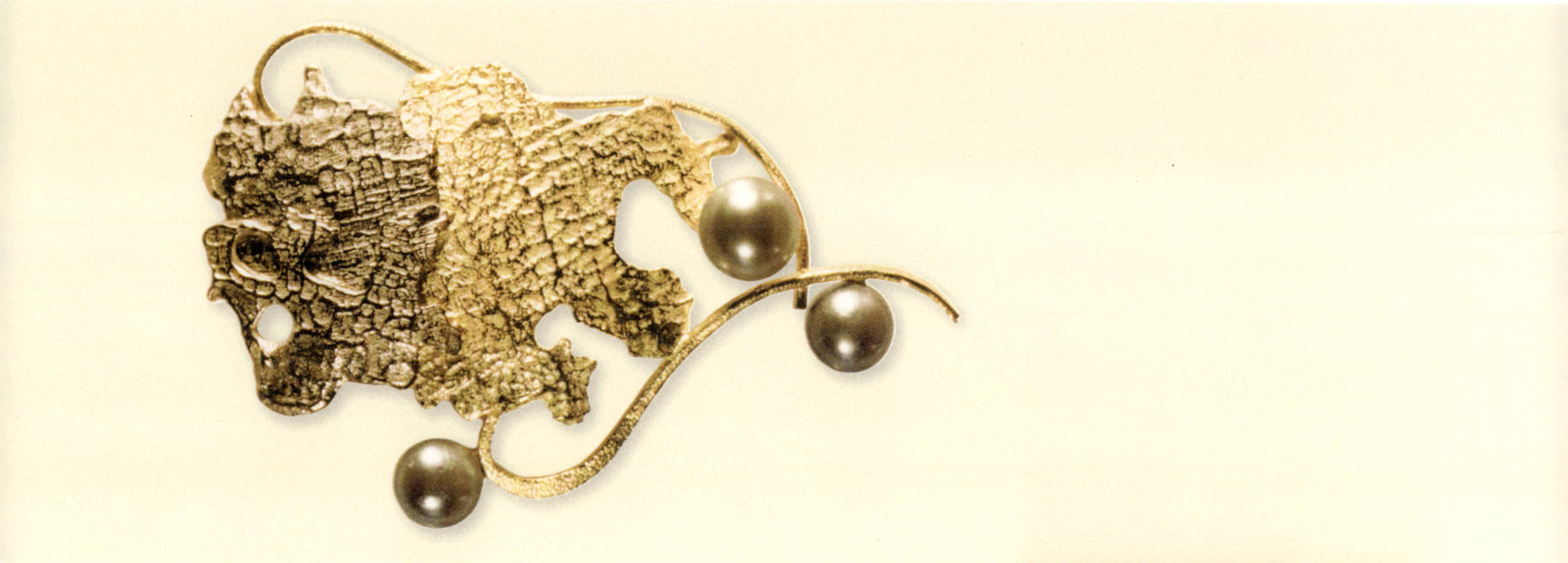

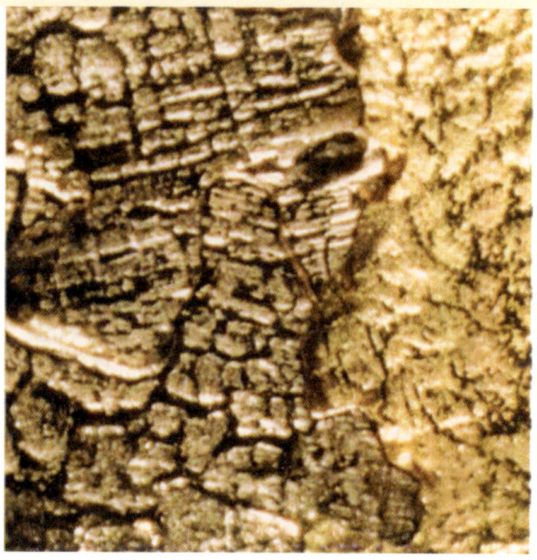

Pin in rough-cast 18-karat gold and South Sea black pearls

OPPOSITE: Pin and pendant, 18-karat gold, diamonds, and peacock feathers

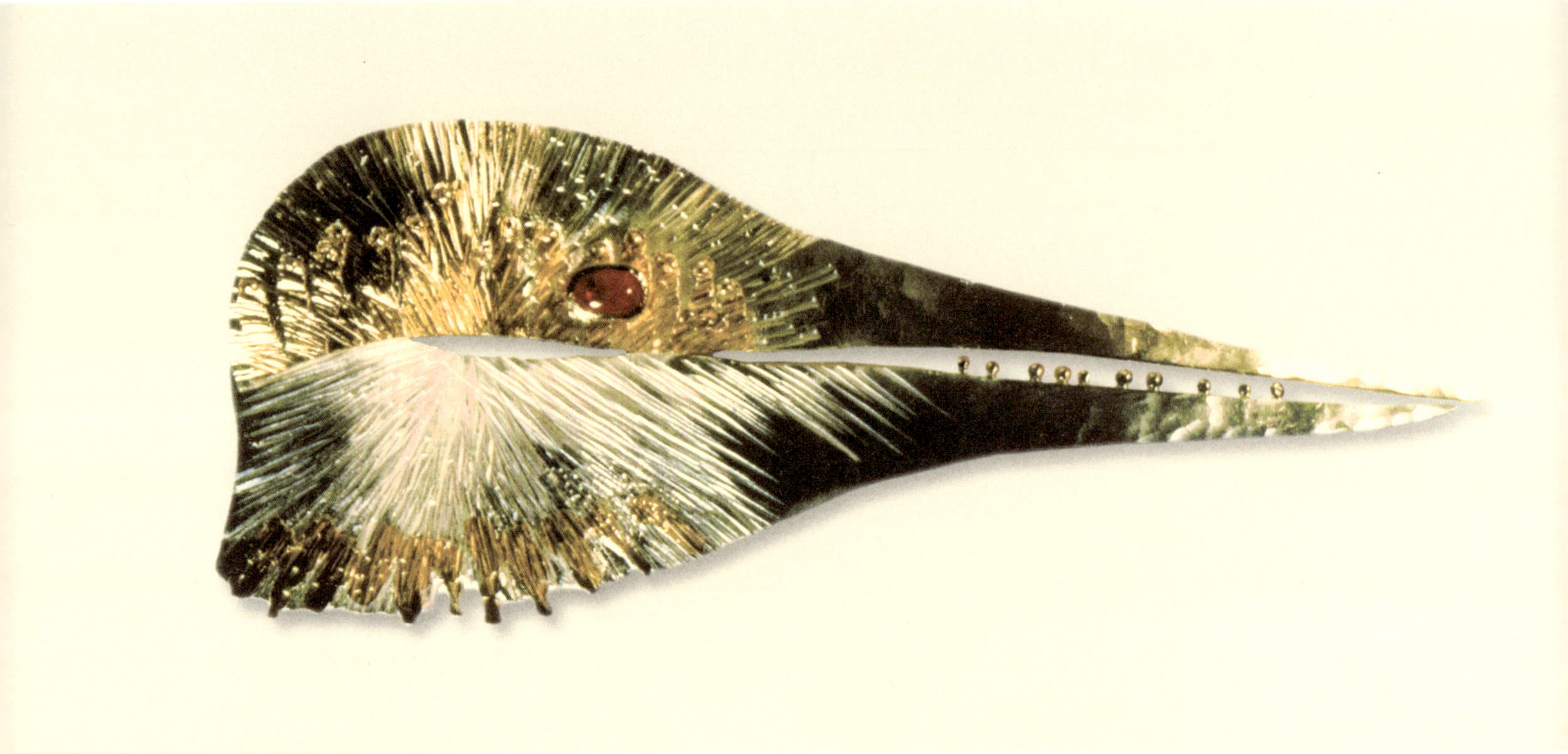

Prehistoric bird pin, fine silver, 24-karat gold, and Burma ruby

OPPOSITE: Opal pin in 18-karat gold

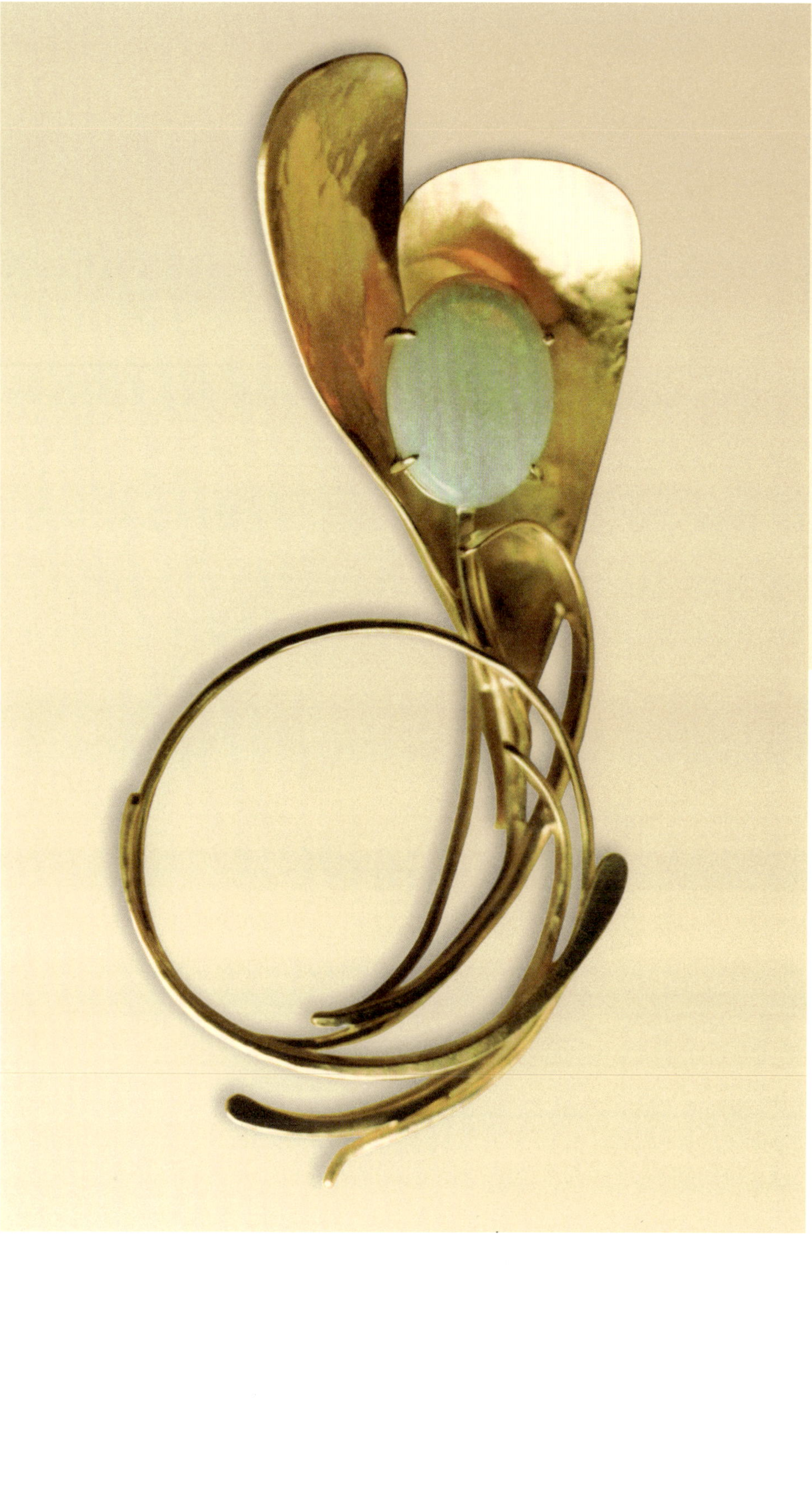

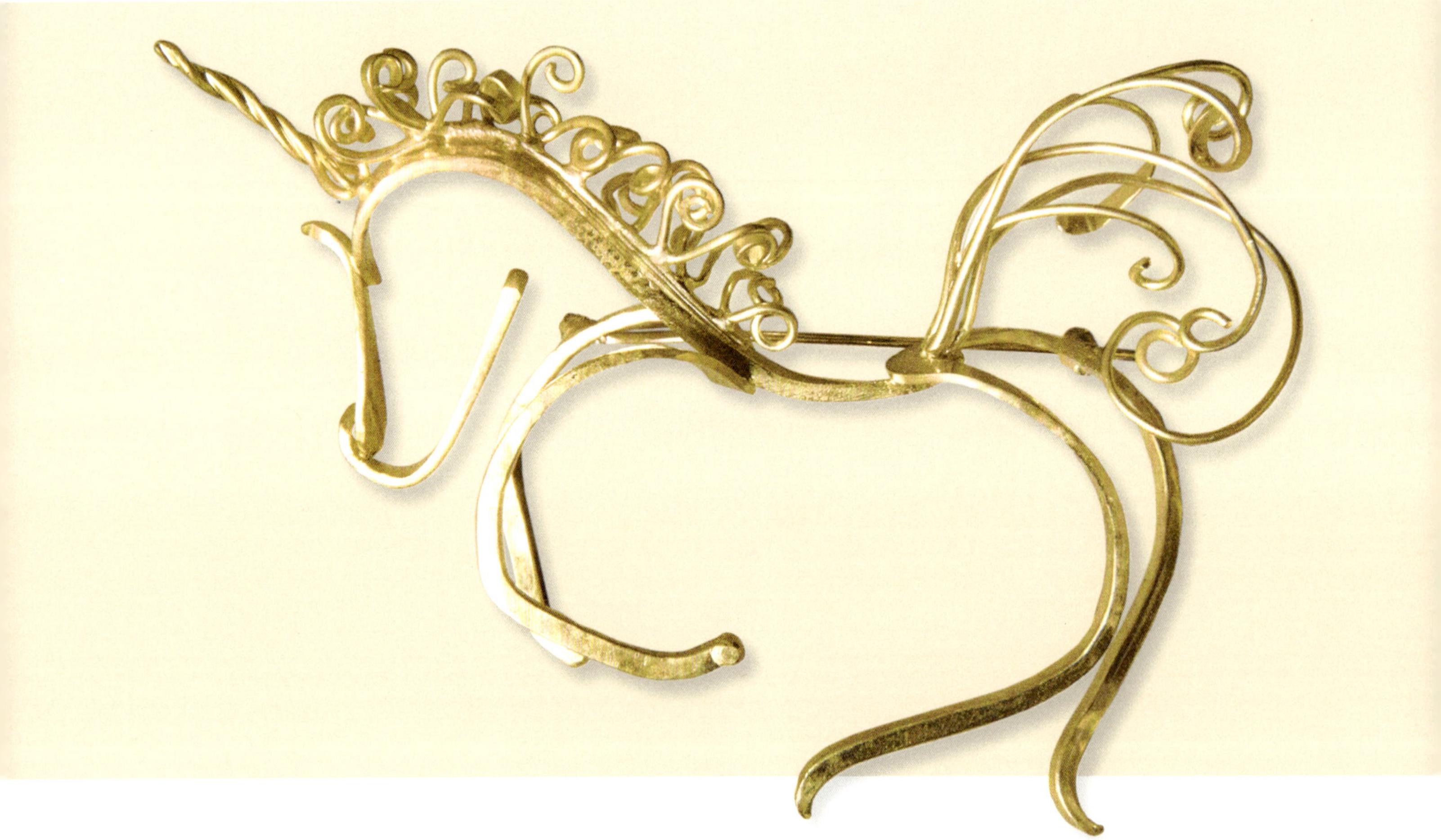

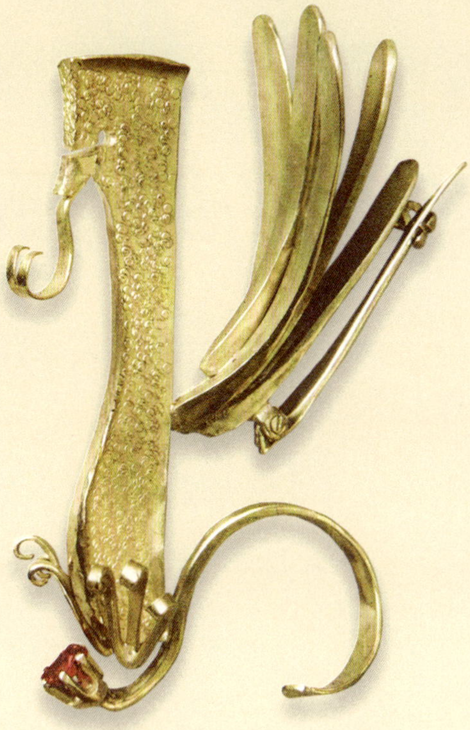

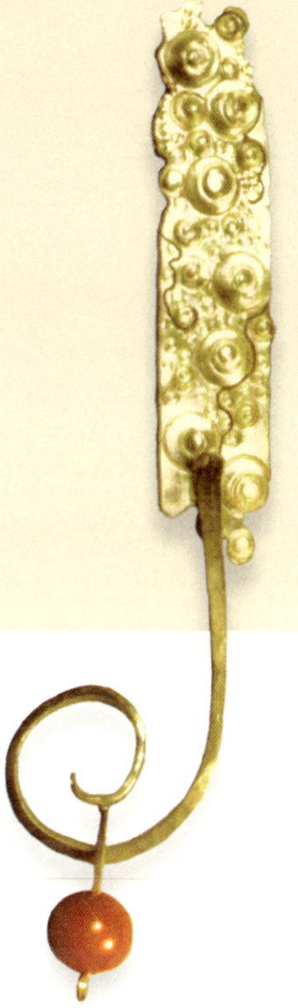

ABOVE: *Mendel the Griffin,* 18-karat gold and Burma ruby

RIGHT: Pin of 18-karat carved gold and red coral, c. 1955

OPPOSITE: *The Unicorn,* 18-karat gold pin, c. 1953

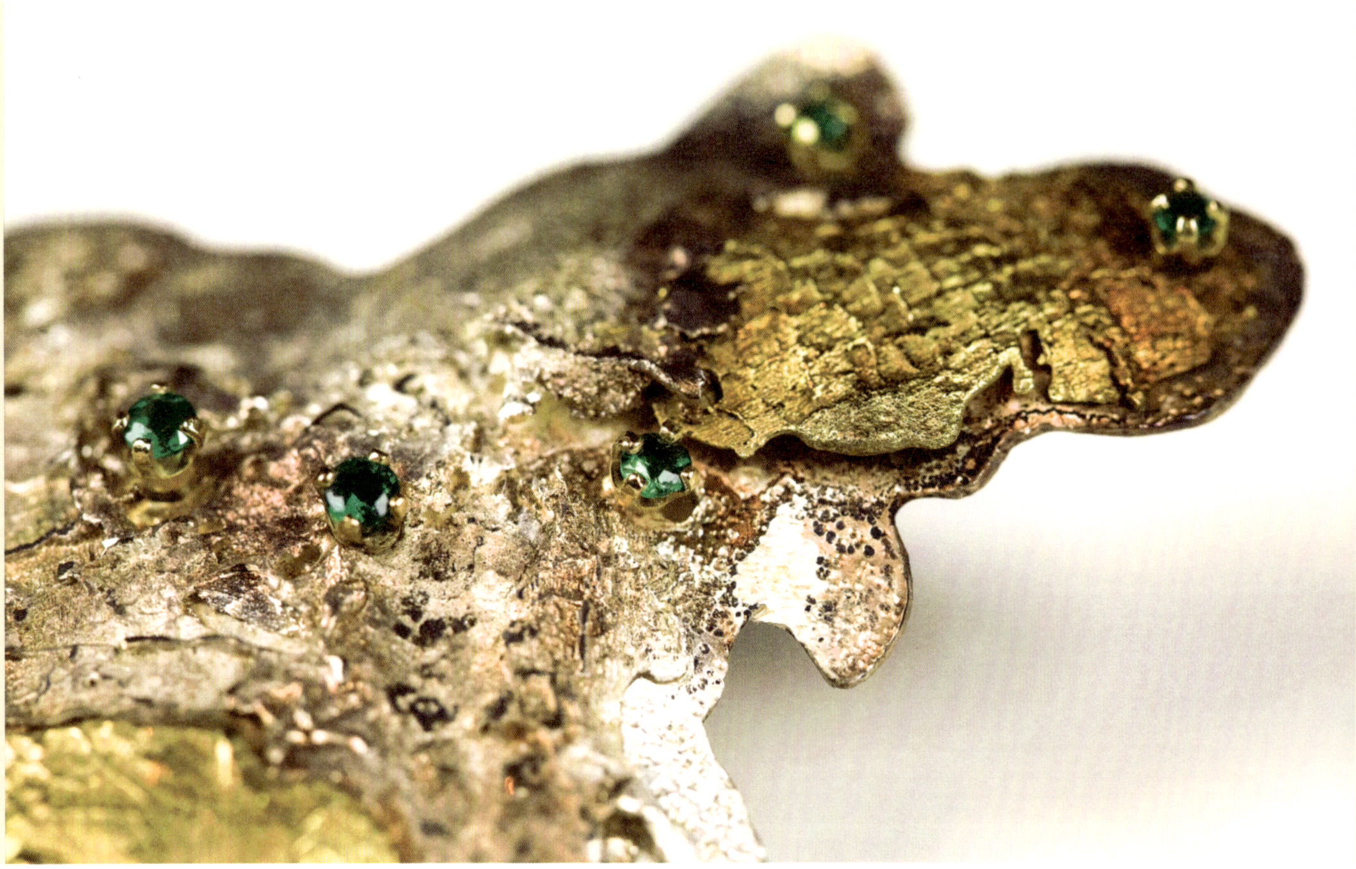

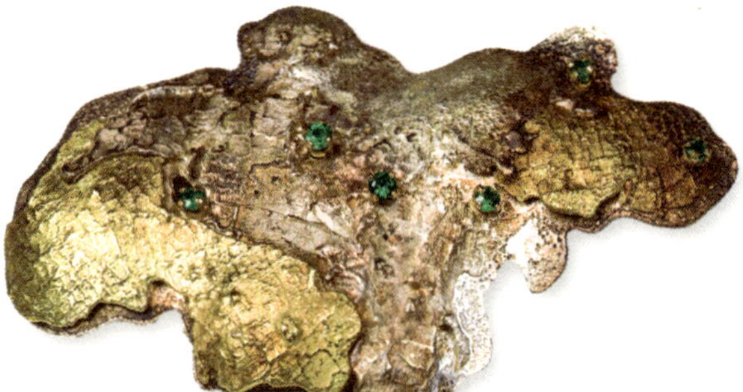

Free-form pin of rough-cast fine silver and 24-karat gold with emeralds

OPPOSITE: *The Ram,* 18-karat gold and emerald. Approximately 6″ long

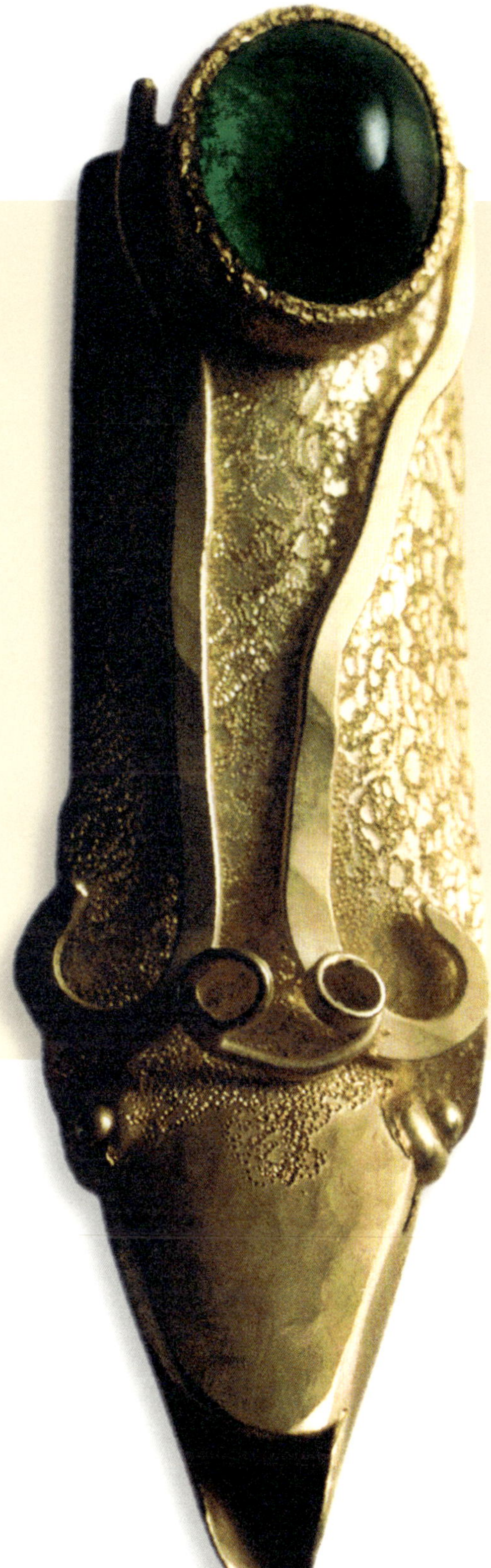

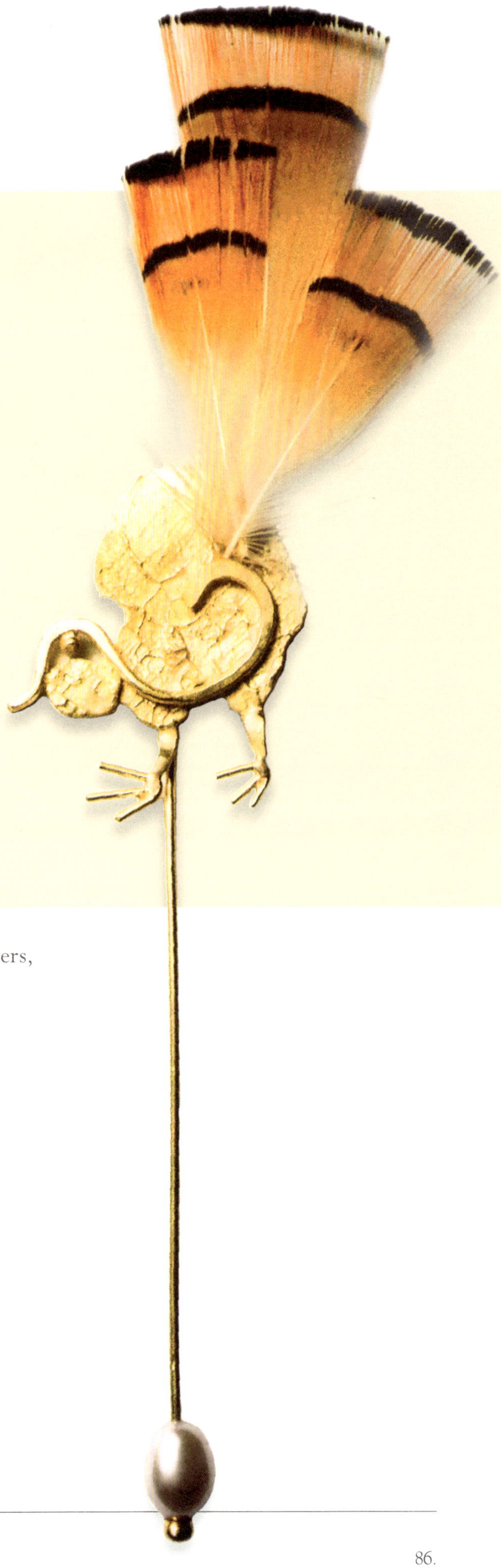

Ms. Chick, 18-karat gold and feathers, with pearl clasp

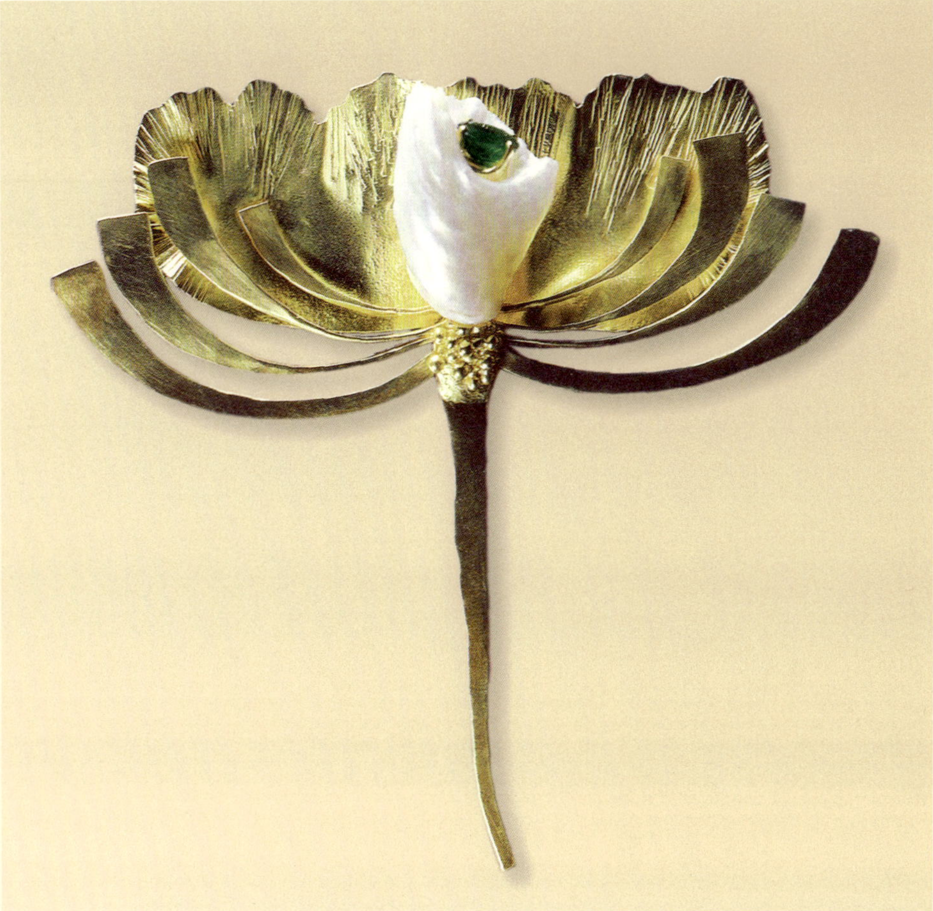

The Lotus, 18-karat gold, freshwater pearl, and emerald pin

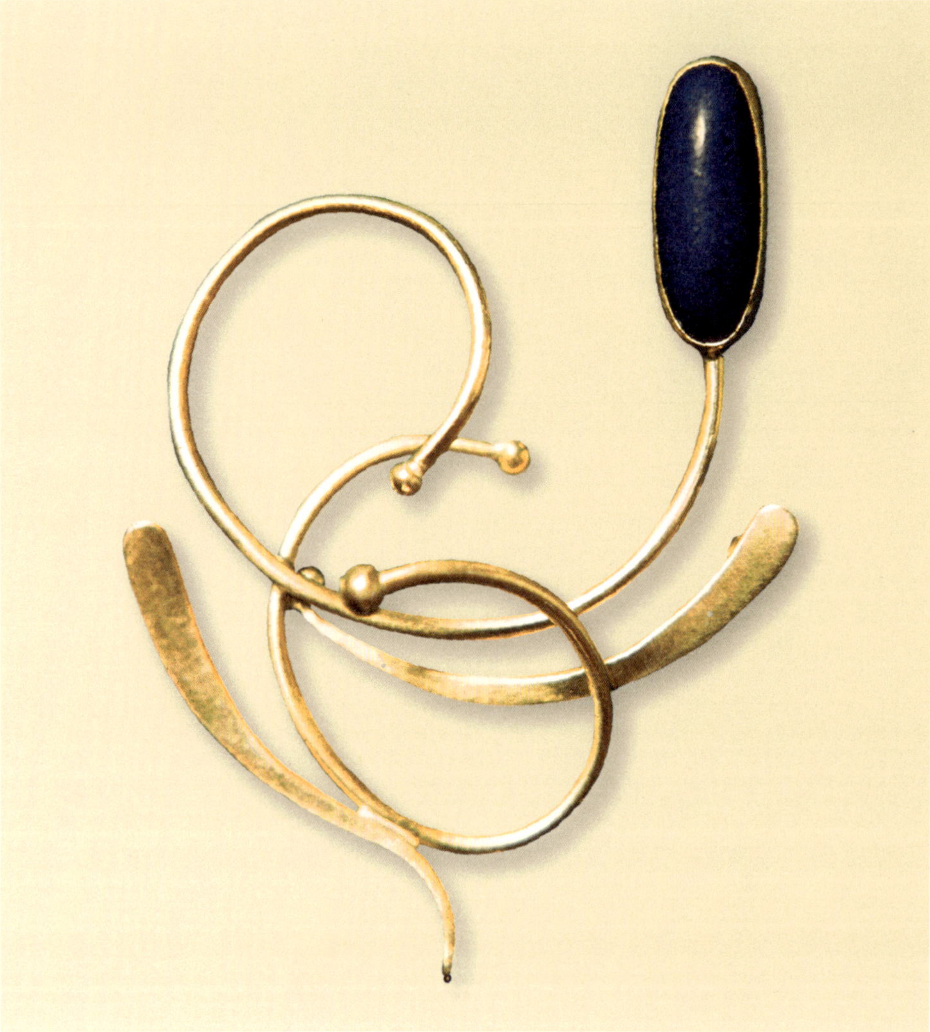

Pin of 18-karat gold with lapis lazuli, c. 1956

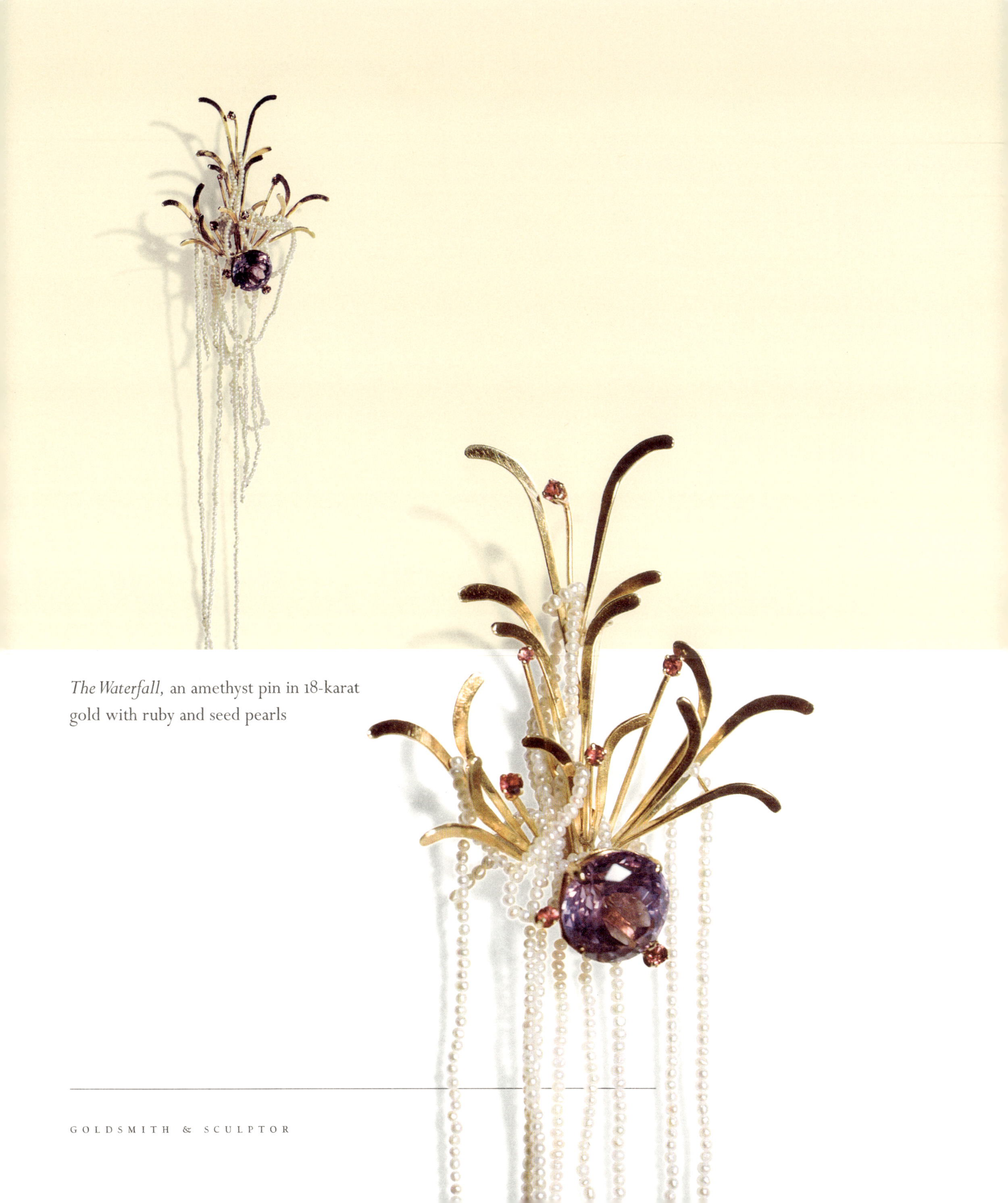

The Waterfall, an amethyst pin in 18-karat gold with ruby and seed pearls

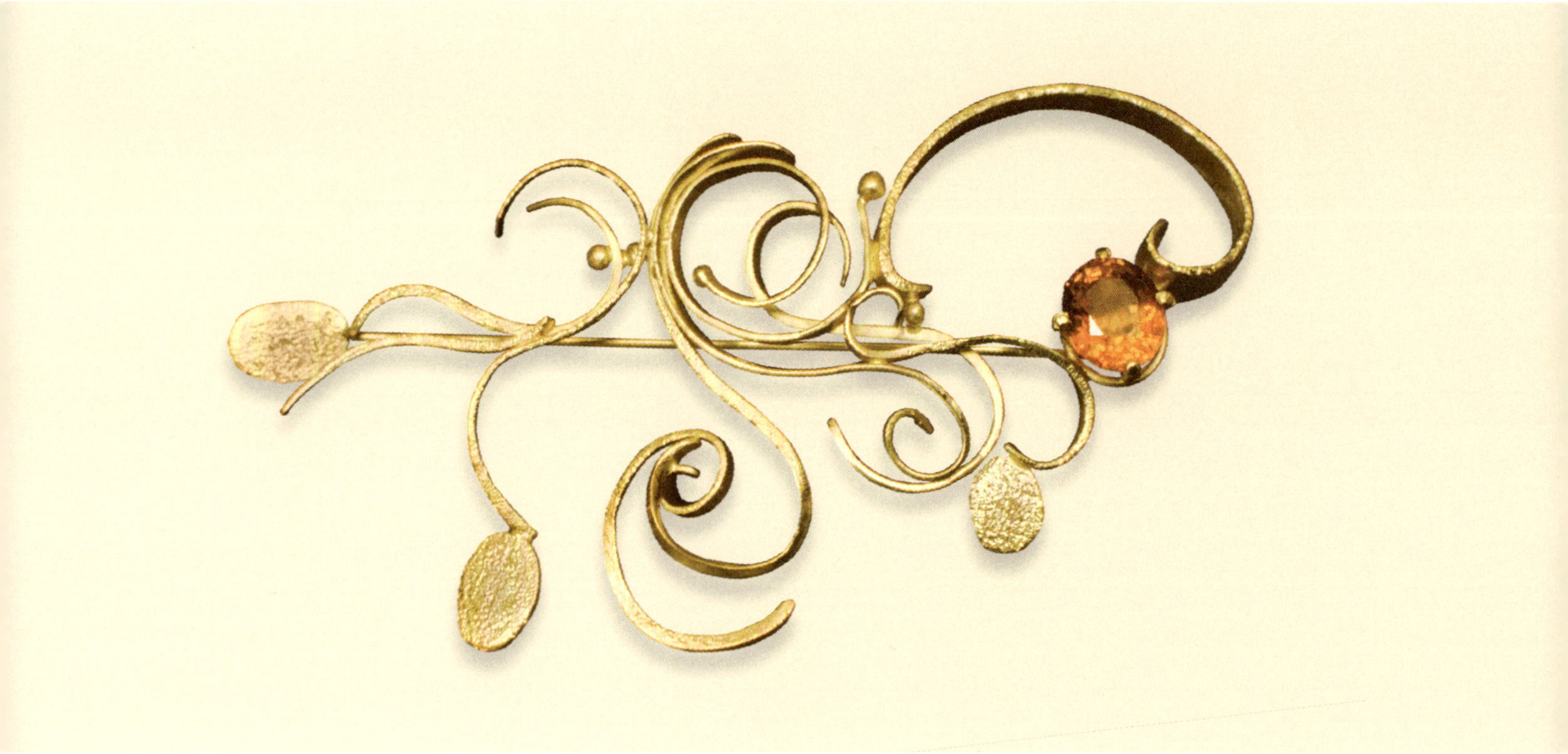

Orange sapphire pin, 18-karat gold

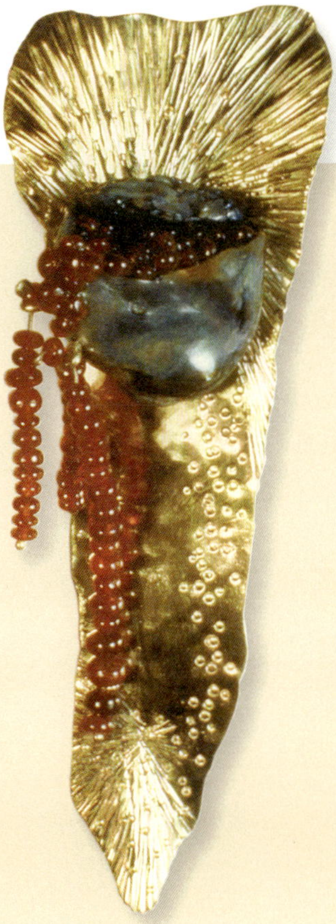

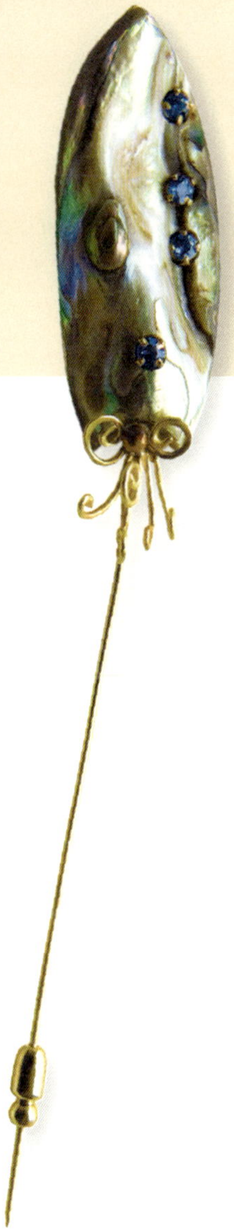

ABOVE: Pin of 18-karat gold, abalone pearl, and ruby beads

RIGHT: Abalone and sapphire pin, 18-karat gold (Nina Fuller Photography)

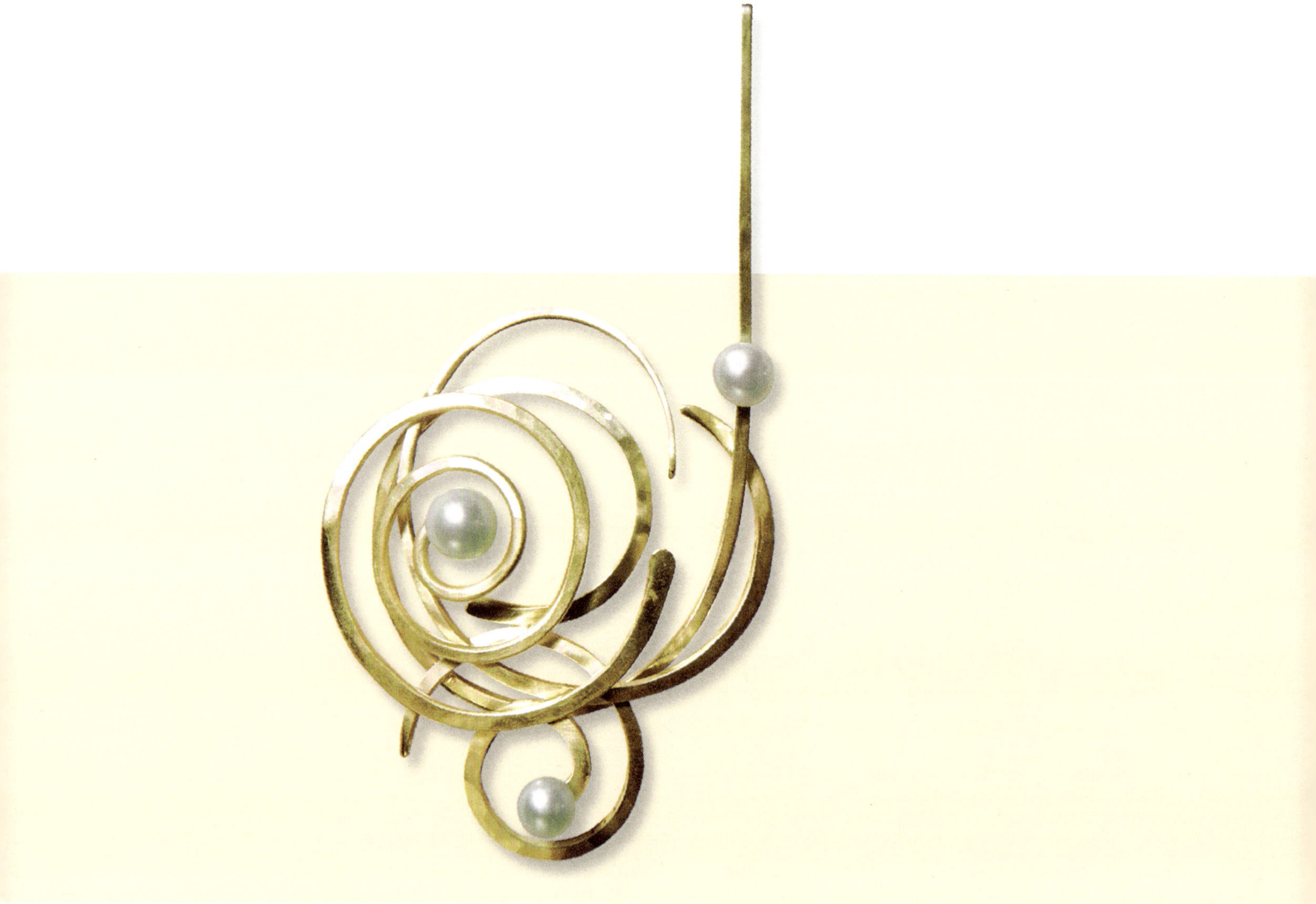

Pin of 18-karat gold and freshwater pearls

OPPOSITE: Sapphire starburst pin,
18-karat gold, c. 1955

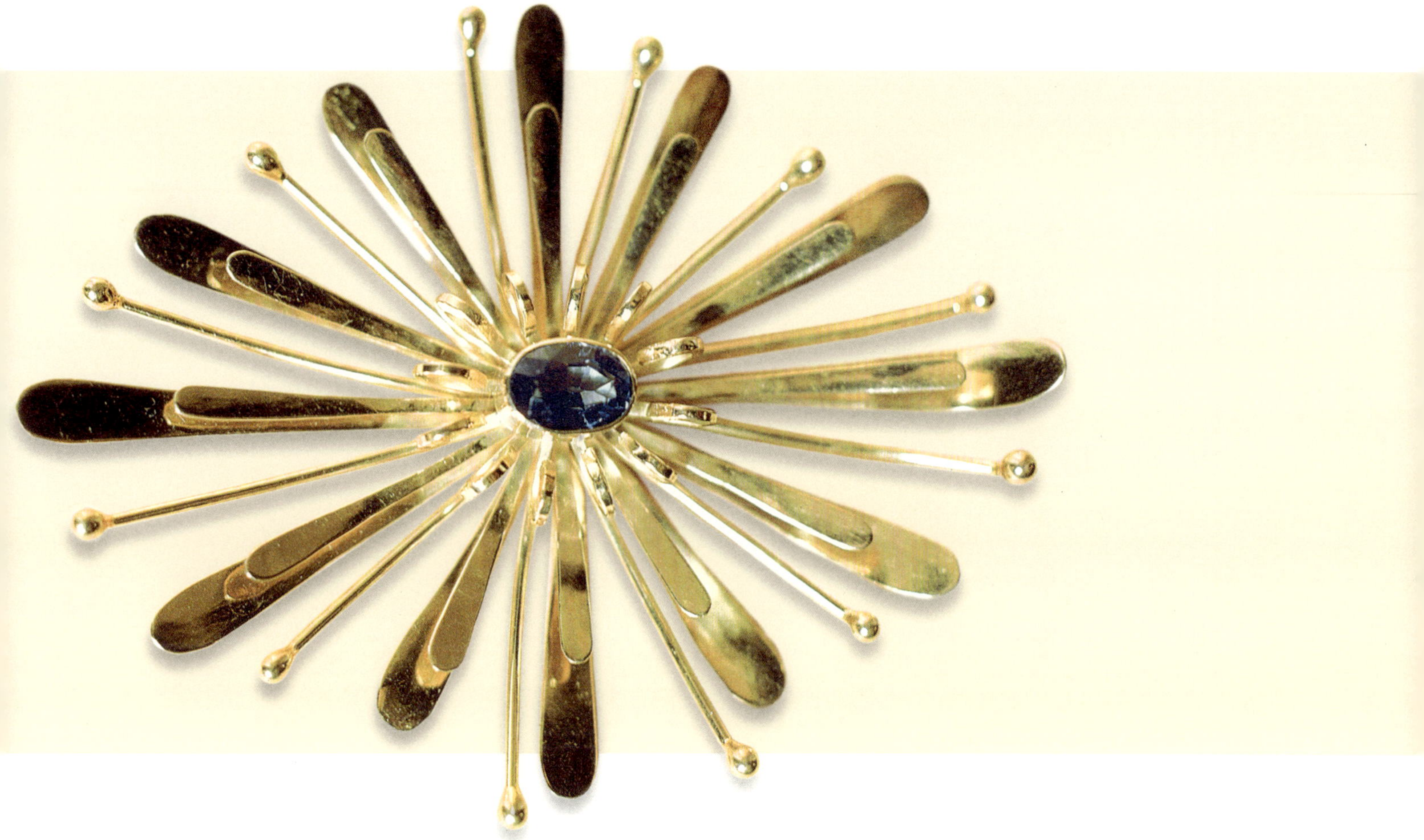

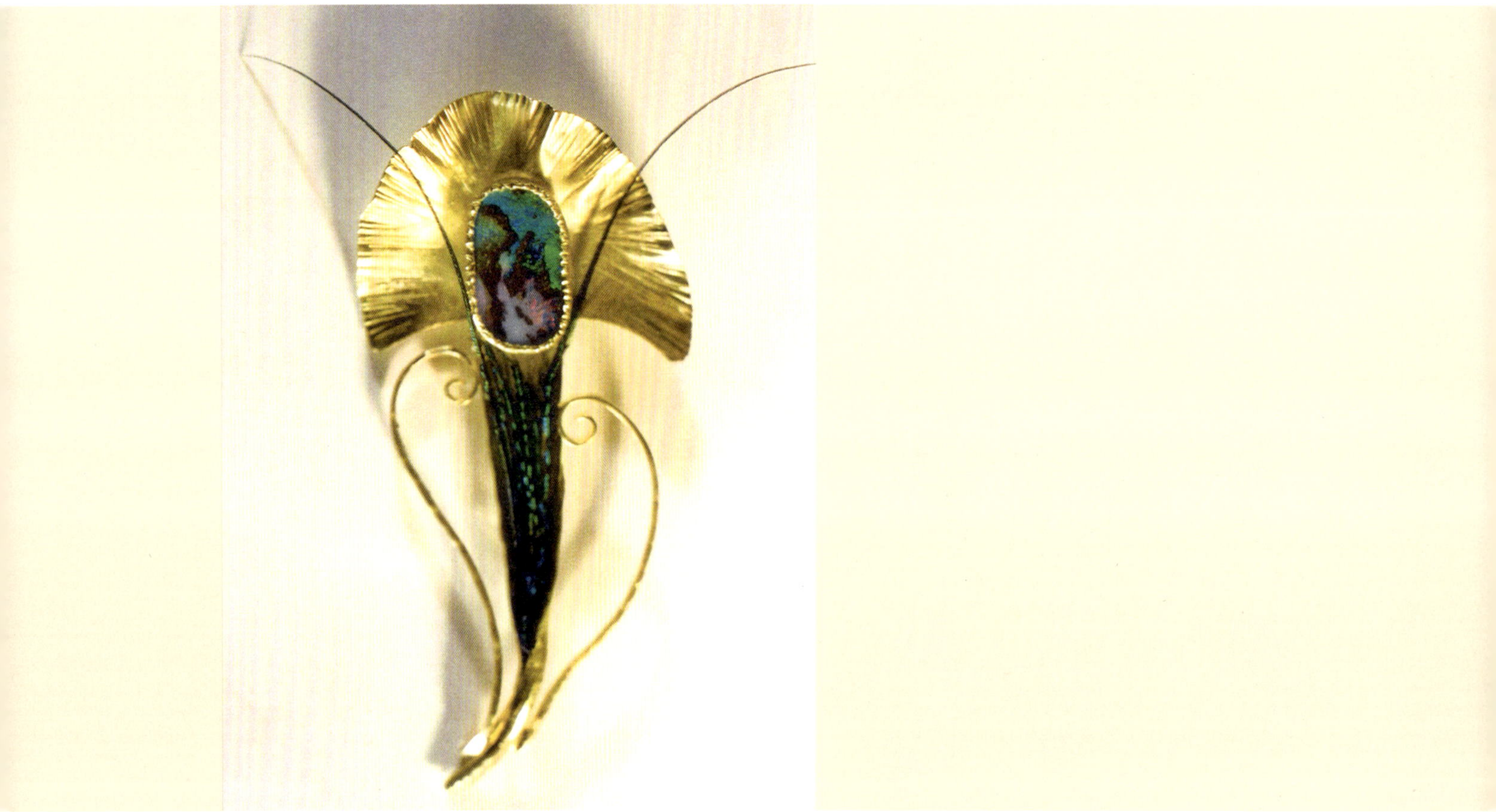

Pin in 18-karat gold with boulder opal and peacock feathers

OPPOSITE: *The Fire Boat,* 18-karat gold and diamonds, celebrating the Tall Ships coming into Boston Harbor, 1976

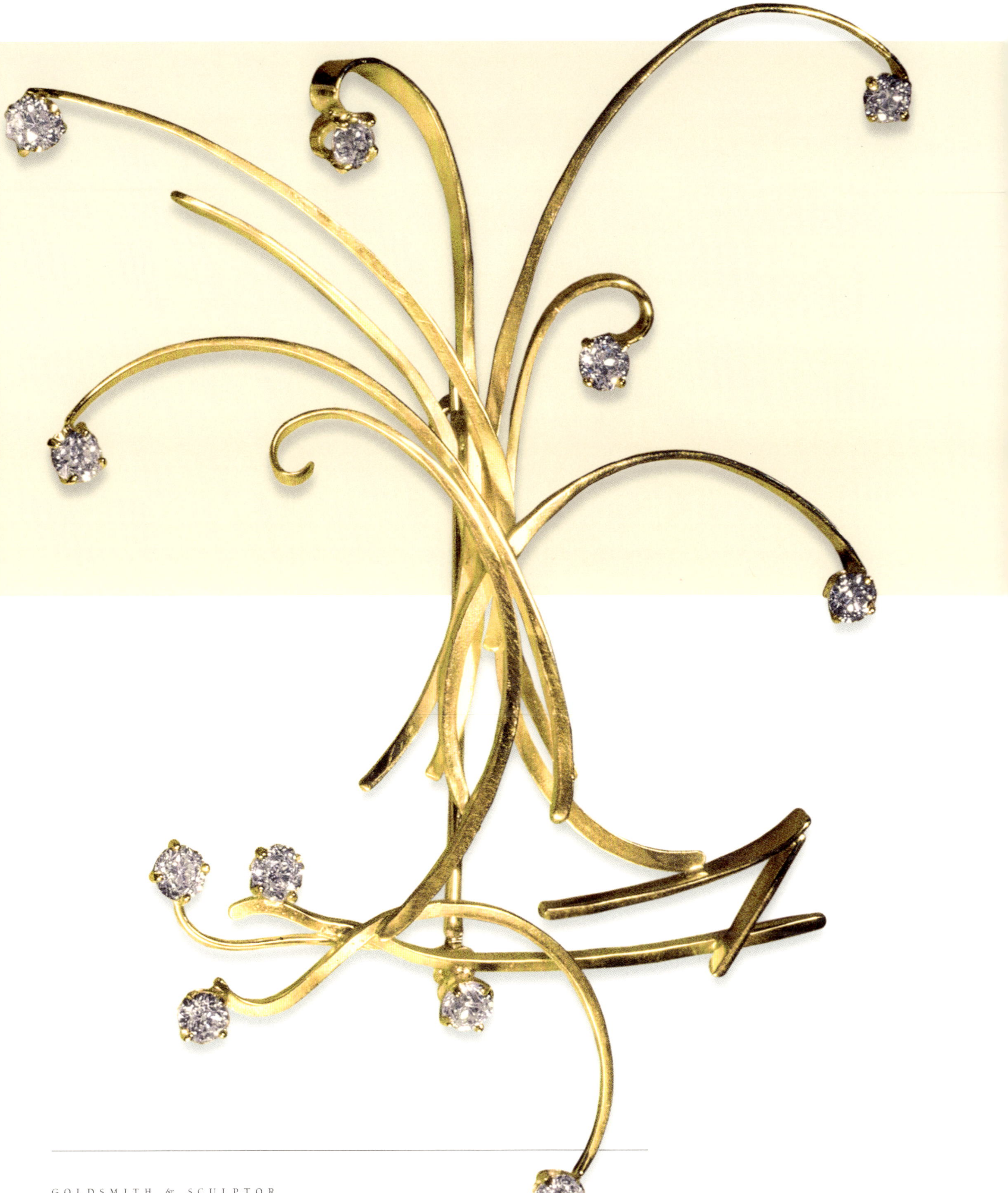

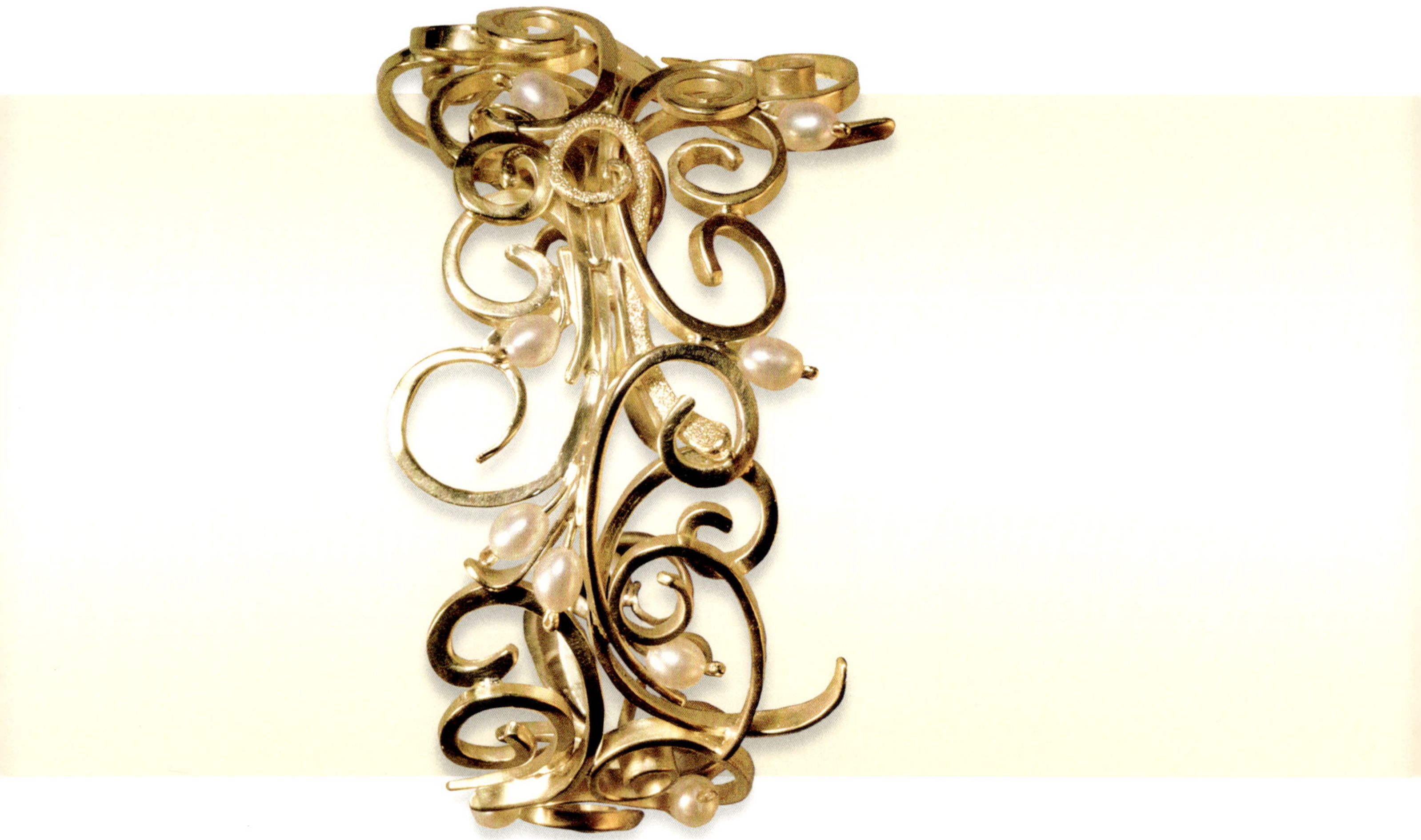

Openwork bracelet of 18-karat gold and freshwater pearls

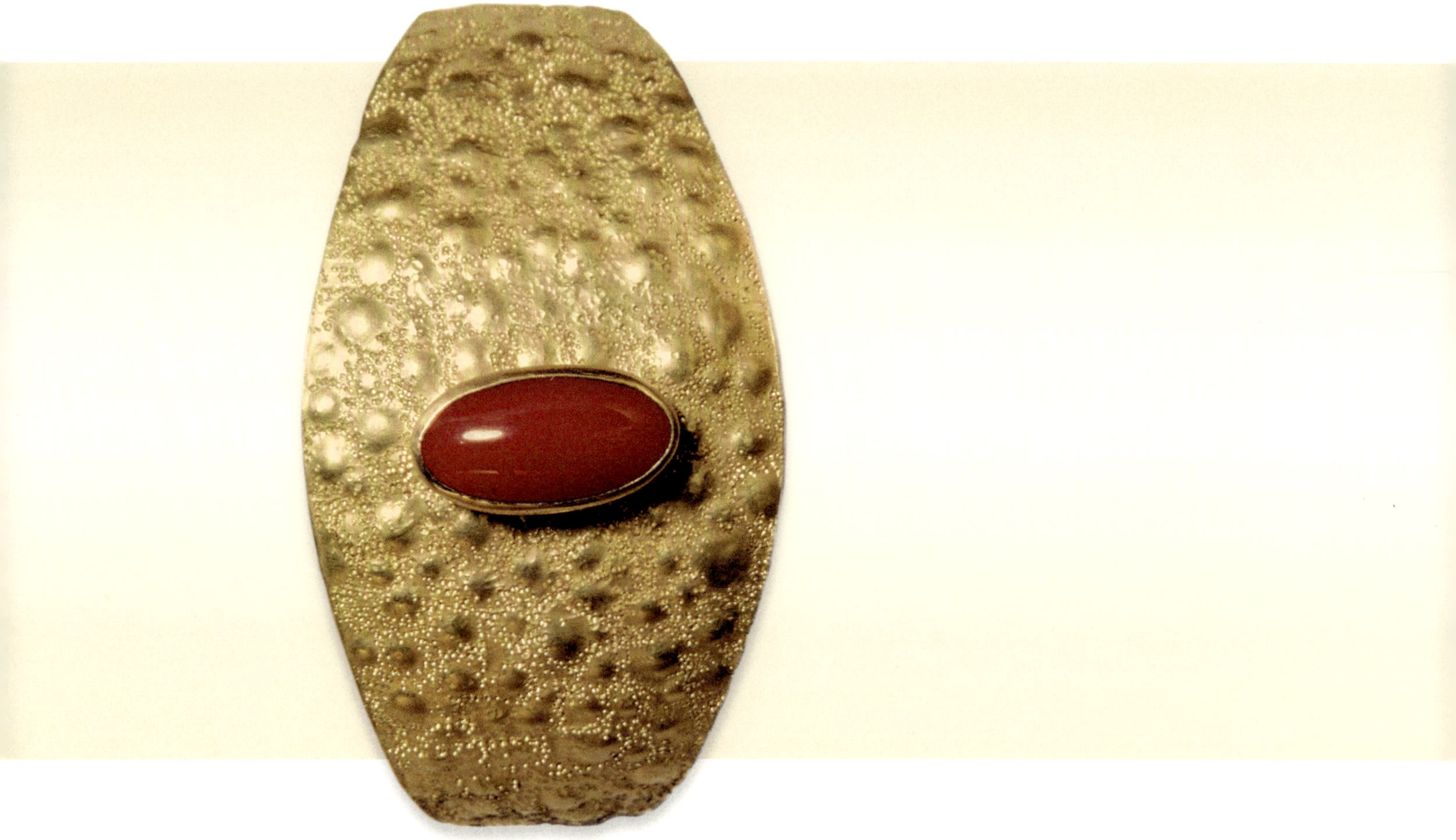

Hammered 18- and 24-karat gold
bracelet with coral

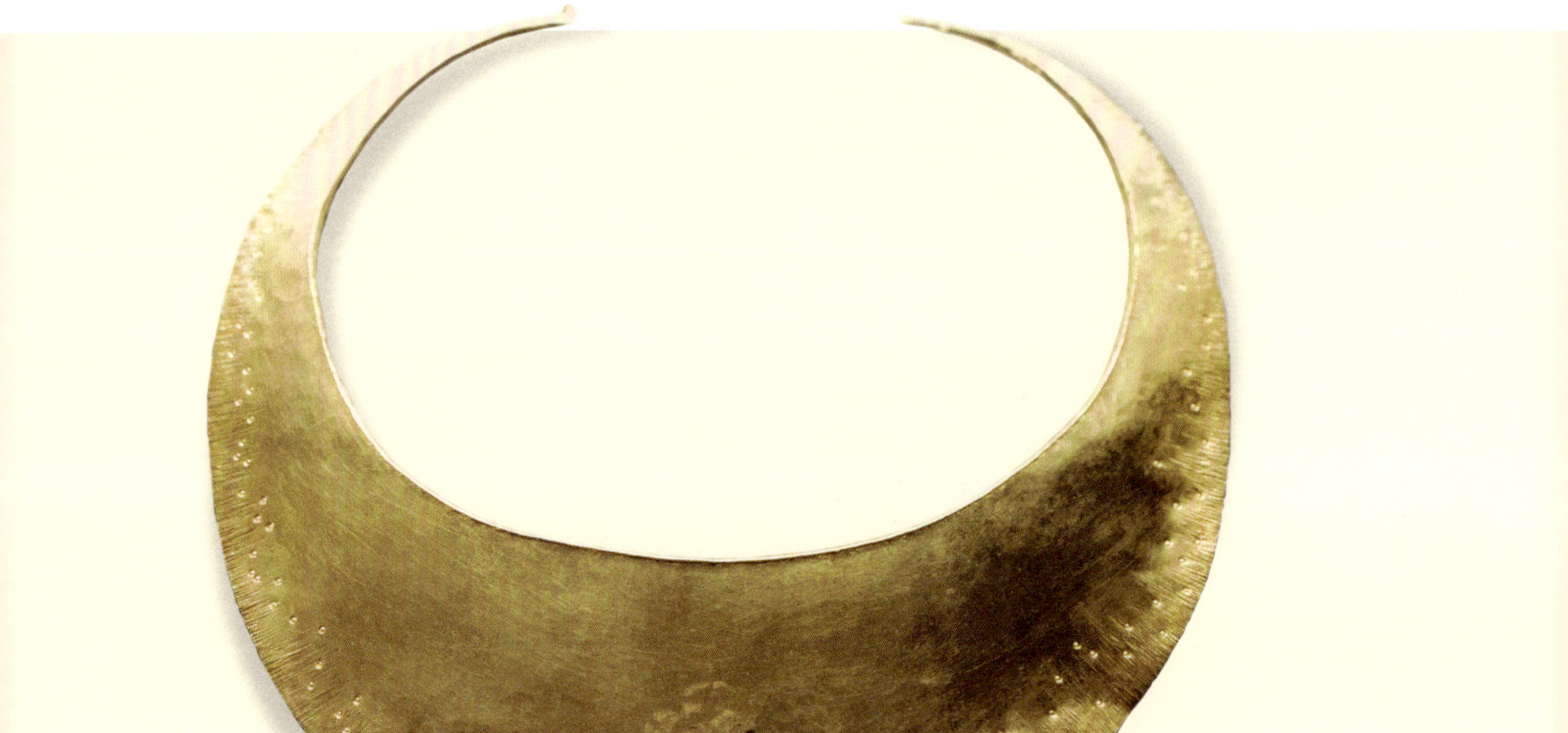

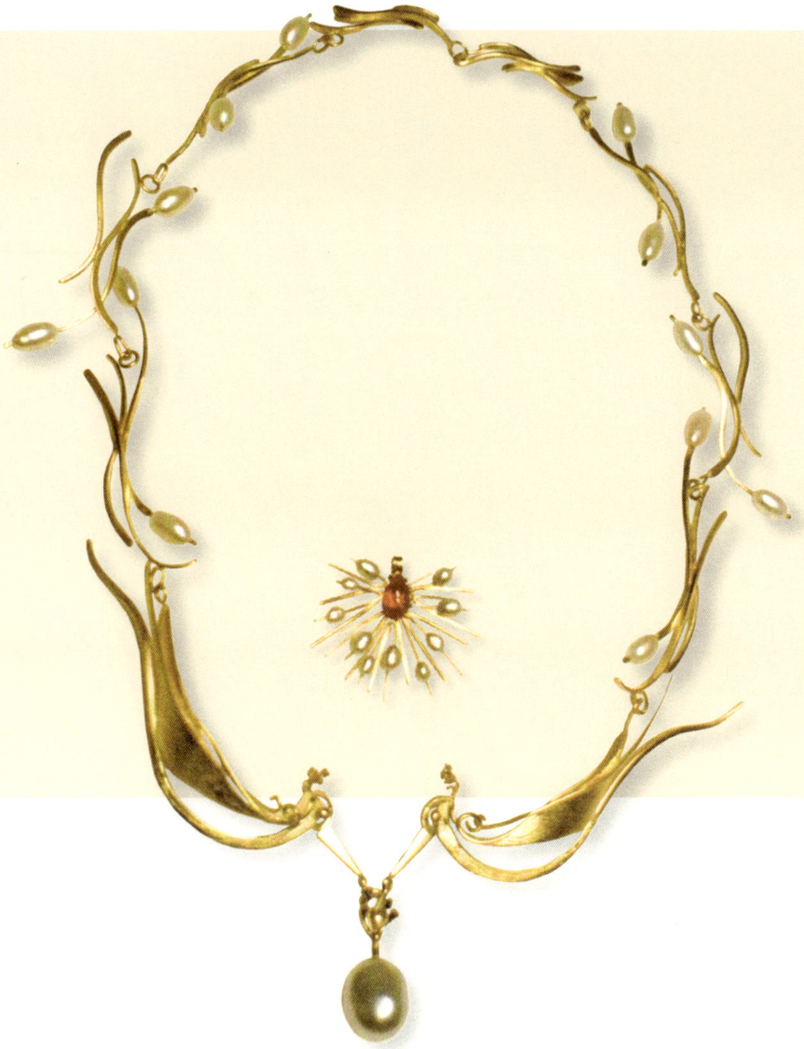

Bird necklace, 18-karat gold, Lake Biwa freshwater pearls, baroque pearl, diamonds, and ruby; necklace may be worn with either the pearl or starburst ruby pendant

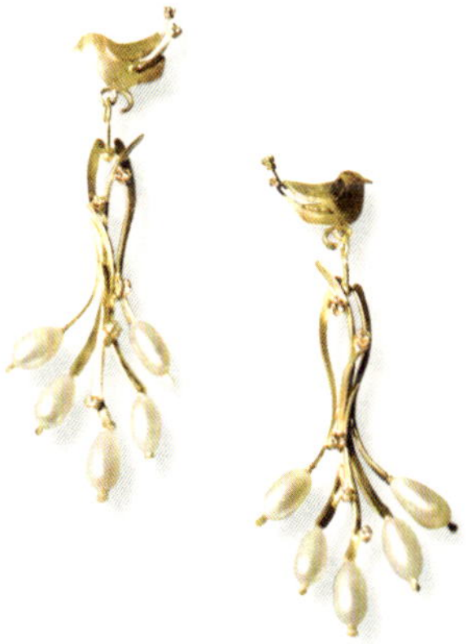

RIGHT: Bird earrings, 18-karat gold, Lake Biwa freshwater pearls, and diamonds

OPPOSITE: Lunule, 18-karat gold, made as a replica for the exhibition *The Treasures of Early Irish Art* at the Museum of Fine Arts, Boston, in 1977

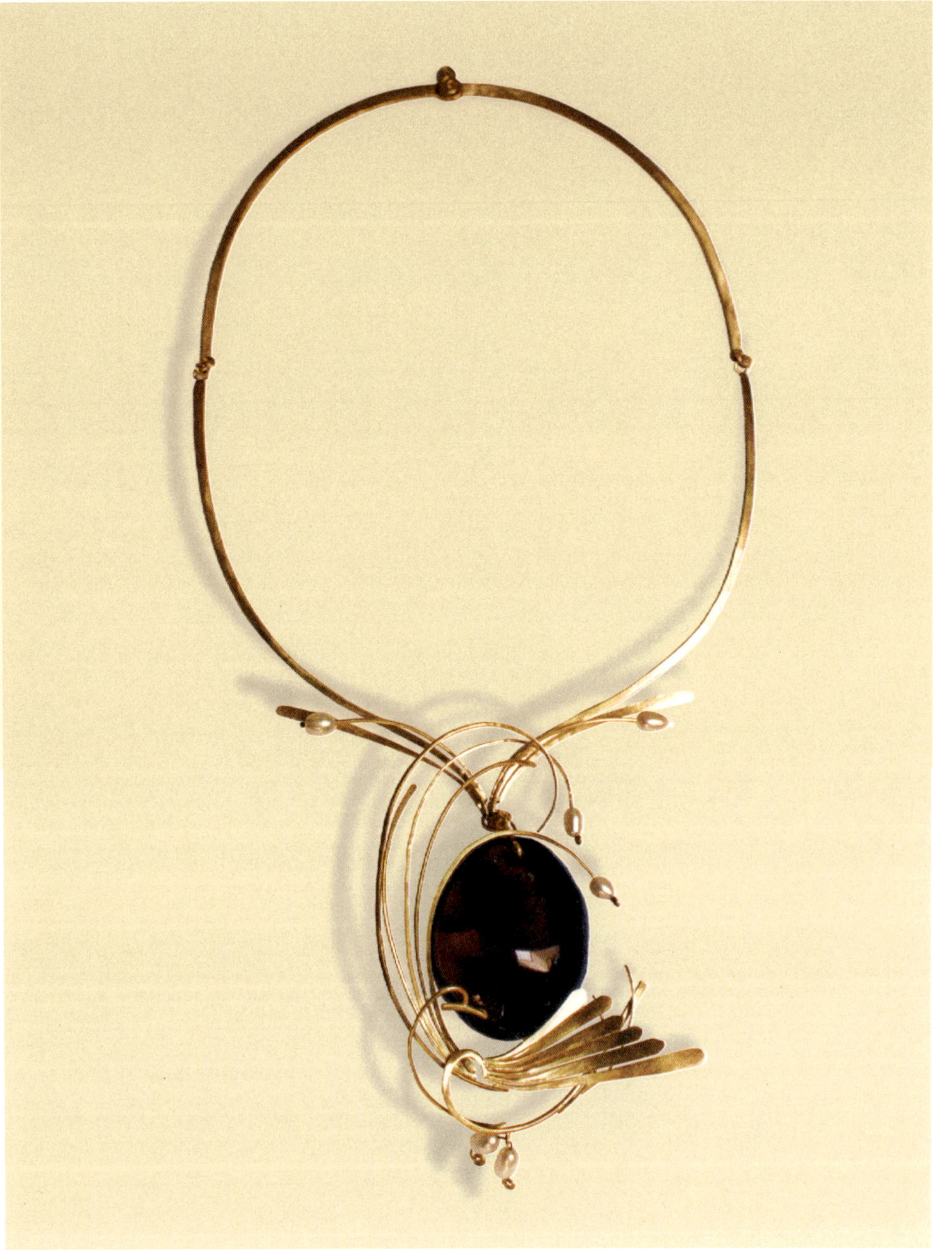

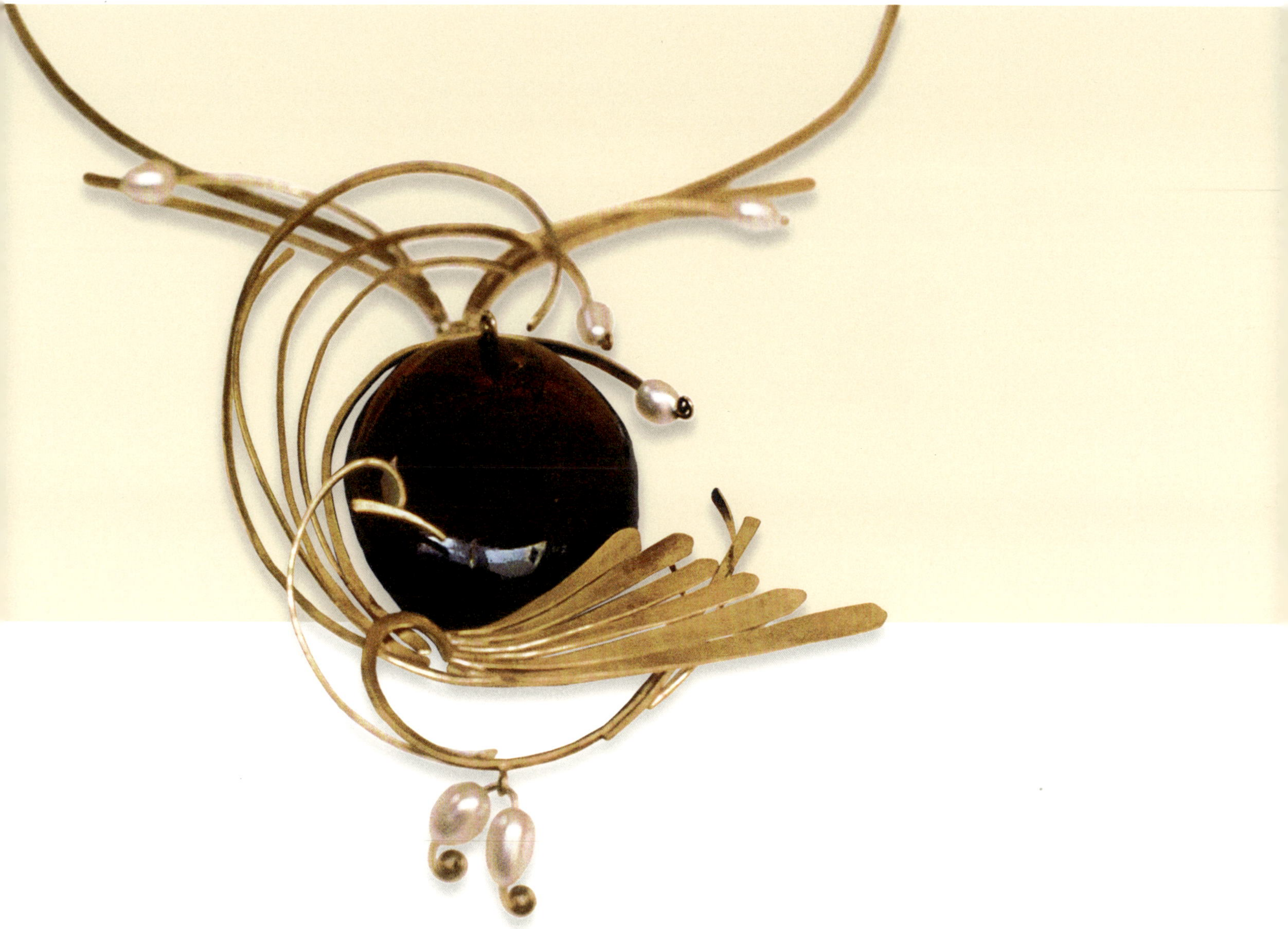

Necklace with amber, 18-karat gold, and freshwater pearls

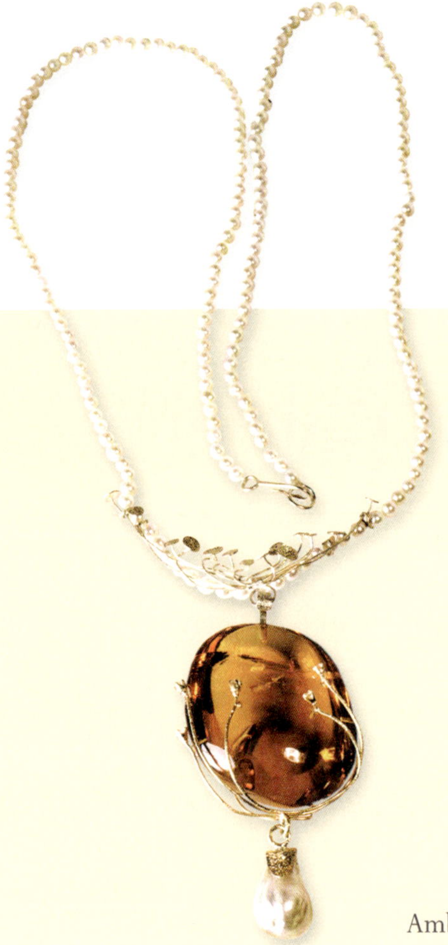

Amber and pearl necklace

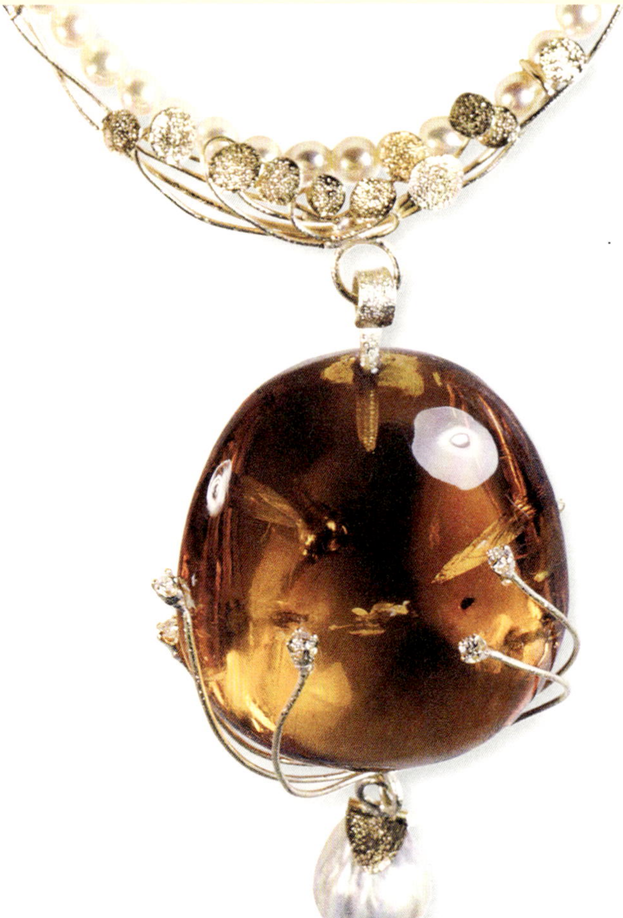

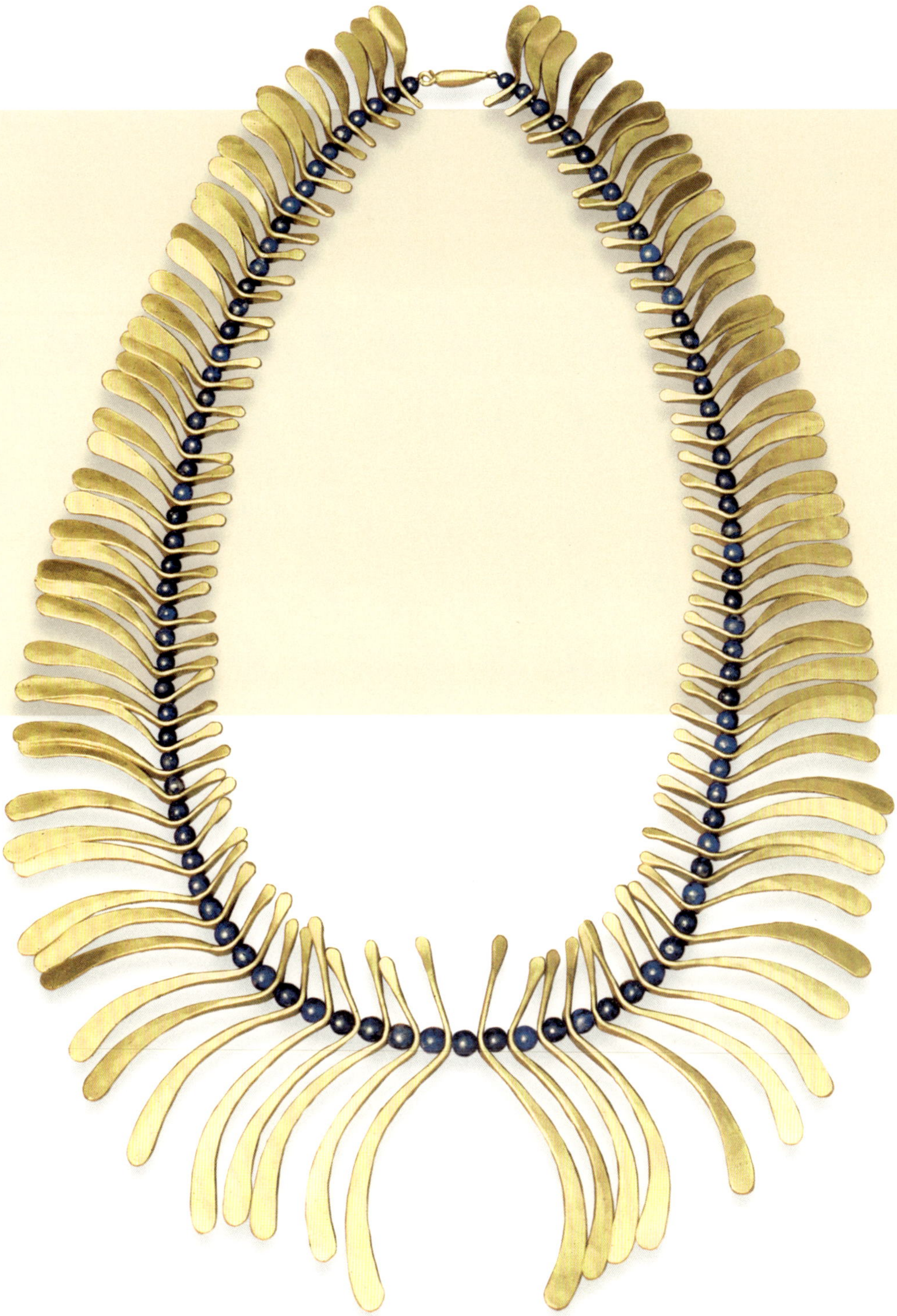

Necklace, 22-karat gold and
lapis lazuli, c. 1954

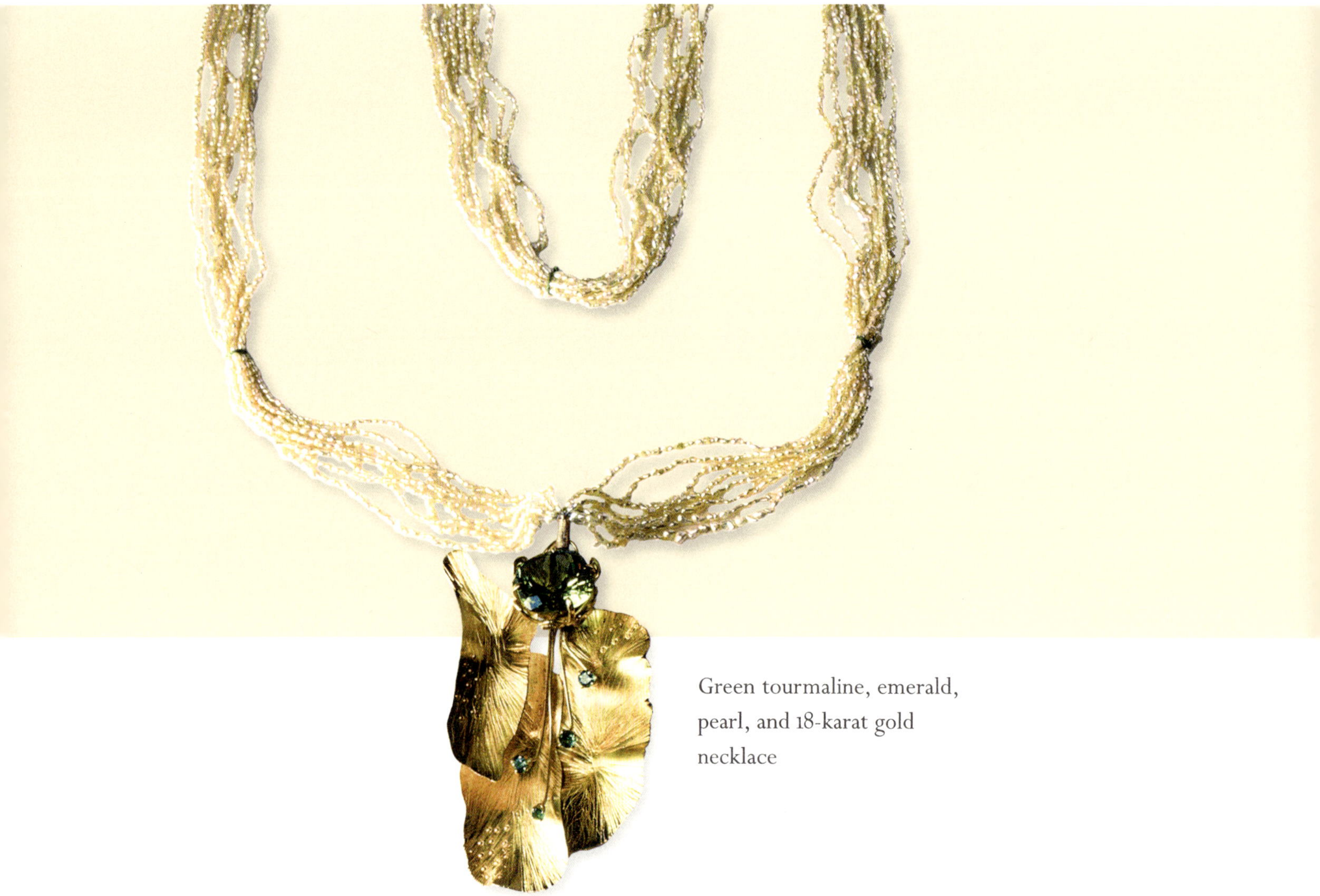

Green tourmaline, emerald, pearl, and 18-karat gold necklace

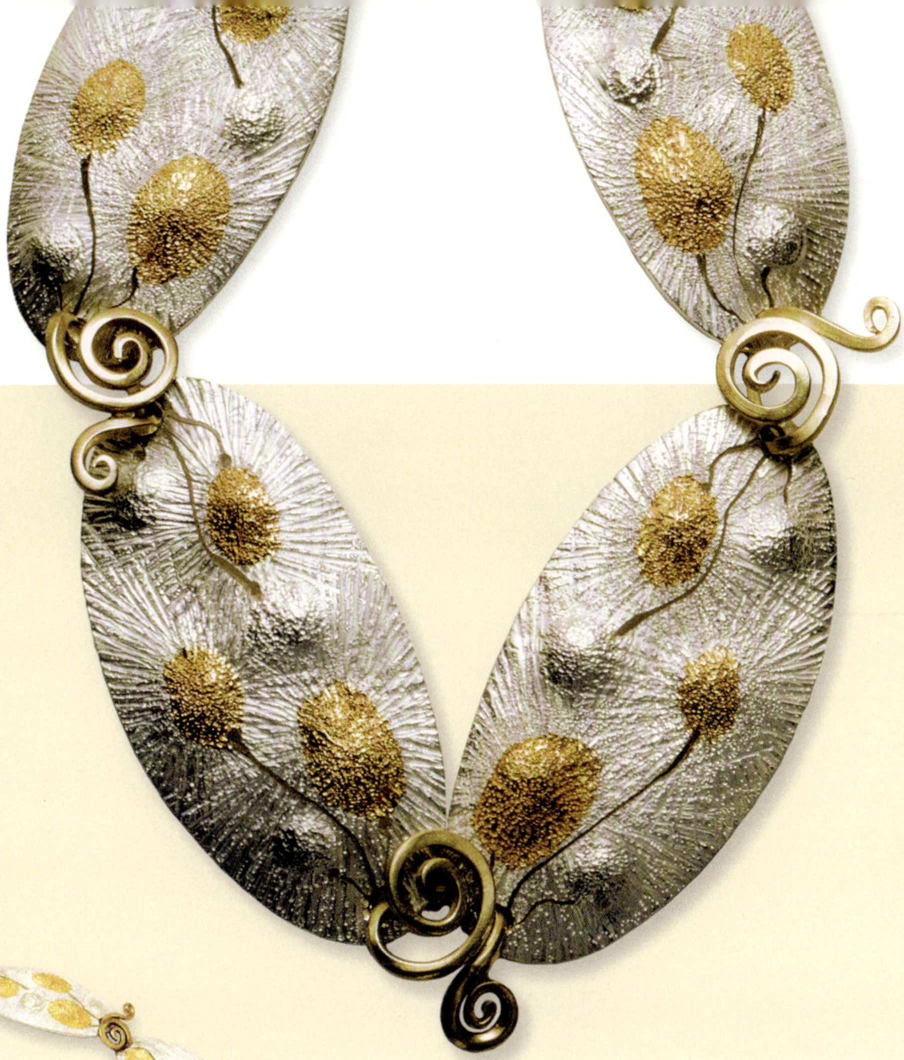

Fine silver and fused
24-karat gold necklace

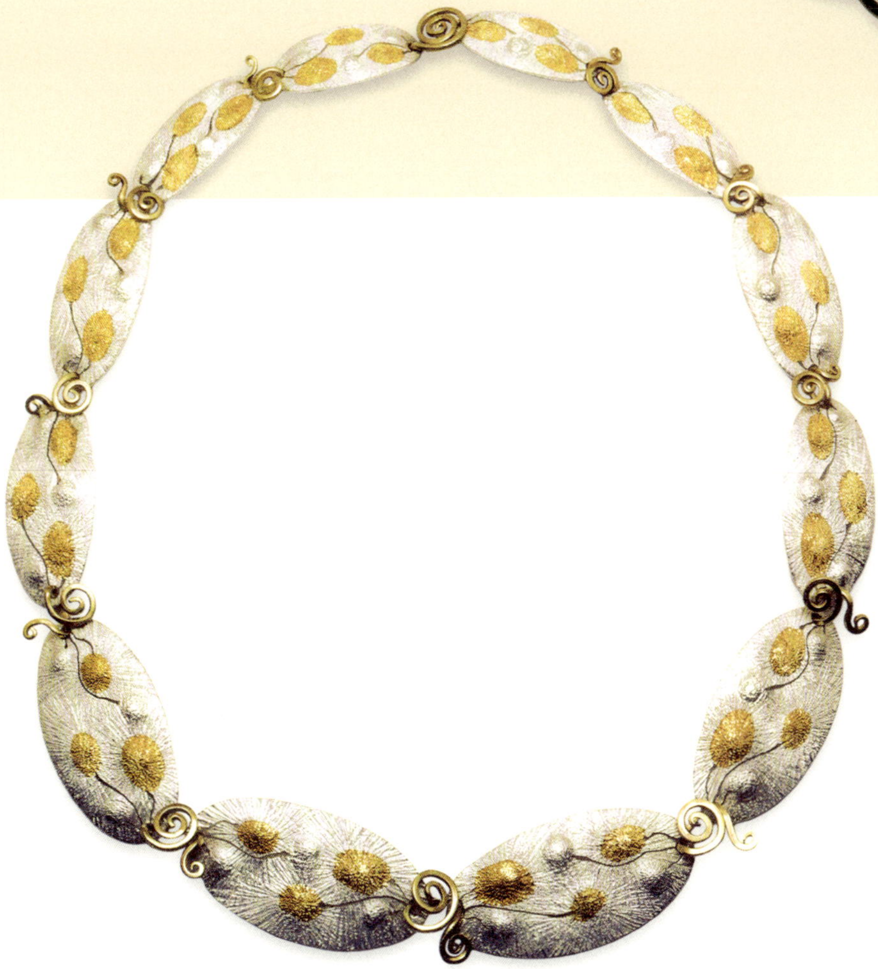

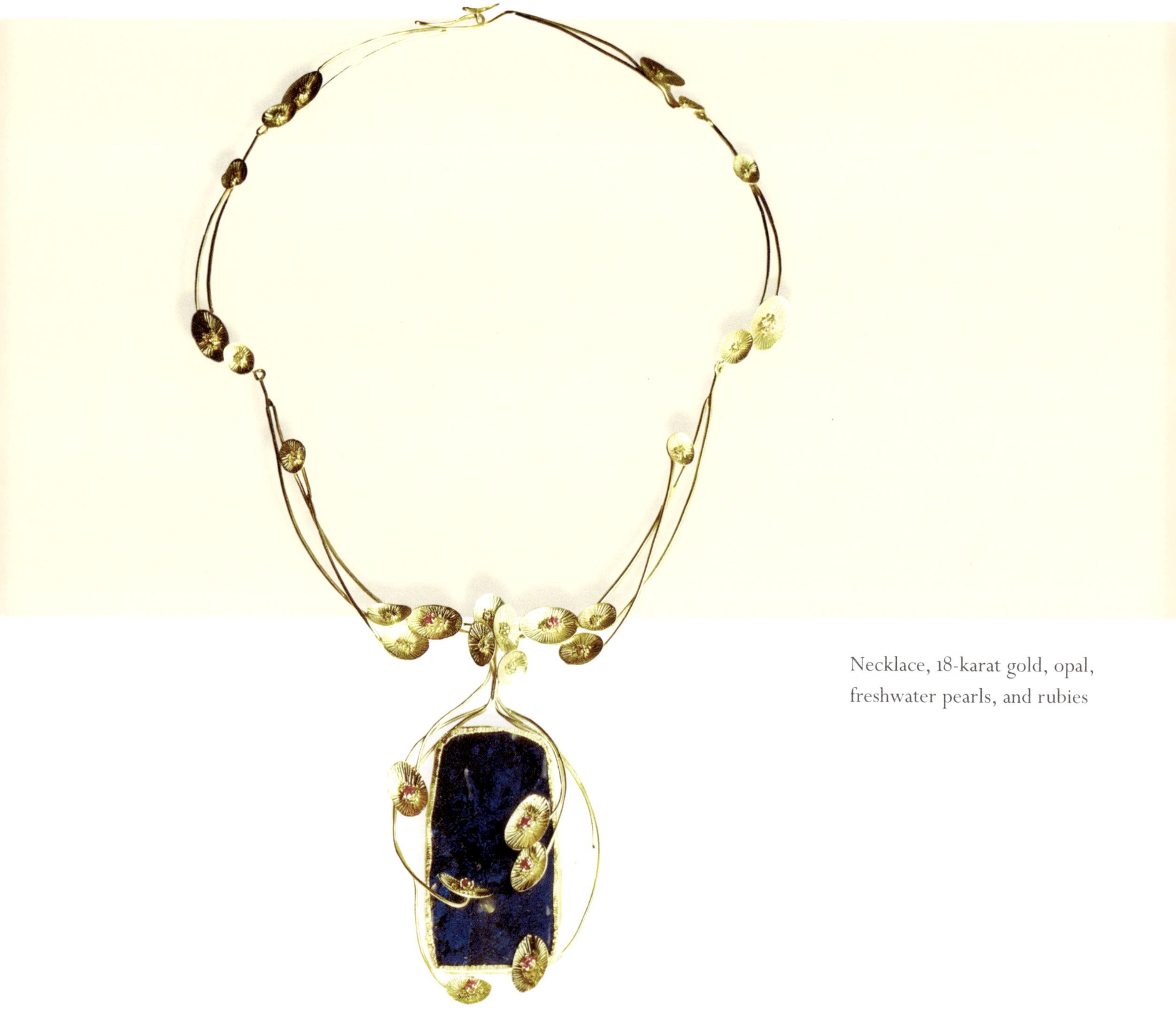

Necklace, 18-karat gold, opal, freshwater pearls, and rubies

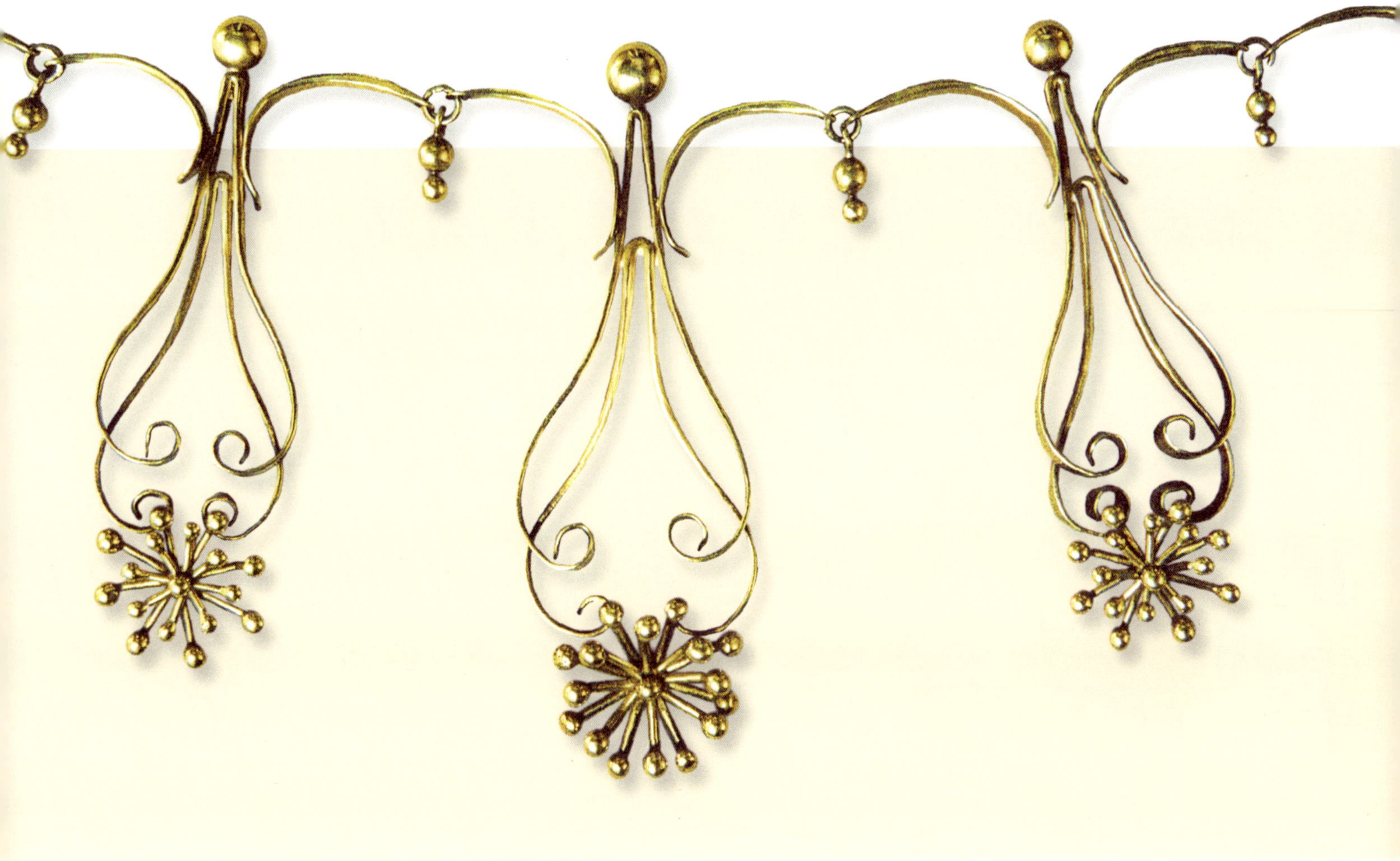

Necklace, 18-karat gold, c. 1955

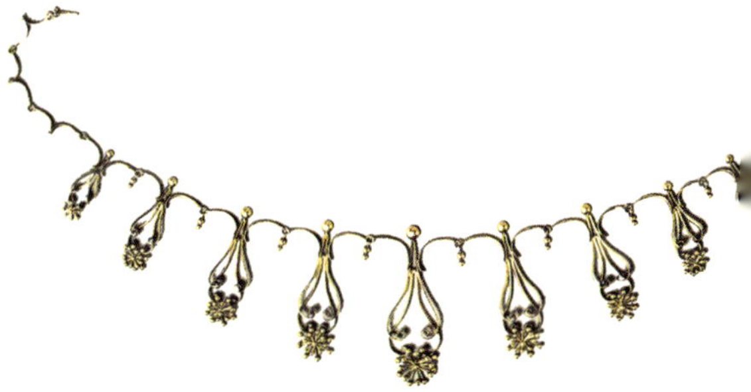

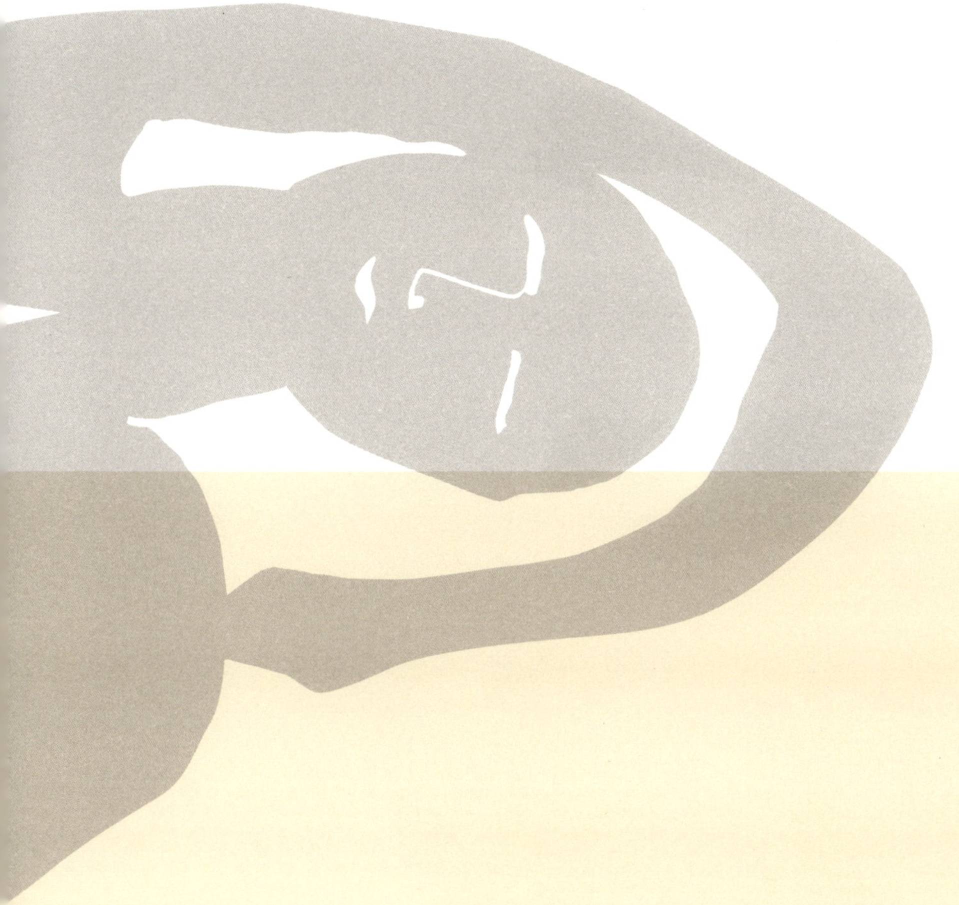

SCULPTURE & OBJECTS

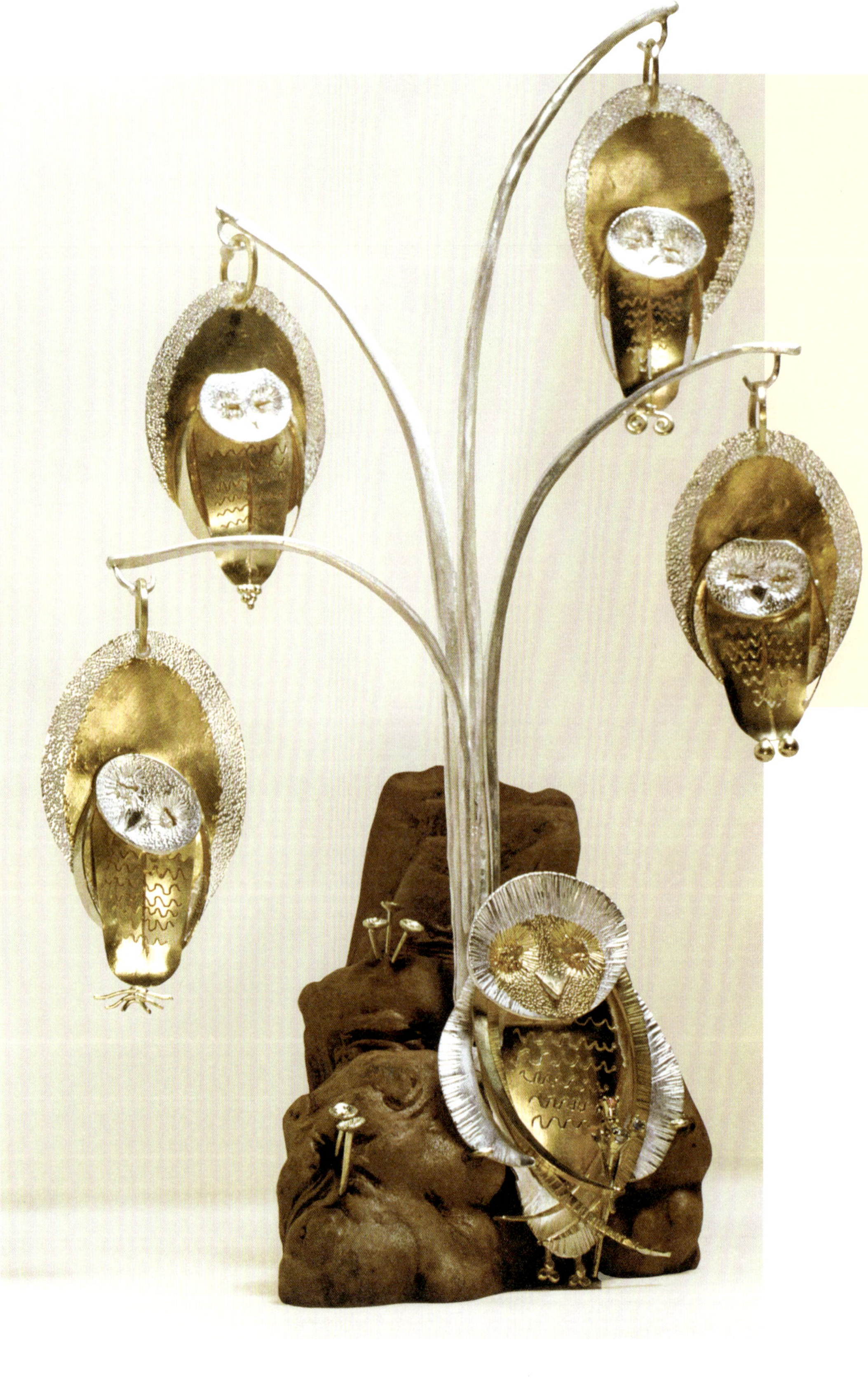

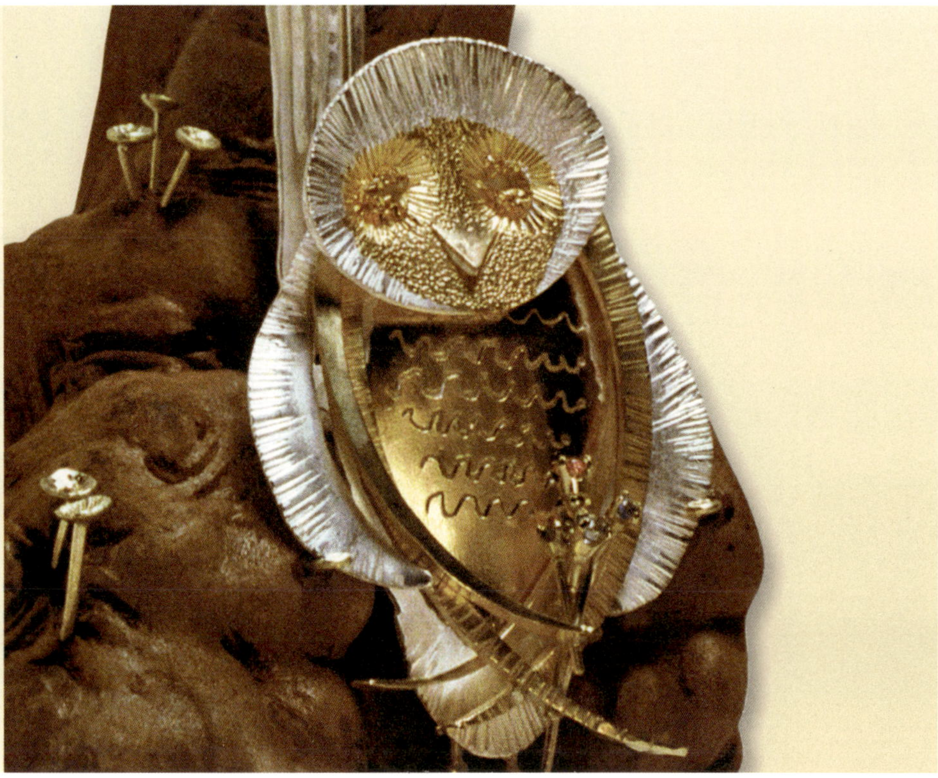

The Owls, mother and four owlets, 18- and 24-karat gold, fine silver, Montana sapphires, mounted on manzanita root. Owlets may be worn as pendants, and mother owl may be worn as a pin. Approximately 10″ high

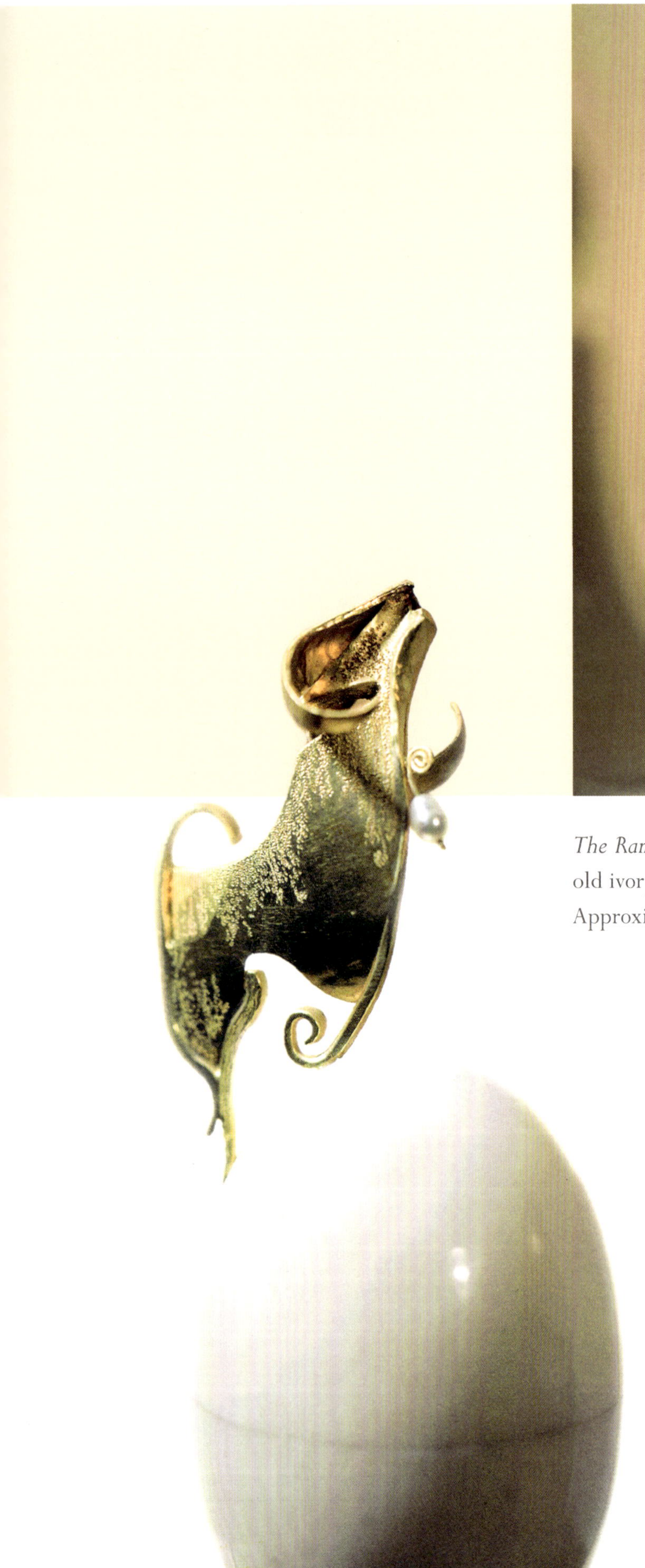

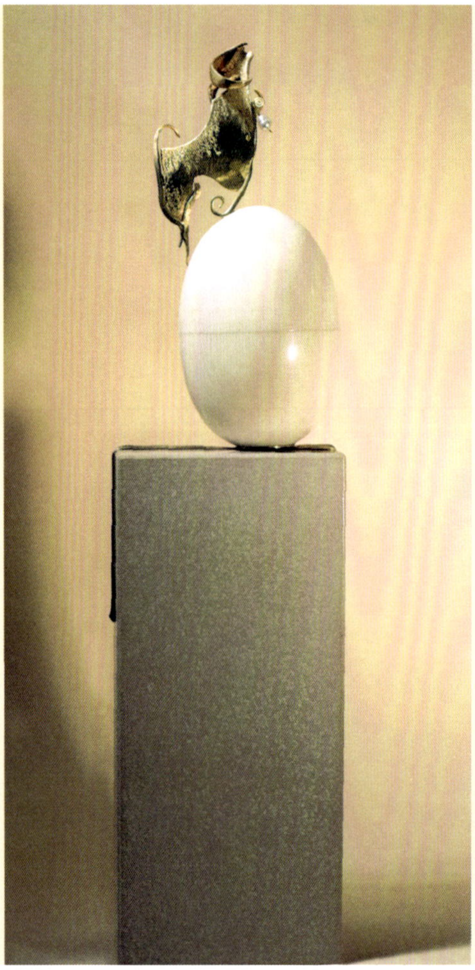

The Ram, 18-karat gold, pearl,
old ivory on plinth of antique marble.
Approximately 5¼″ high

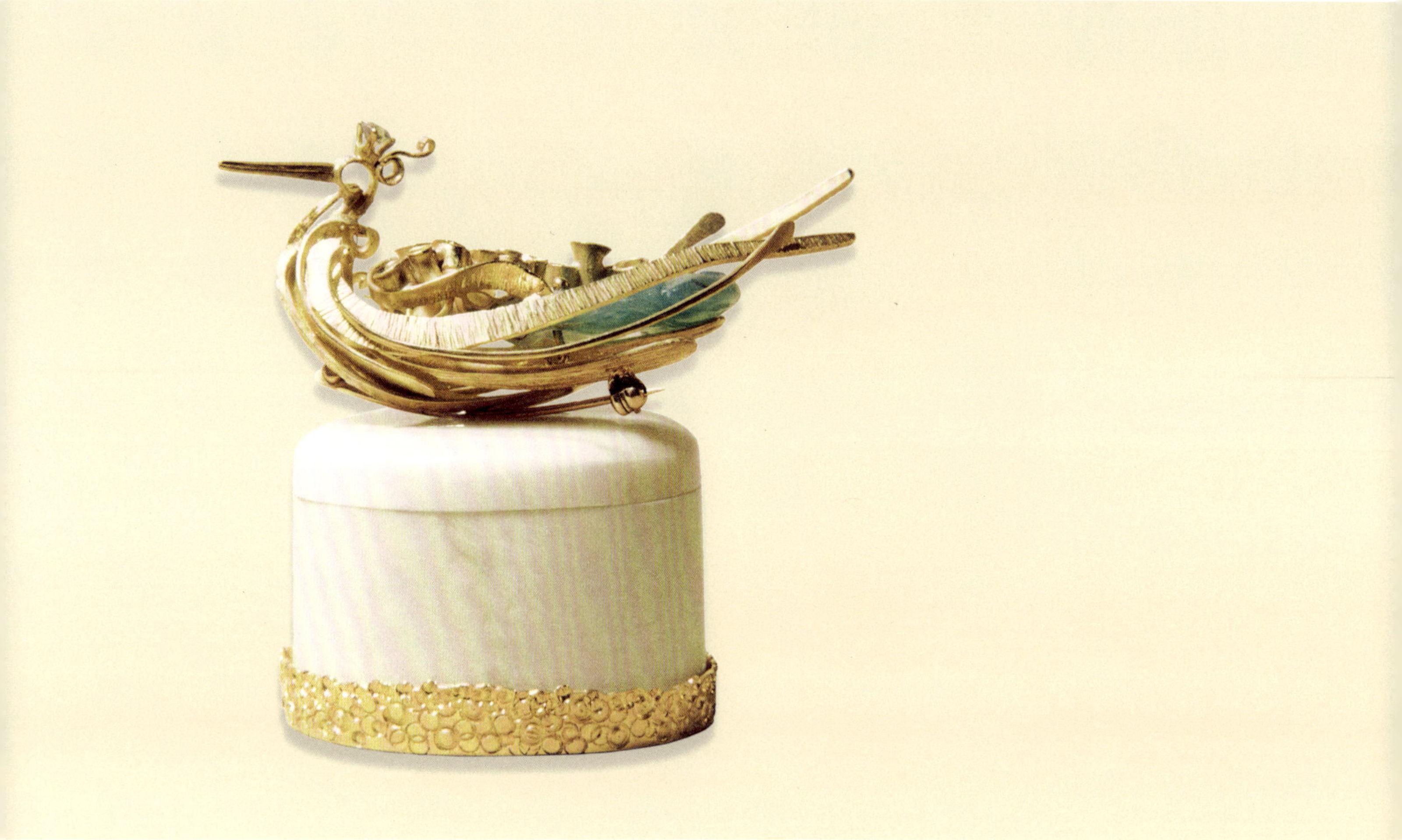

Shoulder pin of 18-karat gold with jade and diamonds mounted on an antique ivory box with 18-karat gold border, c. 1968. Approximately 2″ high

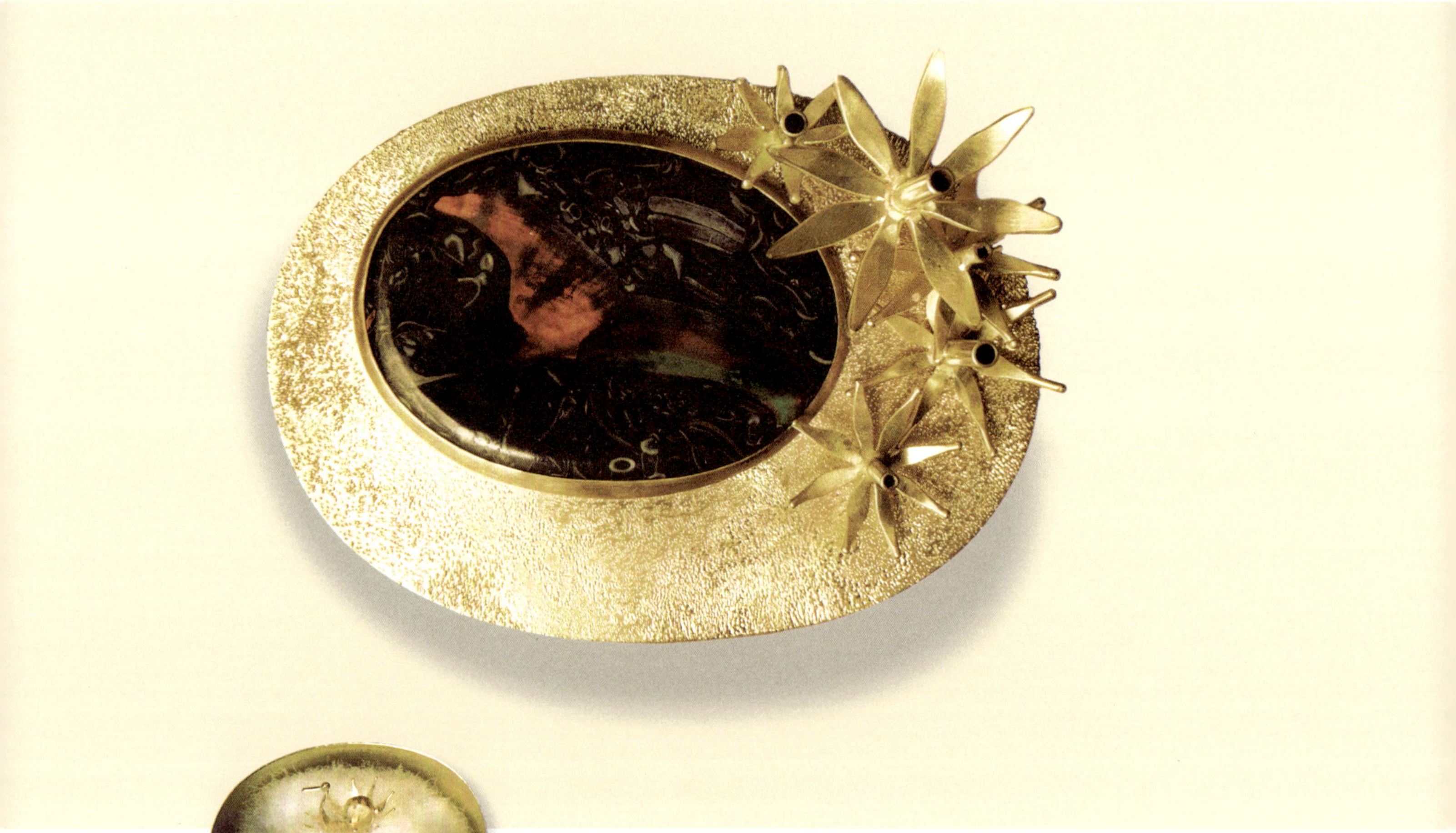

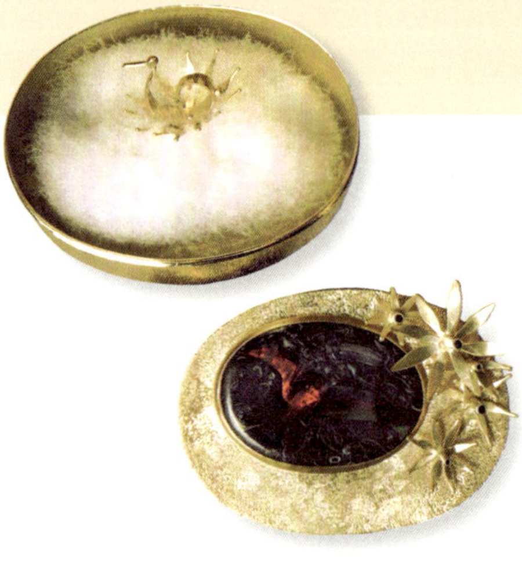

Powder box, 18-karat gold
and black opal

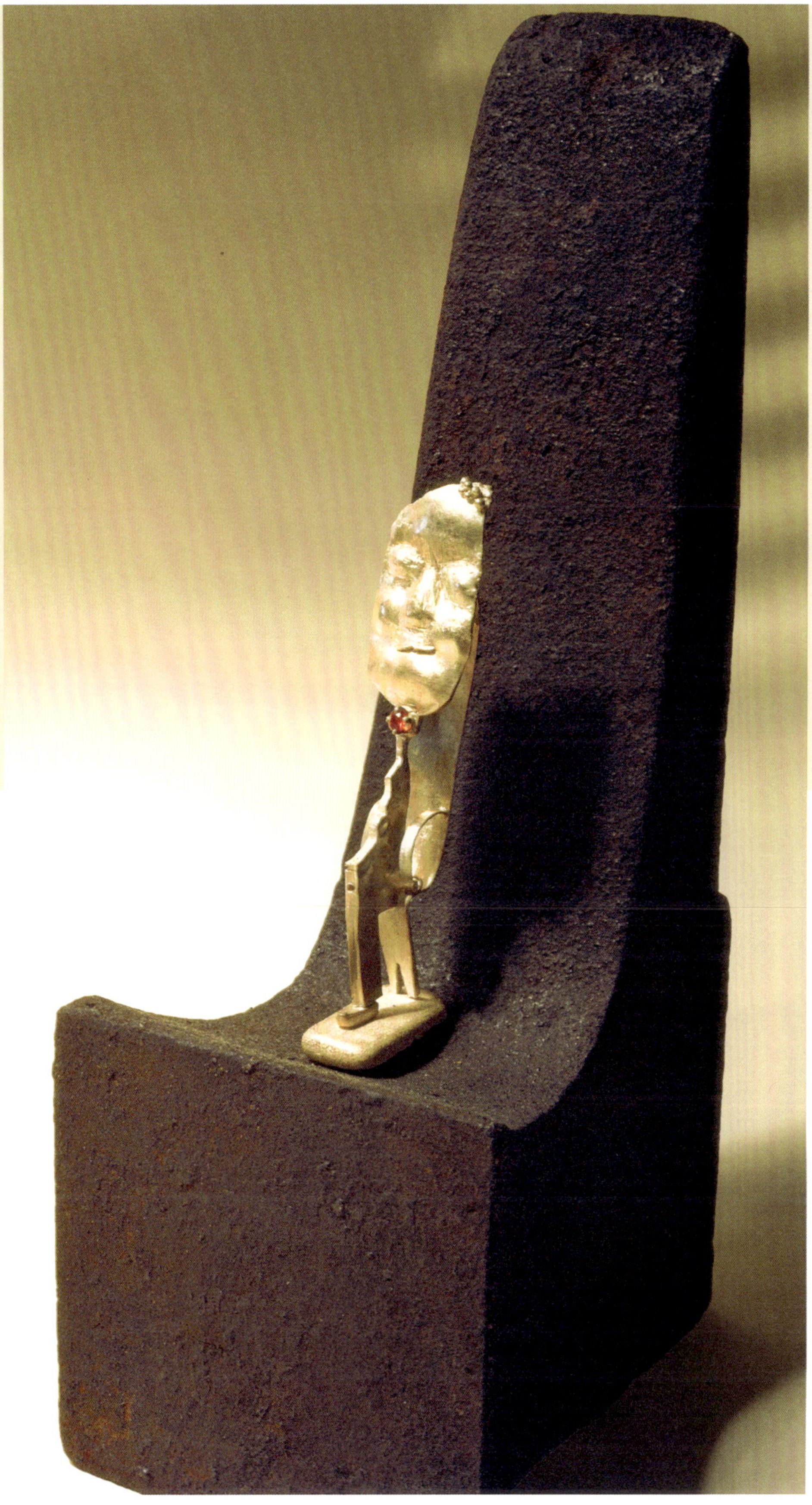

The Doge of Detroit, 18-karat gold, ruby, on a rusted iron plinth. Approximately 6″ high

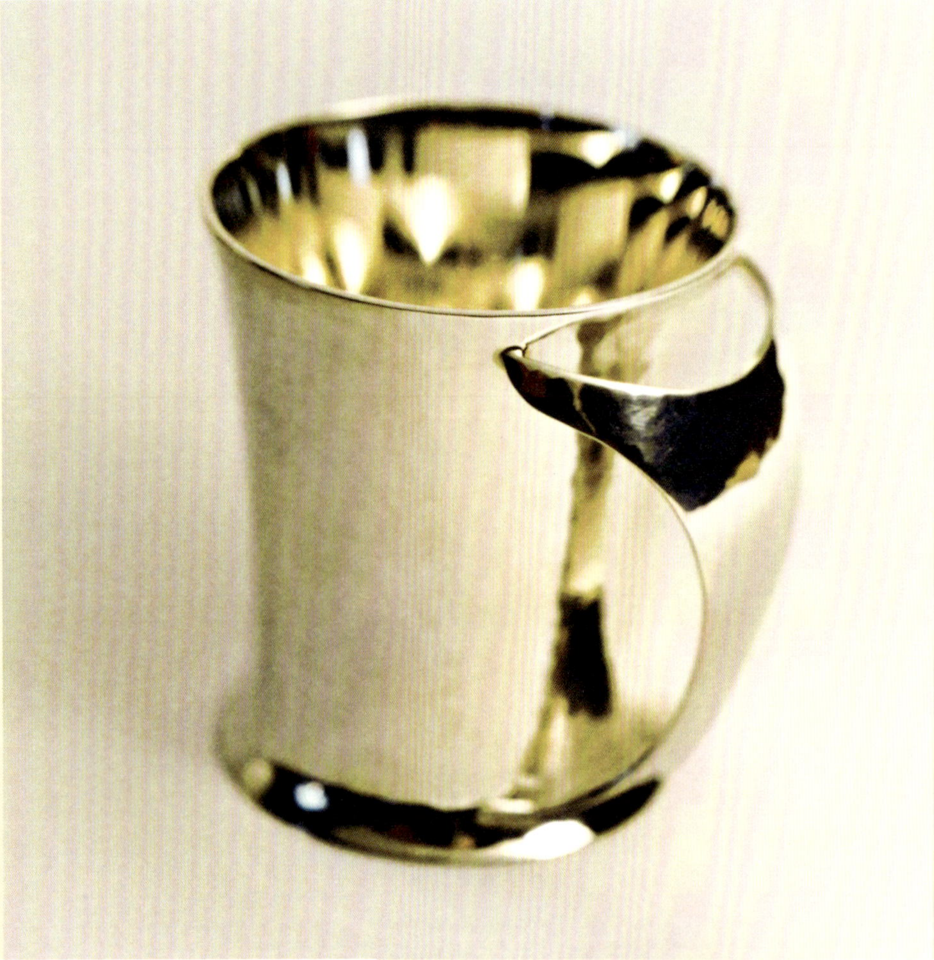

Baby cup, sterling silver, 18-karat gold inside. Approximately 2¼″ diameter

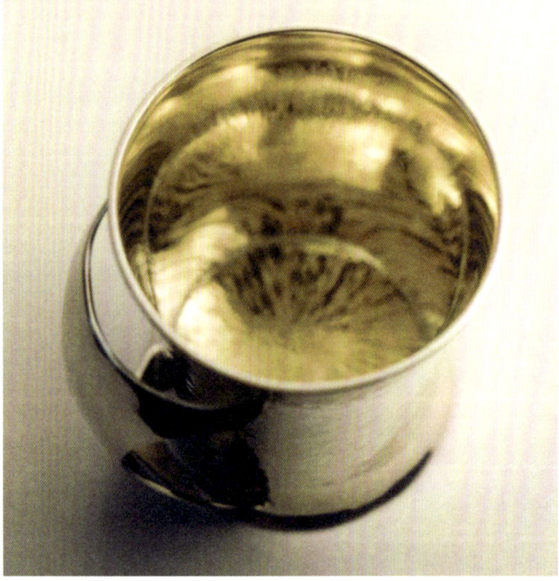

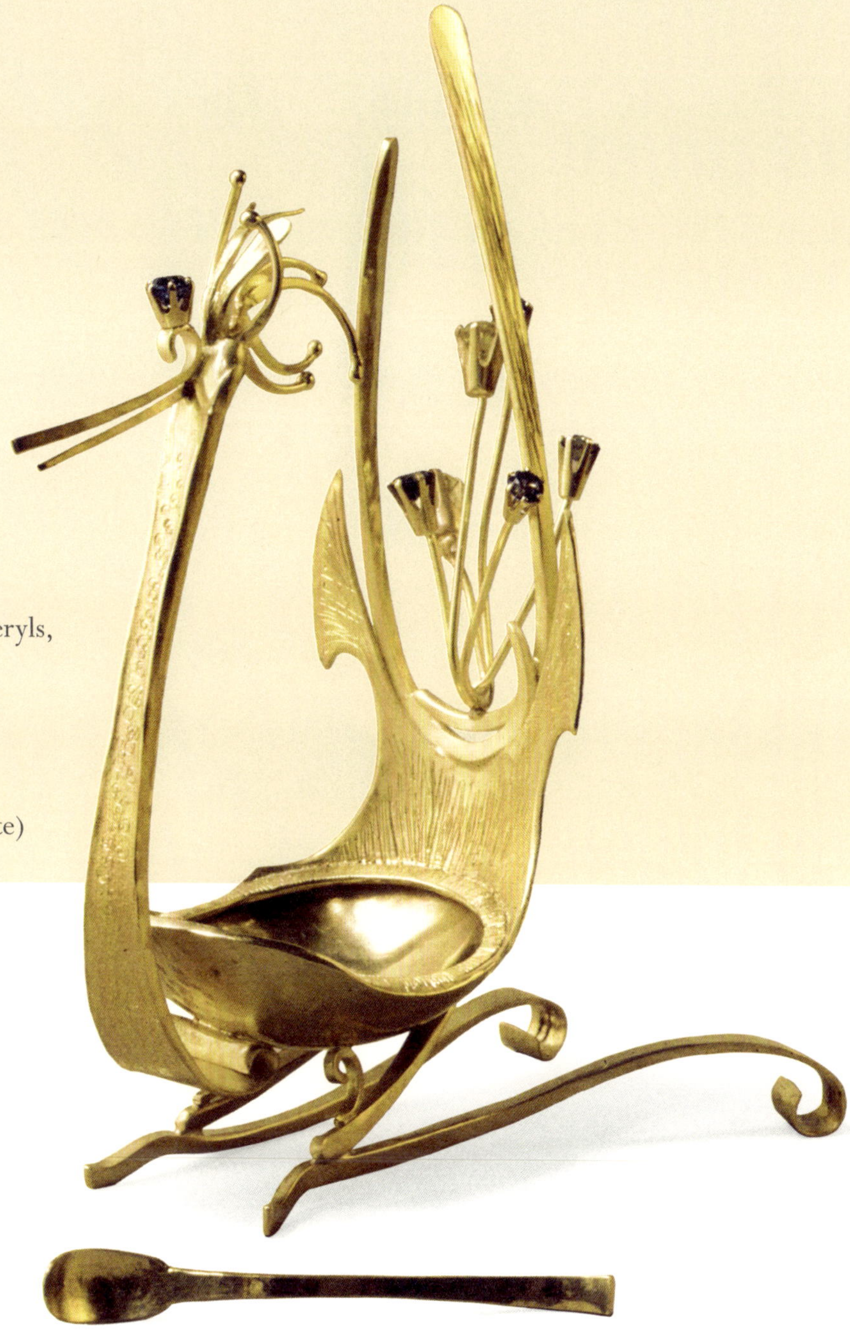

Salt cellar and spoon, 18-karat gold, blue and green sapphires, and chrysoberyls, made to honor Julia Child, c. 1968. Approximately 3½″ high

BELOW: Julia Child admiring Henry's salt cellar (Photograph: Conrad J. White)

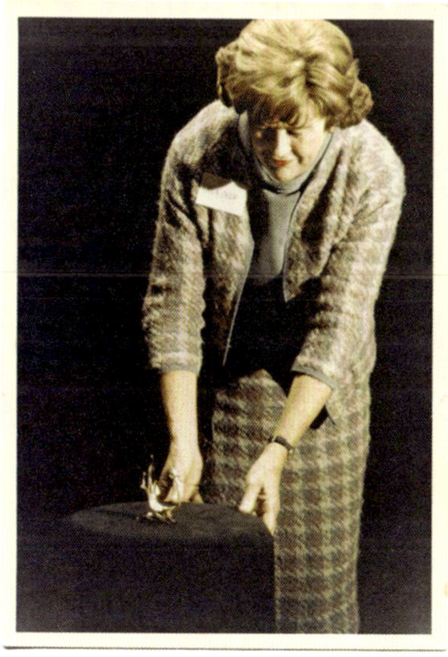

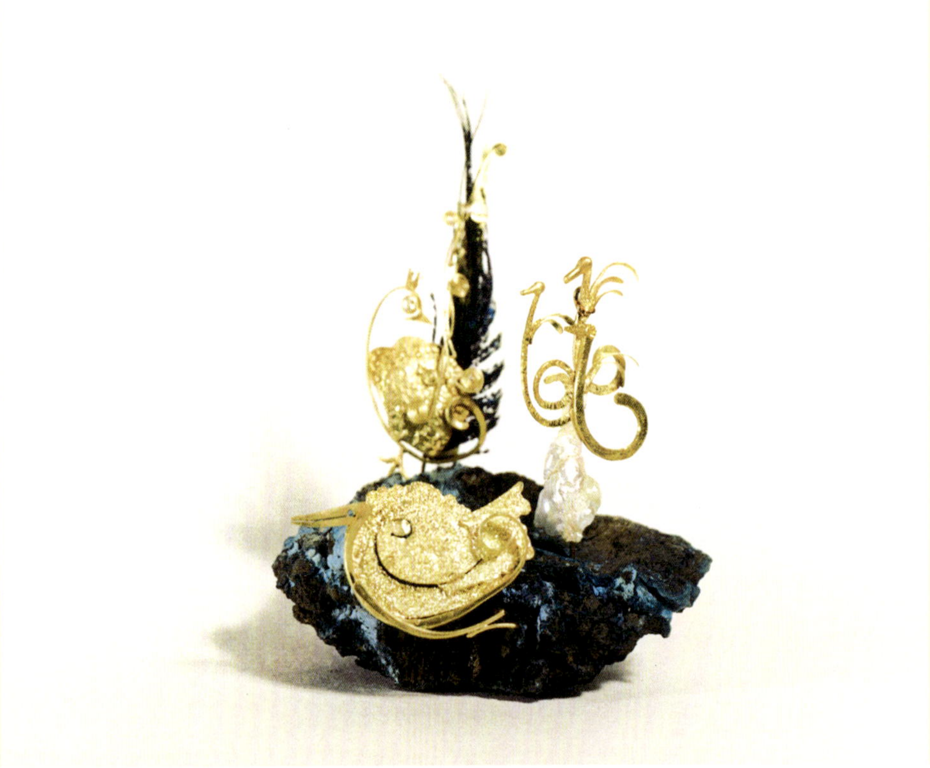

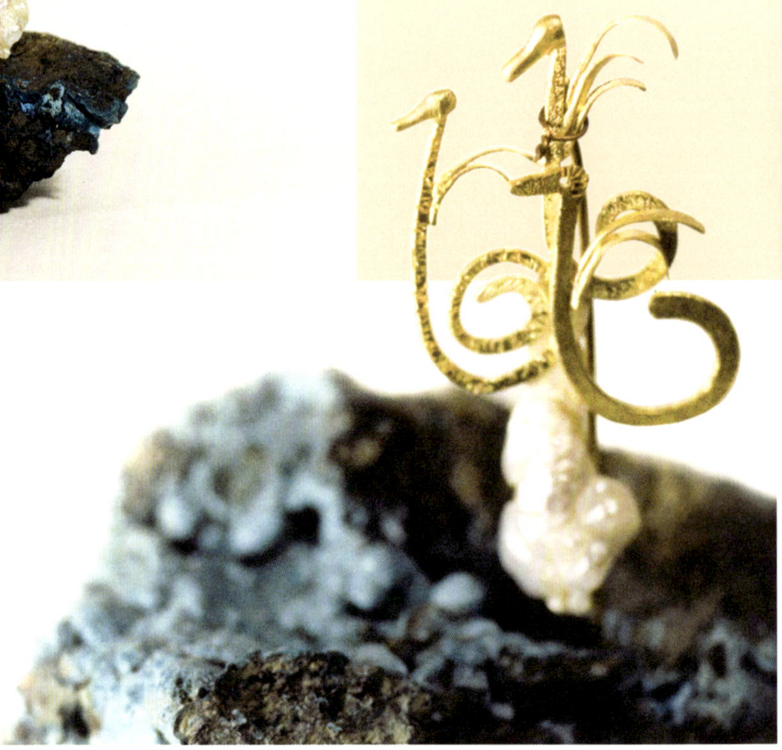

Birds of a Feather, 18-karat gold, freshwater pearls, peacock feathers, on a plinth of azurite-malachite, with three removable bird pins. Approximately 5″ high

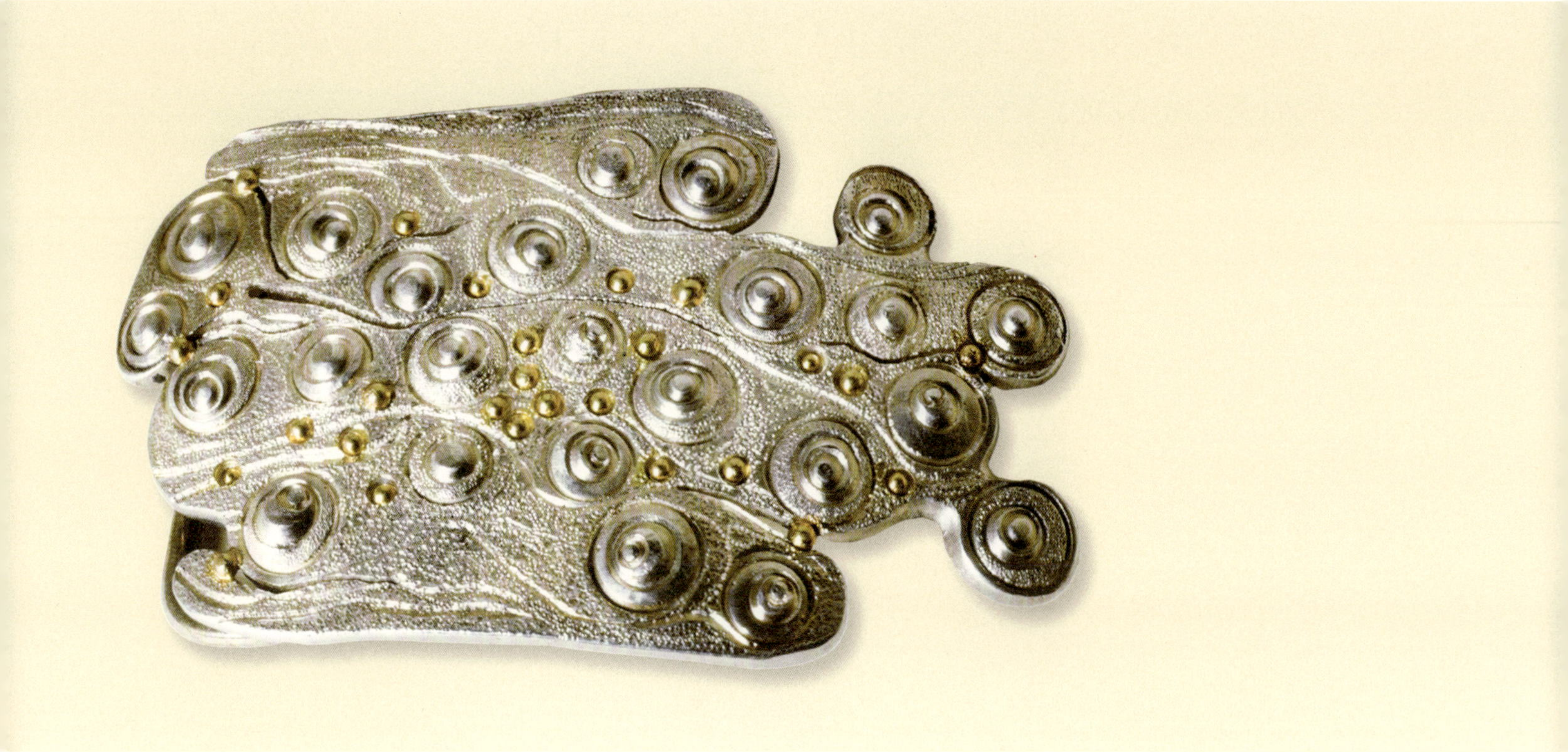

Free-form belt buckle, fine silver,
18-karat gold

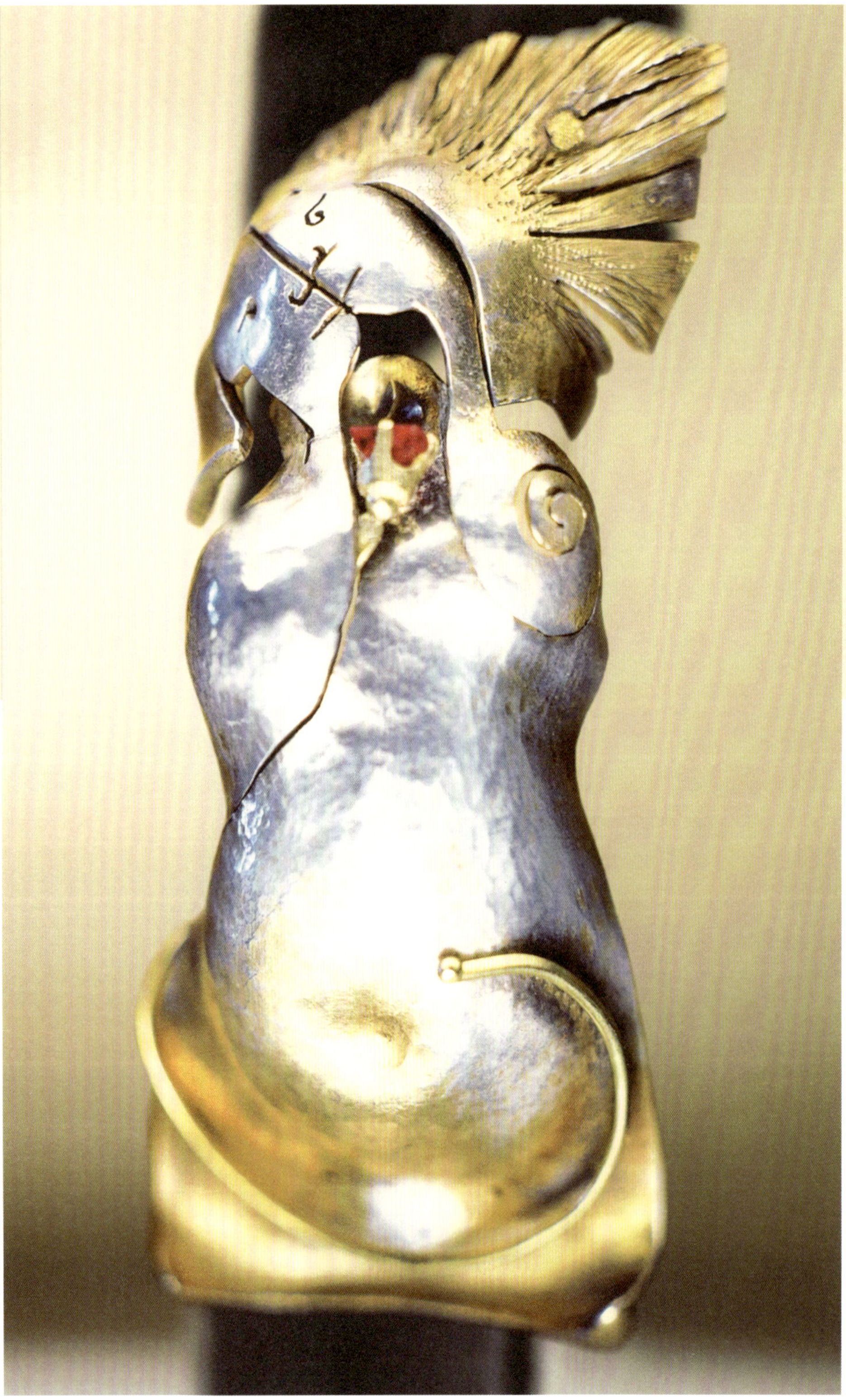

Love in the Afternoon, fine silver, 18- and 24-karat gold on a plinth of ebony, c. 1959. Removable as a pin. Approximately 3½″ high

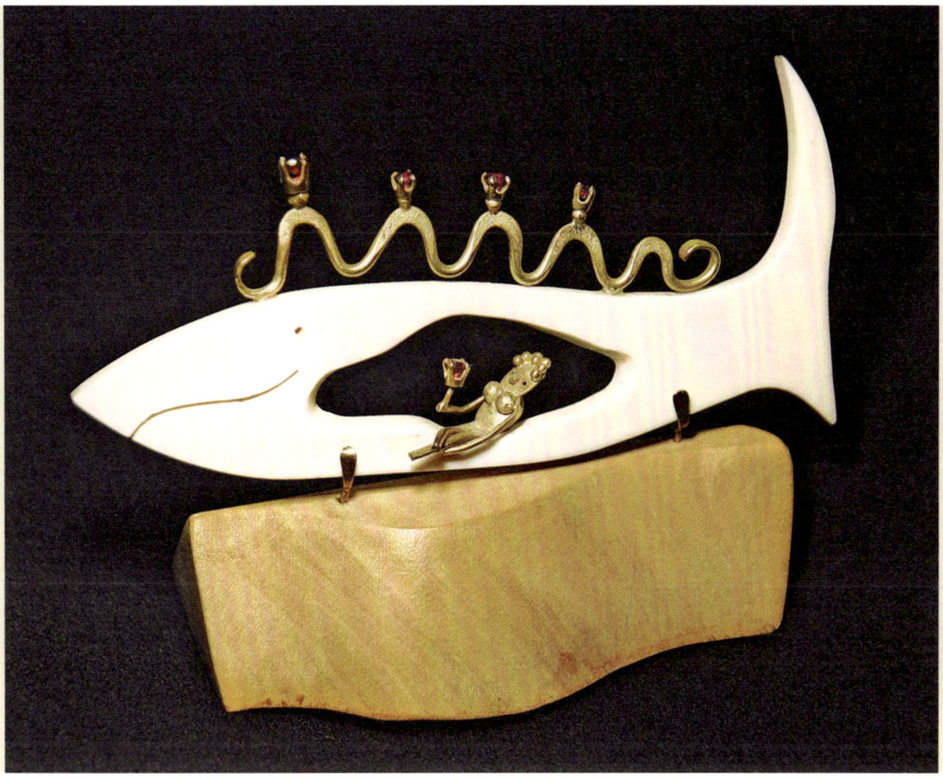

Joan in the Whale, 18-karat gold, antique ivory, and rubies mounted on a boxwood base; Joan clutches a bouquet of sapphires. Approximately 2″ high, 3¼″ long (Sarah Cucinelli Photography)

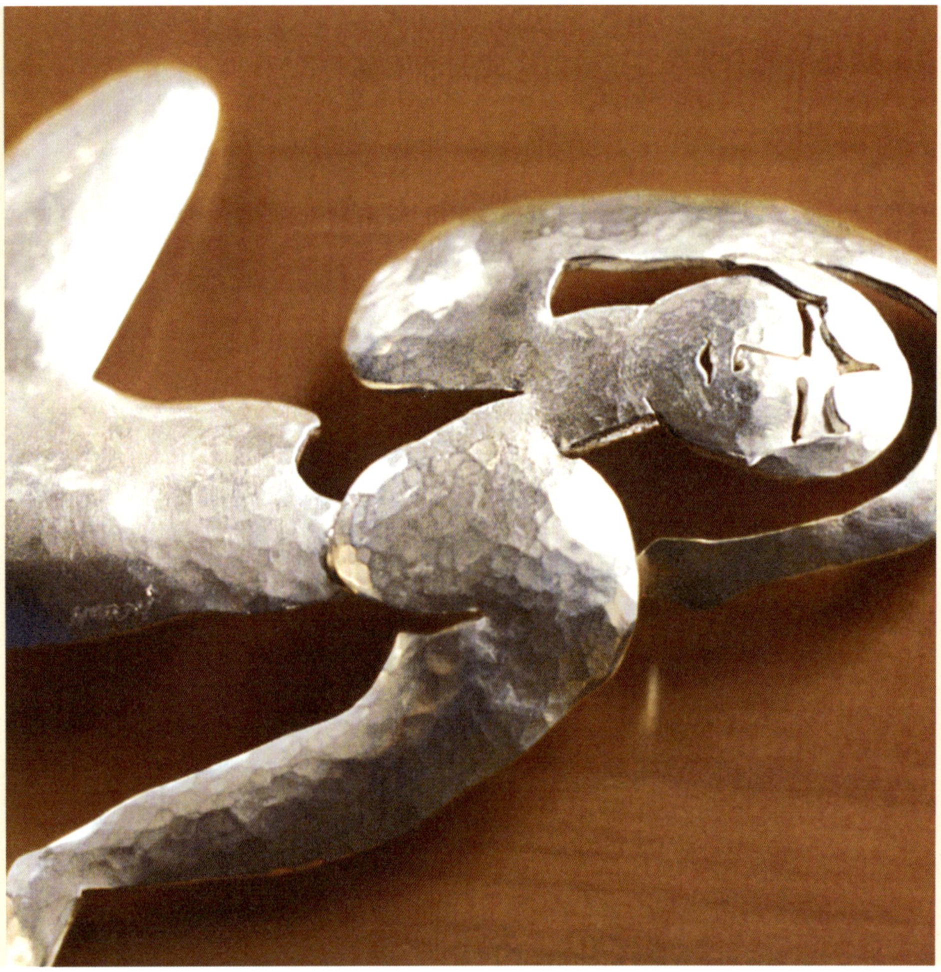

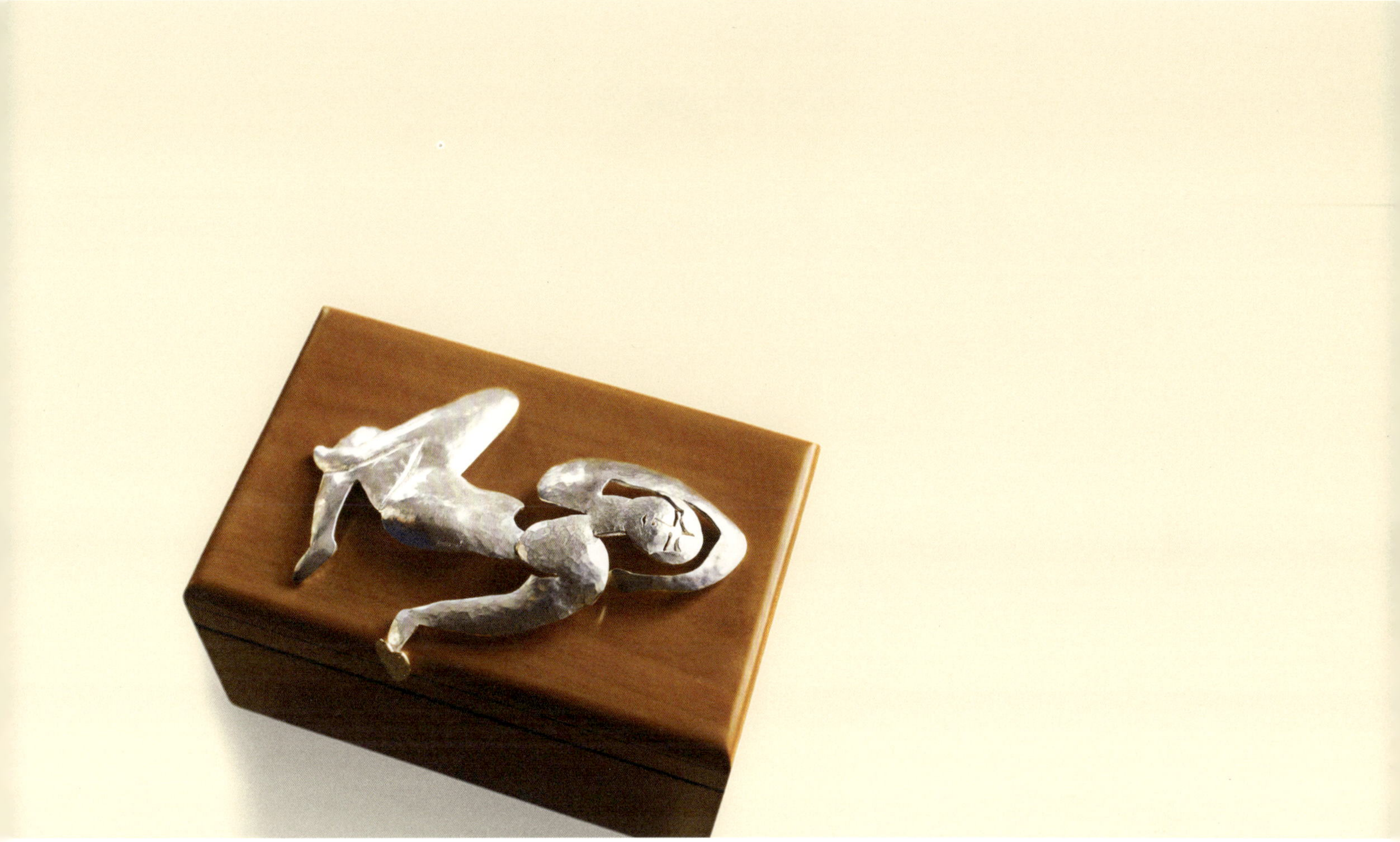

Pearwood box with odalisque
of fine silver clutching an 18-karat
gold heart, in celebration of
Matisse exhibition at MoMA
in 1992. Odalisque approximately 4½″ long

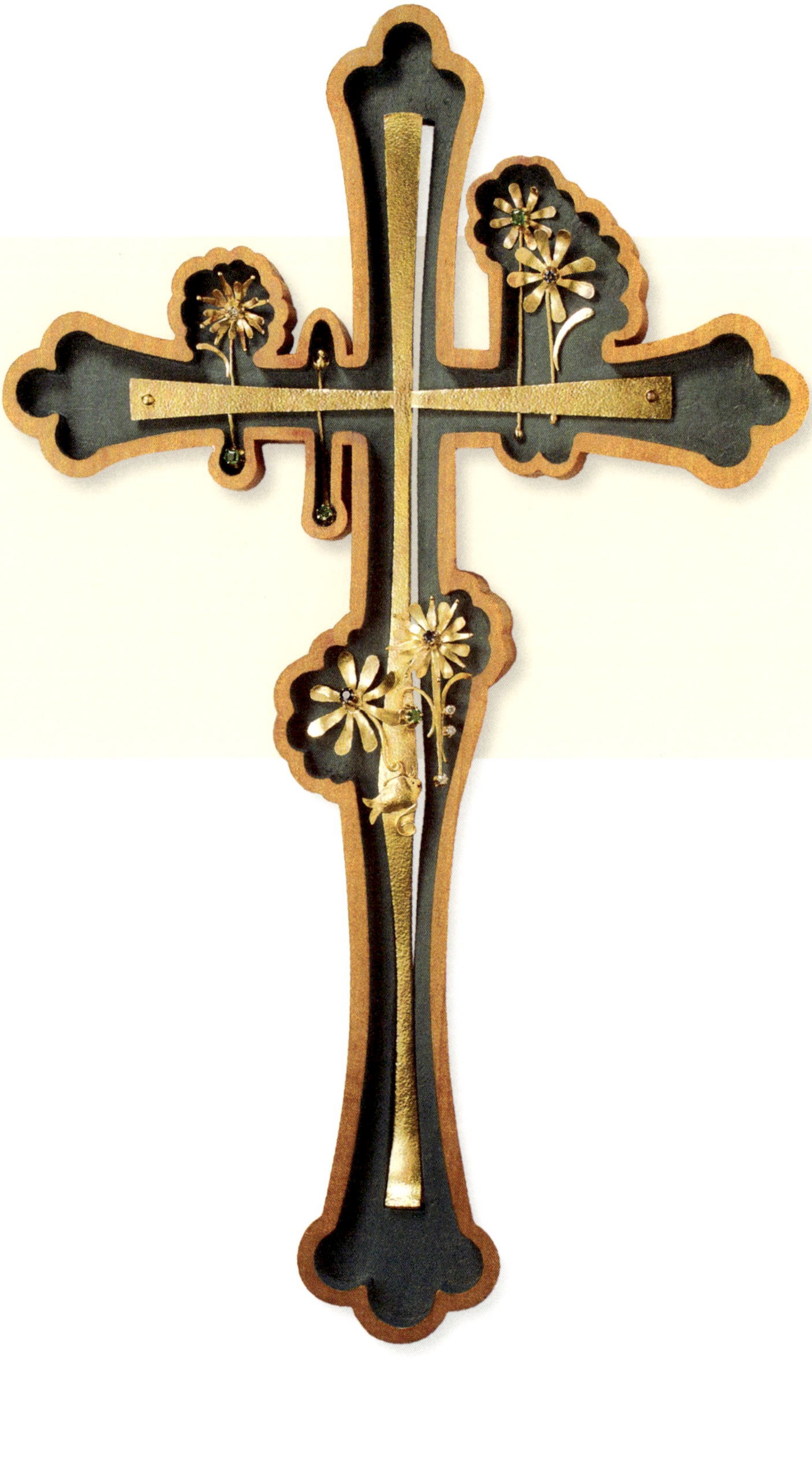

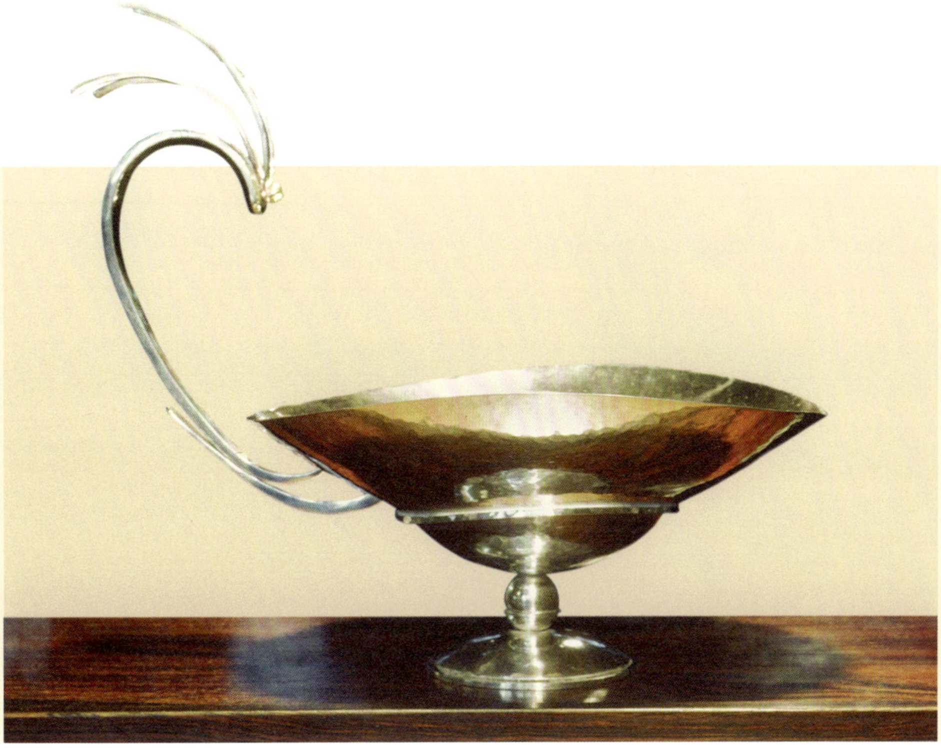

Baptismal water holder, sterling silver, 18-karat gold cross inside bowl. Approximately 6″ high, 8¾″ wide

OPPOSITE: Children's cross, 18-karat gold with rubies, sapphires, and colored diamonds, in natural and painted aged pearwood. Approximately 10″ high, 6″ wide

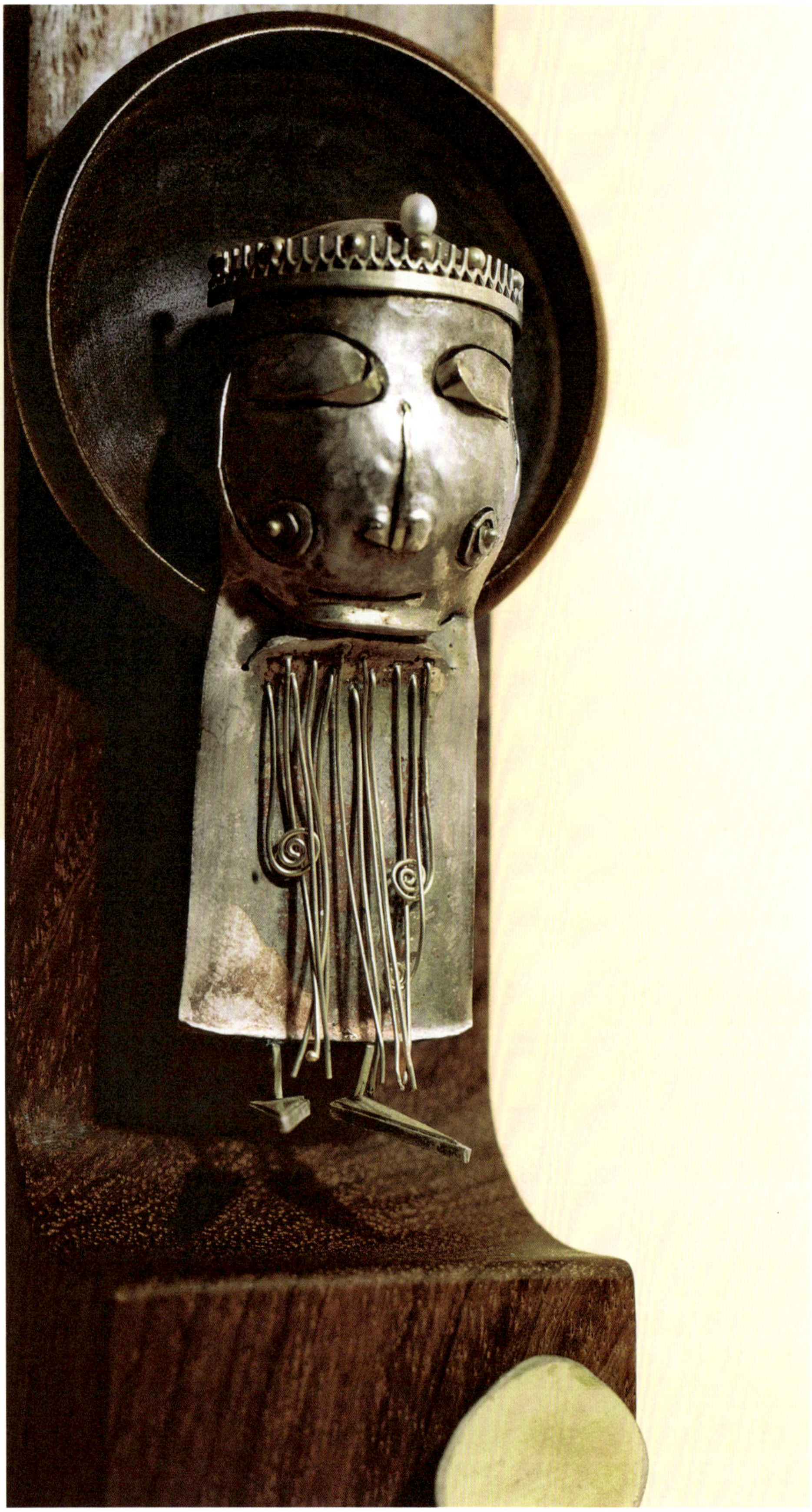

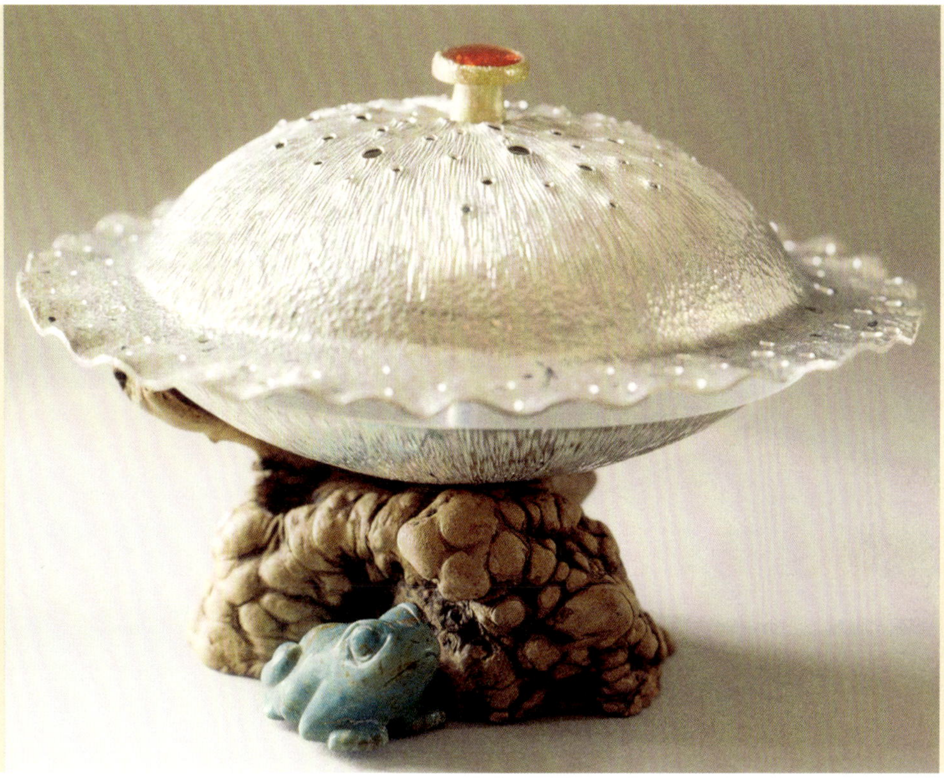

Time for Love Again, fine silver, with opal finial, mounted on manzanita root with turquoise toad. Electronic timer is activated when two people touch the unit and kiss, producing a chime for the hour. Approximately 5½″ high, 6½″ diameter

OPPOSITE: *St. Warumba,* fine silver, 14- and 18-karat gold, rosewood, with freshwater pearl and 24-karat gold leaf. Approximately 12½″ high, 2″ wide

CHRONOLOGY

September 20, 1920	Born in Danbury, Connecticut, son of John A. Shawah and Mary Shawah, brother of George (1913) and Ann (1915); raised and schooled in Norwalk, Connecticut.
1942–1945	Serves in the United States Navy as a torpedo man on a PT boat in the South Pacific.
1946–1949	Attends Pratt Institute and receives a three-year certificate in interior design.
1949–1952	Moves to Boston, designs ship interiors at Irving and Casson A. H. Davenport, then commercial interiors at T. B. Epps architectural firm. Teaches evening design courses at Vesper George School of Art. Enrolls at Boston University and completes a BS in art education, staying on at the university to teach design courses.
1952	Receives a free copy of *How To Make Modern Jewelry,* published the Museum of Modern Art in 1949, and is taken with the notion of "making miniature sculpture called jewelry."
Summer 1953	Opens first workshop in Nantucket at the back of a friend's gift shop and begins making jewelry in earnest.
1956–1959	In New York, with summers in Nantucket. Receives MFA degree from Columbia University in 1957. Has several one-man shows and begins selling work to Georg Jensen.

November 1959	Moves to Cambridge, Massachusetts, and opens goldsmith shop at 14B Eliot Street, just off Harvard Square.
1961	Invited by the Worshipful Company of Goldsmiths in London to participate in exhibition *Modern Jewelry, 1890–1961.*
1965/1966	Works exhibited in the New England Pavilion of the New York World's Fair.
1967–1969	Teaches design courses at Boston University and the Polaroid Corporation.
March 9–16, 1970	First American to have a one-man show at Goldsmiths' Hall in London.
1972–present	Leaves Harvard Square studio and moves to current studio and residence in Cambridge.
1975–1976	Creates Bicentennial medallion, reviving an ancient technique of coining.
April 1, 1981	Inducted as an Associate of the Worshipful Company of Goldsmiths, London. At the time, one of just forty others in the world granted this title.
1980s	Active as a community organizer to save Porter Square and a trustee of the Boston Society of Arts and Crafts, the oldest craft society in the country.
1998–2000	Creates *The Eagle and the Rose* for millennium celebration at the White House; now in the National Archives.
To the present	Actively working as a goldsmith on private commissions.

ACKNOWLEDGMENTS

I owe a special debt of gratitude to Daniel Shapiro and Agnes (Aggie) Gund, whose patronage over the years has coaxed me beyond what I thought were my capabilities. I also acknowledge with heartfelt thanks the very generous support of the Agnes Gund Foundation in the production of this book. My thanks go as well to other supporters of my work and close family members who helped make this book a reality.

I am ever grateful to my niece Judy Metro for her encouragement, publishing expertise, and gentle prodding that helped move this book forward.

And I thank especially my grand-niece Dr. Ann Skelton Ludwig, who turned my scribbled writing and unreal spelling into a coherent manuscript. Instead of knitting during her downtime in the obstetric waiting room, she spent many hours on a laptop trying to make sense of her uncle's words.

The idea for this book came from my longtime friend, Dr. Virginia "Ginger" Saba, a respected leader in our government's health programs. I took her advice to heart: "If I can write five books, you can write one."

Henry Shawah

COLOPHON

Designed by Lisa Carey & Matthew Hirschmann, Lisa Carey Design LLC, Alexandria, Virginia, with support from Gene Shaffer

Typeset in Perpetua & Californian, designed by Eric Gill & Frederic Goudy respectively

Printed on Mohawk Superfine Softwhite Eggshell 100 lb. text & Beckett Expressions Radiance White 100 lb. text, both acid-free

Printed by Capital Offset, Concord, New Hampshire

Cover foil stamped & embossed by Matheson Higgins Congress Press, Woburn, Massachusetts

Bound by Acme Bookbinding, Charlestown, Massachusetts

Unless otherwise credited, all photographs are by Henry Shawah.

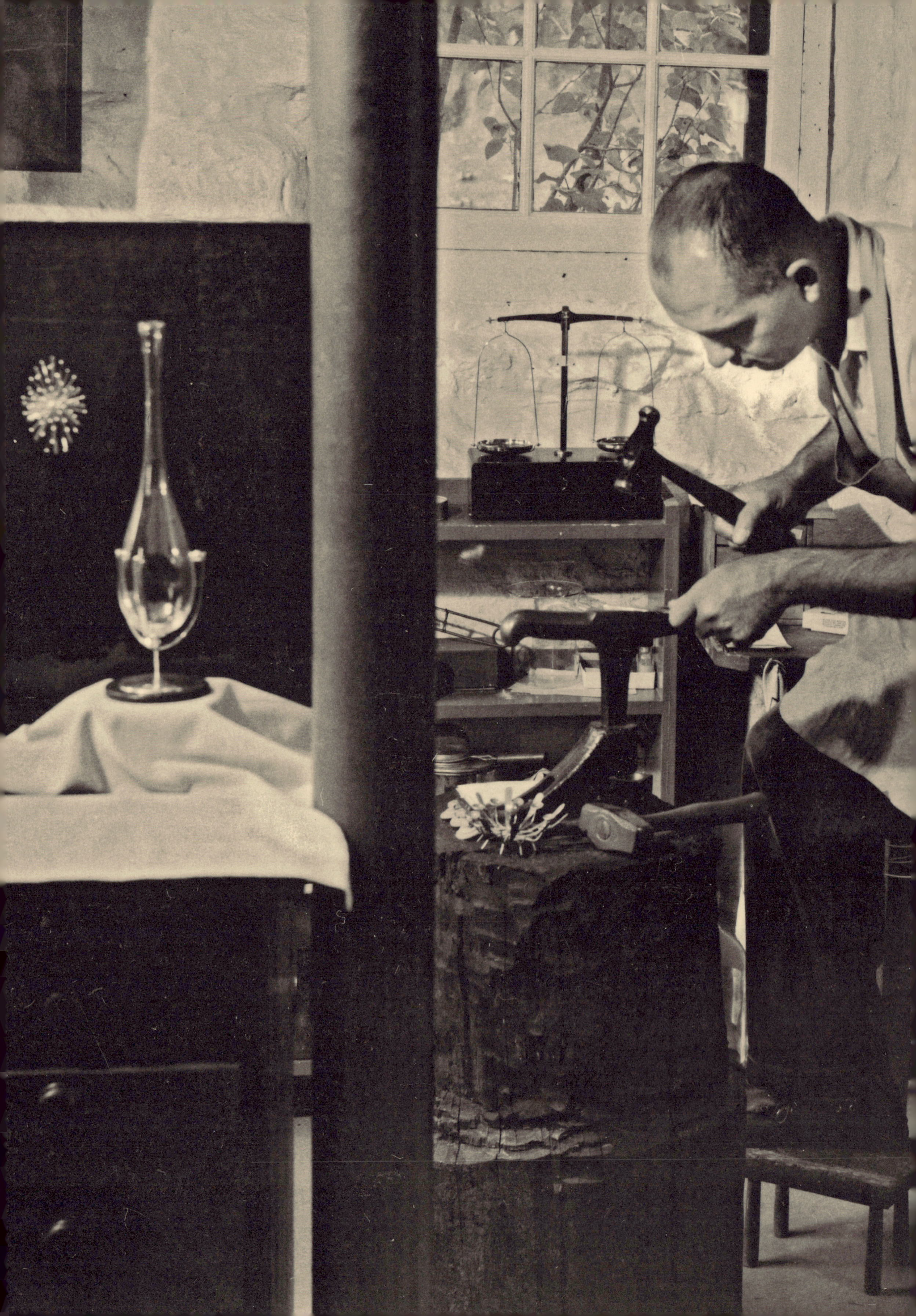